1a

McDOUGAL LITTELL

¡En español!

AUTHORS

Estella Gahala

Patricia Hamilton Carlin

Audrey L. Heining-Boynton

Ricardo Otheguy

Barbara J. Rupert

CULTURE CONSULTANT

Jorge A. Capetillo-Ponce

McDougal Littell
A HOUGHTON MIFFLIN COMPANY
Evanston, Illinois • Boston • Dallas

Cover Photography

Foreground: Photo by Martha Granger/EDGE Productions.

Background: El Morro Castle, San Juan, Puerto Rico, Bruce Adams/CORBIS.

Back cover, top: School Division, Houghton Mifflin Co.; from left to right: El Morro Castle, San Juan, Puerto Rico, Bruce Adams/CORBIS; Quito, Ecuador, Joseph F. Viesti/The Viesti Collection; Pyramid of the Sun at Teotihuacán, Mexico City, Michael T. Sedam/CORBIS; View of Arenal Volcano from Tabacón Hot Springs, Costa Rica, Kevin Schafer; Aerial view of Las Ramblas, Barcelona, Spain, age fotostock; Machu Picchu, Urubamba Valley, Peru, Robert Fried.

Front Matter Photography

iii School Division, Houghton Mifflin Company (t); **v** Nancy Sheehan (b); School Division, Houghton Mifflin Company (tr); **vi** DC Photos/Dee Cullency/Visuals Unlimited (tr); **ix** Robert Frerck/Odyssey Productions/ Chicago (b); **x** RMIP/Richard Haynes; **xi** David Sanger (t); *El cumpleaños de Lala y Tudi* by Carmen Lomas Garza. Reprinted with permission of the publisher, Children's Book Press, San Francisco, CA. Copyright, 1990 by Carmen Lomas Garza (cl); **xiii** RMIP/Richard Haynes (bl); Andrew Wallace/Reuters News Media, Inc. (bc); John Todd/AP Photo (br); **xiv** Katsuyoshi Tanaka/Woodfin Camp & Associates (cl); RMIP/Richard Haynes (bl); John Marshall/Getty Images (t); **xviii** School Division, Houghton Mifflin Company (b); **xxvi** courtesy, *¡Qué onda!* Magazine (tl); **xxvii** Patricia A. Eynon (tr); **xxix** Larry Bussaca/Retna Ltd. (cr).

Illustration

vii Fian Arroyo; **viii, x** Catherine Leary; **xxx-xxxv** Gary Antonetti/Ortelius Design.

ISBN: 0-618-25059-X   3 4 5 6 7 8 9   – VJM – 06 05 04

Internet: www.mcdougallittell.com

1a

McDOUGAL LITTELL

¡En español!

Contenido

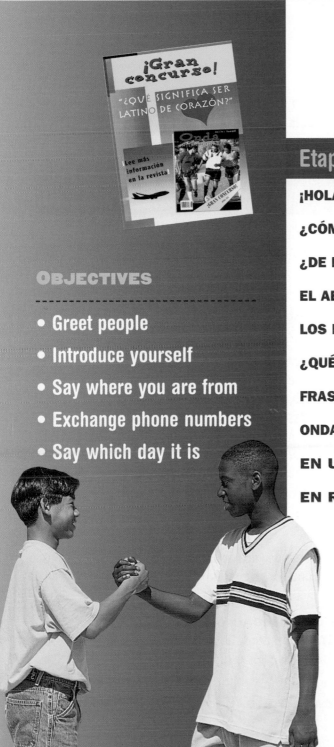

OBJECTIVES

- Greet people
- Introduce yourself
- Say where you are from
- Exchange phone numbers
- Say which day it is

ETAPA
1

OBJECTIVES

- Greet others
- Introduce others
- Say where people are from
- Express likes

OBJECTIVES

- **Describe others**
- **Give others' likes and dislikes**
- **Describe clothing**

UNIDAD 1

ETAPA 3

OBJECTIVES

- Describe family
- Ask and tell ages
- Talk about birthdays
- Give dates
- Express possession

LOS ÁNGELES - Te presento a mi familia 78

UNIDAD 2

ETAPA 1

OBJECTIVES

- **Describe classes and classroom objects**
- **Say how often you do something**
- **Discuss obligations**

CIUDAD DE MÉXICO
MÉXICO

UNA SEMANA TÍPICA

Explore exciting Mexico City with Isabel and Ricardo, two Mexican teenagers.

UNIDAD 2

ETAPA 2

UNIDAD 2

ETAPA 3

OBJECTIVES

- Discuss plans
- Sequence events
- Talk about places and people you know

Mis actividades 164

UNIDAD 3

SAN JUAN
PUERTO RICO

EL FIN DE SEMANA

Enjoy the weather and the landscape of Puerto Rico with three friends.

ETAPA 1

OBJECTIVES

- Extend invitations
- Talk on the phone
- Express feelings
- Say where you are coming from
- Say what just happened

UNIDAD 3

ETAPA 2

OBJECTIVES

- Talk about sports
- Express preferences
- Say what you know
- Make comparisons

¡Deportes para todos! 224

José Cruz, Jr.

Iván Rodríguez

UNIDAD 3

ETAPA 3

OBJECTIVES

- Describe the weather
- Discuss clothing and accessories
- State an opinion
- Describe how you feel
- Say what is happening

PUERTO RICO

El tiempo en El Yunque — 250

About the Authors

Estella Gahala holds a Ph.D. in Educational Administration and Curriculum from Northwestern University. A career teacher of Spanish and French, she has worked with a wide range of students at the secondary level. She has also served as foreign language department chair and district director of curriculum and instruction. Her workshops at national, regional, and state conferences as well as numerous published articles draw upon the current research in language learning, learning strategies, articulation of foreign language sequences, and implications of the national Standards for Foreign Language Learning upon curriculum, instruction, and assessment. She has coauthored nine basal textbooks.

Patricia Hamilton Carlin completed her M.A. in Spanish at the University of California, Davis, where she also taught as a lecturer. Previously she had earned a Master of Secondary Education with specialization in foreign languages from the University of Arkansas and had taught Spanish and French at levels K–12. Her secondary programs in Arkansas received national recognition. A coauthor of the *¡DIME! UNO* and *¡DIME! DOS* secondary textbooks, Patricia currently teaches Spanish and foreign language/ESL methodology at the University of Central Arkansas, where she coordinates the second language teacher education program. In addition, Patricia is a frequent presenter at local, regional, and national foreign language conferences.

Audrey L. Heining-Boynton received her Ph.D. in Curriculum and Instruction from Michigan State University. She is a Professor of Education and Romance Languages at The University of North Carolina at Chapel Hill, where she is a second language teacher educator and Professor of Spanish. She has also taught Spanish, French, and ESL at the K–12 level. Dr. Heining-Boynton was the president of the National Network for Early Language Learning, has been on the Executive Council of ACTFL, and involved with AATSP, Phi Delta Kappa, and state foreign language associations. She has presented both nationally and internationally, and has published over forty books, articles, and curricula.

Ricardo Otheguy received his Ph.D. in Linguistics from the City University of New York, where he is currently Professor of Linguistics at the Graduate School and University Center. He has written extensively on topics related to Spanish grammar as well as on bilingual education and the Spanish of the United States. He is coauthor of *Tu mundo: Curso para hispanohablantes,* a Spanish high school textbook for Spanish speakers, and of *Prueba de ubicación para hispanohablantes,* a high school Spanish placement test.

Barbara J. Rupert has taught Level 1 through A.P. Spanish and has implemented a FLES program in her district. She completed her M.A. at Pacific Lutheran University. Barbara is the author of CD-ROM activities for the *iBravo!* series and has presented at local, regional, and national foreign language conferences. She is the president of the Washington Association for Language Teaching. In 1996, Barbara received the Christa McAuliffe Award for Excellence in Education, and in 1999, she was selected Washington's "Spanish Teacher of the Year" by the Juan de Fuca Chapter of the AATSP.

Culture Consultant

Jorge A. Capetillo-Ponce is currently Assistant Professor of Sociology at University of Massachusetts, Boston, and Researcher at the Mauricio Gastón Institute for Latino Community Development and Public Policy. His graduate studies include an M.A. and a Ph.D. in Sociology from the New School for Social Research in New York City, and an M.A. in Area Studies at El Colegio de México in Mexico City. He is the editor of the book *Images of Mexico in the U.S. News Media,* and has published essays on a wide range of subjects such as media, art, politics, religion, international relations, and cultural theory. Dr. Capetillo's geographical areas of expertise are Latin America, the United States, and the Middle East. During the years 2000 and 2001 he was the Executive Director of the Mexican Cultural Institute of New York. He has also worked as an advisor to politicians and public figures, as a researcher and an editor, and as a university professor and television producer in Mexico, the United States, and Central America.

Contributors

Consulting Authors

Dan Battisti
Dr. Teresa Carrera-Hanley
Bill Lionetti
Patty Murguía Bohannan
Lorena Richins Layser

Regional Language Reviewers

Dolores Acosta (Mexico)
Jaime M. Fatás Cabeza (Spain)
Grisel Lozano-Garcini (Puerto Rico)
Isabel Picado (Costa Rica)
Juan Pablo Rovayo (Ecuador)

Contributing Writers

Ronni L. Gordon
Christa Harris
Debra Lowry
Sylvia Madrigal Velasco
Sandra Rosenstiel
David M. Stillman
Jill K. Welch

Senior Reviewers

O. Lynn Bolton
Dr. Jane Govoni
Elías G. Rodríguez
Ann Tollefson

Middle School Reviewers

Mary Jo Aronica
Springman School
Glenview, IL

Laura Bertrand
Explorer Middle School
Phoenix, AZ

Amy Brewer
Stonewall Jackson Middle School
Mechanicsville, VA

María Corcoran
Sacred Heart Model School
Louisville, KY

Diane Drear
Brown Middle School
Hillsboro, OR

Beverly Fessenden
Carwise Middle School
Palm Harbor, FL

Alma Hernández
Alamo Junior High School
Midland, TX

Robert Hughes
Martha Brown Middle School
Fairport, NY

Nancy Lawrence
Cross Cultural Education Unit
Albuquerque, NM

Lucille Madrid
Taylor Junior High School
Mesa, AZ

Barbara Mortanian
Tenaya Middle School
Fresno, CA

Sally Nickerson
Broadview Middle School
Burlington, NC

Lynn Perdue
Fuller Junior High School
Little Rock, AR

Leela Scanlon
West Middle School
Andover, MA

Kathleen Solórzano
Homestead High School
Mequon, WI

Carol Sparks
Foothill Middle School
Walnut Creek, CA

Elizabeth Torosian
Doherty Middle School
Andover, MA

Jaya Vijayasekar
Griswold Middle School
Rocky Hill, CT

Janet Wohlers
Weston Middle School
Weston, MA

Colleen Yarbrough
Canon McMillan Middle School
Canonsburg, PA

Teacher Reviewers

Linda Amour
Highland High School
Bakersfield, CA

Susan Arbuckle
Mahomet-Seymour High School
Mahomet, IL

Dawne Ashton
Sequoia High School
Redwood City, CA

Sheila Bayles
Rogers High School
Rogers, AR

Warren Bender
Duluth East High School
Duluth, MN

Gail Block
Daly City, CA

Amy Brewer
Stonewall Jackson Middle School
Mechanicsville, VA

William Brill
Hollidaysburg Area Junior High School
Hollidaysburg, PA

Adrienne Chamberlain-Parris
Mariner High School
Everett, WA

Norma Coto
Bishop Moore High School
Orlando, FL

Roberto del Valle
Shorecrest High School
Shoreline, WA

Art Edwards
Canyon High School
Santa Clarita, CA

Rubén D. Elías
Roosevelt High School
Fresno, CA

José Esparza
Curie Metropolitan High School
Chicago, IL

Lorraine A. Estrada
Cabarrus County Schools
Concord, NC

Vincent Fazzolari
East Boston High School
East Boston, MA

Alberto Ferreiro
Harrisburg High School
Harrisburg, PA

Judith C. Floyd
Henry Foss High School
Tacoma, WA

Valarie L. Forster
Jefferson Davis High School
Montgomery, AL

Michael Garber
Boston Latin Academy
Boston, MA

Becky Hay de García
James Madison Memorial High School
Madison, WI

Lucy H. García
Pueblo East High School
Pueblo, CO

Marco García
Lincoln Park High School
Chicago, IL

Raquel R. González
Odessa High School
Odessa, TX

Linda Grau
Shorecrest Preparatory School
St. Petersburg, FL

Myriam Gutiérrez
John O'Bryant School
Roxbury, MA

Deborah Hagen
Ionia High School
Ionia, MI

Sandra Hammond
St. Petersburg High School
St. Petersburg, FL

Bill Heller
Perry Junior/Senior High School
Perry, NY

Joan Heller
Lake Braddock Secondary School
Burke, VA

Paula Hirsch
Windward School
Los Angeles, CA

Ann Hively
Orangevale, CA

Robert Hughes
Martha Brown Middle School
Fairport, NY

Janet King
Long Beach Polytechnic High School
Long Beach, CA

Jody Klopp
Oklahoma State Department
   of Education
Edmond, OK

Richard Ladd
Ipswich High School
Ipswich, MA

Carol Leach
Francis Scott Key High School
Union Bridge, MD

Teacher Reviewers (continued)

Maria Leinenweber
Crescenta Valley High School
La Crescenta, CA

Sandra Martín
Palisades Charter High School
Pacific Palisades, CA

Laura McCormick
East Seneca Senior High School
West Seneca, NY

Karen McDowell
Aptos, CA

Sue McKee
Tustin, CA

Rafaela McLeod
Southeast Raleigh High School
Raleigh, NC

Kathleen L. Michaels
Palm Harbor University High School
Palm Harbor, FL

Vickie A. Mike
Horseheads High School
Horseheads, NY

Robert Miller
Woodcreek High School
Roseville, CA

Barbara Mortanian
Tenaya Middle School
Fresno, CA

Patty Murray
Cretin-Derham Hall High School
St. Paul, MN

Linda Nanos
West Roxbury High School
West Roxbury, MA

Terri Nies
Mannford High School
Mannford, OK

María Emma Nunn
John Tyler High School
Tyler, TX

Leslie Ogden
Nordhoff High School
Ojai, CA

Teri Olsen
Alameda High School
Alameda, CA

Lewis Olvera
Hiram Johnson West Campus
   High School
Sacramento, CA

Judith Pasco
Sequim High School
Sequim, WA

Anne-Marie Quihuis
Paradise Valley High School
Phoenix, AZ

Rita Risco
Palm Harbor University High School
Palm Harbor, FL

James J. Rudy, Jr.
Glen Este High School
Cincinnati, OH

Kathleen Solórzano
Homestead High School
Mequon, WI

Margery Sotomayor
Ferndale, CA

Carol Sparks
Foothill Middle School
Walnut Creek, CA

Sarah Spiesman
Whitmer High School
Toledo, OH

M. Mercedes Stephenson
Hazelwood Central High School
Florissant, MO

Carol Thorp
East Mecklenburg High School
Charlotte, NC

Elizabeth Torosian
Doherty Middle School
Andover, MA

Pamela Urdal Silva
East Lake High School
Tarpon Springs, FL

Dana Valverde
Arroyo Grande High School
Arroyo Grande, CA

Wendy Villanueva
Lakeville High School
Lakeville, MN

Helen Webb
Arkadelphia High School
Arkadelphia, AR

Jena Williams
Jonesboro High School
Jonesboro, AR

Janet Wohlers
Weston Middle School
Weston, MA

Teacher Panel

Linda Amour
Highland High School
Bakersfield, CA

Jeanne Aréchiga
Northbrook High School
Houston, TX

Dena Bachman
Lafayette Senior High School
St. Joseph, MO

Sharon Barnes
J. C. Harmon High School
Kansas City, KS

Ben Barrientos
Calvin Simmons Junior High School
Oakland, CA

Paula Biggar
Sumner Academy of Arts & Science
Kansas City, KS

Hercilia Breton
Highlands High School
San Antonio, TX

Gwen Cannell
Cajon High School
San Bernardino, CA

Edda Cárdenas
Blue Valley North High School
Leawood, KS

Joyce Chow
Crespi Junior High School
Richmond, CA

Laura Cook
Evans Junior High School
Lubbock, TX

Mike Cooperider
Truman High School
Independence, MO

Judy Dozier
Shawnee Mission South High School
Shawnee Mission, KS

Maggie Elliott
Bell Junior High School
San Diego, CA

Terri Frésquez
Del Valle High School
El Paso, TX

Dana Galloway-Grey
Ontario High School
Ontario, CA

Nieves Gerber
Chatsworth Senior High School
Chatsworth, CA

April Hansen
Livermore High School
Livermore, CA

Rose Jenkins
Clements High School
Sugarland, TX

Janet King
Long Beach Polytechnic High School
Long Beach, CA

Susanne Kissane
Shawnee Mission Northwest
   High School
Shawnee Mission, KS

Ann López
Pala Middle School
San Jose, CA

Anna Marxson
Laguna Creek High School
Elk Grove, CA

Beatrice Marino
Palos Verdes Peninsula High School
Rolling Hills, CA

Rudy Molina
McAllen Memorial High School
McAllen, TX

Barbara Mortanian
Tenaya Middle School
Fresno, CA

Vickie Musni
Pioneer High School
San Jose, CA

Teri Olsen
Alameda High School
Alameda, CA

Rodolfo Orihuela
C. K. McClatchy High School
Sacramento, CA

Rob Ramos
J. T. Hutchinson Junior High School
Lubbock, TX

Montserrat Rey
Hightower High School
Fort Bend, TX

Sandra Rivera
Mary Carroll High School
Corpus Christi, TX

Terrie Rynard
Olathe South High School
Olathe, KS

Beth Slinkard
Lee's Summit High School
Lee's Summit, MO

Rosa Stein
Park Hill High School
Kansas City, MO

Marianne Villalobos
Modesto High School
Modesto, CA

Shannon Zerby
North Garland High School
Garland, TX

Acknowledgments

Urban Panel

Rebecca Carr
William G. Enloe High School
Raleigh, NC

Rita Dooley
Lincoln Park High School
Chicago, IL

Norha Franco
East Side High School
Newark, NJ

Kathryn Gardner
Riverside University High School
Milwaukee, WI

Frank González
Mast Academy
Miami, FL

Eula Glenn
Remtec Center
Detroit, MI

Jeana Harper
Detroit Fine Arts High School
Detroit, MI

Guillermina Jauregui
Los Angeles Senior High School
Los Angeles, CA

Lula Lewis
Hyde Park Career Academy
  High School
Chicago, IL

Florence Meyers
Overbrook High School
Philadelphia, PA

Vivian Selenikas
Long Island City High School
Long Island City, NY

Sadia White
Spingarn Stay Senior High School
Washington, DC

Block Scheduling Panel

Barbara Baker
Wichita Northwest High School
Wichita, KS

Patty Banker
Lexington High School
Lexington, NC

Beverly Blackburn
Reynoldsburg Senior High School
Reynoldsburg, OH

Henry Foust
Northwood High School
Pittsboro, NC

Gloria Hawks
A. L. Brown High School
Kannapolis, NC

Lois Hillman
North Kitsap High School
Poulsbo, WA

Nick Patterson
Central High School
Davenport, IA

Sharyn Petkus
Grafton Memorial High School
Grafton, MA

Cynthia Prieto
Mount Vernon High School
Alexandria, VA

Julie Sanchez
Western High School
Fort Lauderdale, FL

Marilyn Settlemyer
Freedom High School
Morganton, NC

Student Review Board

Why Learn Spanish?

To Appreciate the Importance of Spanish in the U.S.

The influence of Spanish is everywhere. Spanish words like **plaza** and **tornado** have become part of the English language. Just think of U.S. place names that come from Spanish: **Colorado, Florida, Nevada, Los Angeles, San Antonio, La Villita,** etc. You can see Spanish on signs. There are Spanish radio and television stations. Singers such as Jon Secada perform in Spanish as well as English.

To Connect

Spanish will help you **communicate** with other people. Spanish is the second most common language in the U.S. and the third most common in the world. You will be able do things like **ask someone for directions, bargain at a market,** and **order in a restaurant** in Spanish.

To Have Fun

Taking Spanish is a new experience that will expose you to the **food,** the **music,** the **celebrations,** and other aspects of Spanish-speaking cultures. It will make travel to other countries as well as to different places in the United States much more enjoyable and more meaningful.

To Be Challenged

Studying Spanish is a challenge. There is a lot to learn, but it's not just vocabulary and grammar in a textbook. In the future you **will be able to read** Spanish-language **newspapers, magazines,** and **books.** Imagine reading *Don Quijote de la Mancha* by Miguel de Cervantes in the original Spanish someday!

To Help You in the Future

Taking a foreign language like Spanish is an accomplishment to be emphasized on college and job applications. It can also help you fulfill college language requirements. Spanish can be **useful in many careers,** from doctor, bank teller, and social worker to teacher, tour guide, and translator.

How to Study Spanish

Use Strategies

Listening strategies provide a starting point to help you understand.

Speaking strategies will help you express yourself in Spanish.

Reading strategies will show you different ways to approach reading.

Writing strategies help you out with your writing skills.

Cultural strategies help you compare Spanish-speaking cultures of the world to your own culture.

PARA LEER • STRATEGY: READING

Look for cognates These are words that look alike and have similar meanings in both English and Spanish, such as **europeo** and **artificiales**. What other cognates can you find in **"Las celebraciones del año"**?

Use Study Hints

The **Apoyo para estudiar** feature provides study hints that will help you learn Spanish.

APOYO PARA ESTUDIAR

Gender

Knowing the gender of nouns that refer to people is easy. But how do you learn the gender of things? When learning a new word, such as **camiseta**, say it with the definite article: **la camiseta**. Say it to yourself and say it aloud several times.

Build Your Confidence

Everyone learns differently, and there are different ways to achieve a goal. Find out what works for you. Grammar boxes are set up with an explanation, a visual representation, and examples from real-life contexts. Use this combination of words and graphics to help you learn Spanish. Focus on whatever helps you most.

GRAMÁTICA

Expressing Feelings with **estar** and Adjectives

 ¿RECUERDAS? *p. 153* You learned that the verb **estar** is used to say where someone or something is located.

▶ **Estar** is also used with **adjectives** to describe how someone feels at a given moment.

estoy	estamos
estás	estáis
está	están

agrees

Diana **está preocupada** por Ignacio.
*Diana **is worried** about Ignacio.*

agrees

Ignacio **está preocupado** por Roberto.
*Ignacio **is worried** about Roberto.*

Remember that **adjectives** must **agree** in gender and number with the nouns they describe.

Have Fun

Taking a foreign language does not have to be all serious work. The dialogs in this book present the Spanish language in **entertaining, real-life contexts.**

- Pair and group activities give you a chance to **interact with your classmates.**
- Vocabulary and grammar puzzles will test your knowledge, but will also be **fun to do.**

Listen to Spanish
Inside and Outside of Class

Listening to Spanish will help you understand it. Pay attention to the **dialogs** and the **listening activities** in class.

Take advantage of opportunities to **hear Spanish outside of class** as well.

- Do you know someone who speaks Spanish?
- Are there any Spanish-language radio and/or television stations in your area?
- Does your video store have any Spanish-language movies?

Take Risks

The goal of studying a foreign language like Spanish is to **communicate.**

Don't be afraid to **speak.**

Everyone makes mistakes, so don't worry if you make a few. When you do make a mistake, **pause and then try again.**

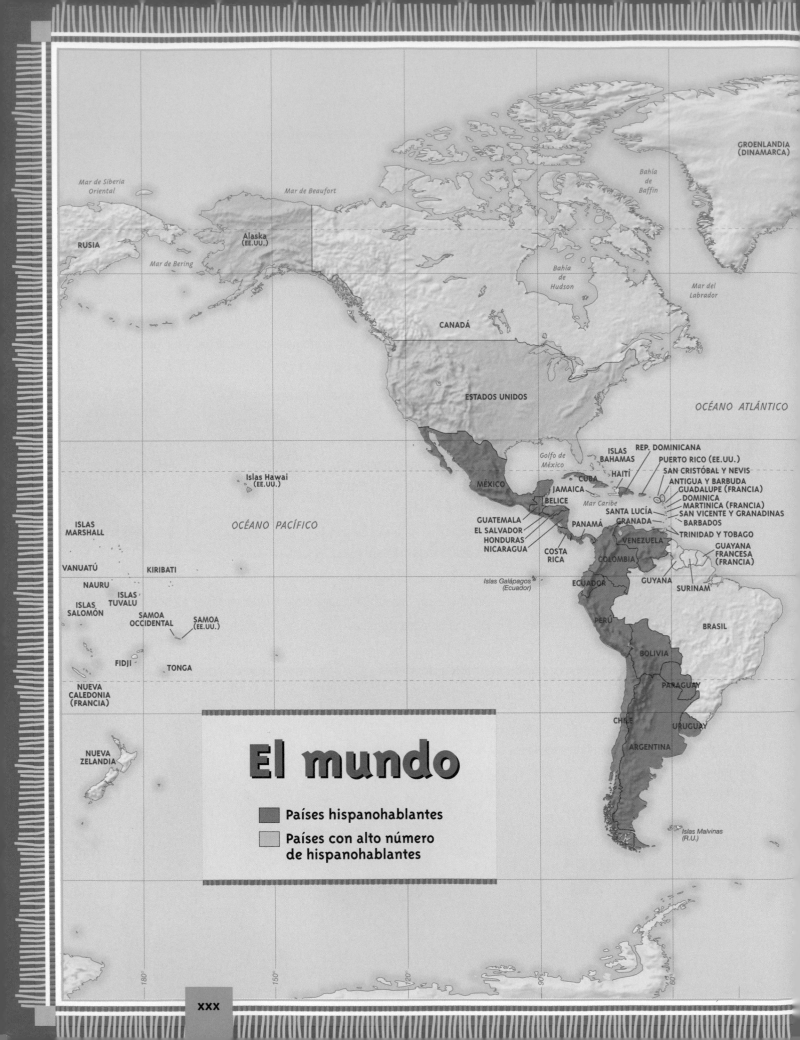

El mundo

■ Países hispanohablantes

■ Países con alto número de hispanohablantes

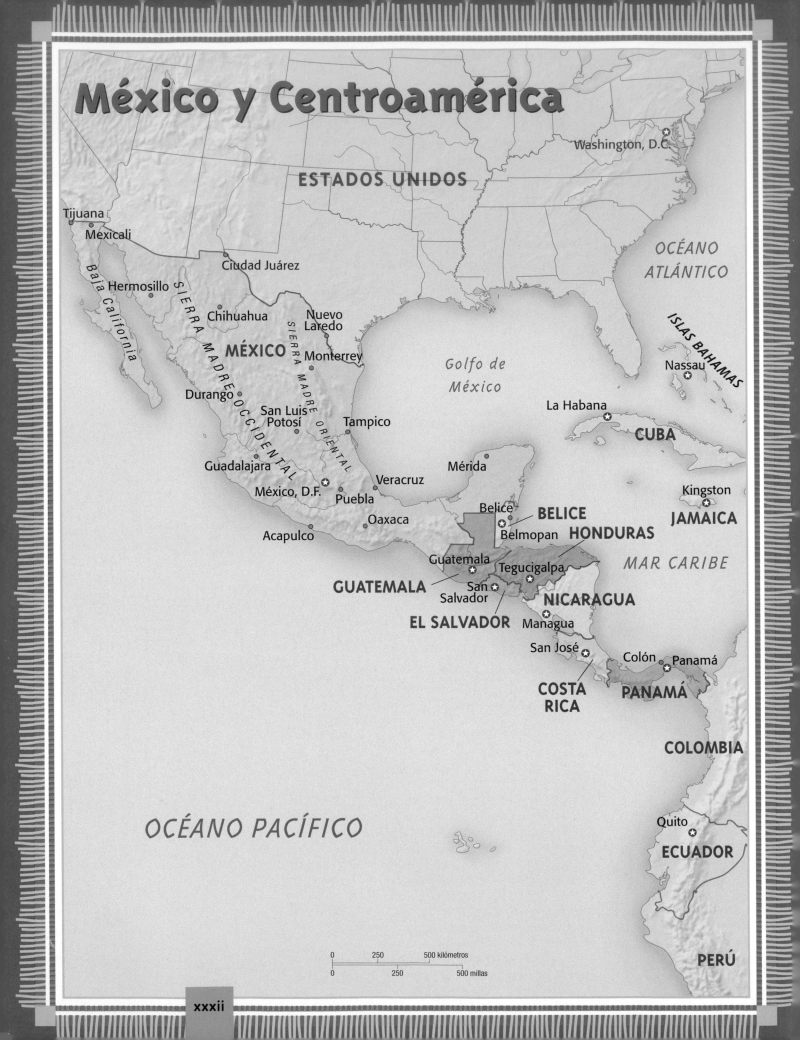

México y Centroamérica

ESTADOS UNIDOS

Washington, D.C.

OCÉANO ATLÁNTICO

Tijuana
Mexicali
Ciudad Juárez
Hermosillo
Baja California
SIERRA MADRE OCCIDENTAL
Chihuahua
Nuevo Laredo
MÉXICO
Monterrey
Durango
San Luis Potosí
SIERRA MADRE ORIENTAL
Guadalajara
Tampico
México, D.F.
Puebla
Veracruz
Acapulco
Oaxaca

Golfo de México

Mérida

La Habana
CUBA

ISLAS BAHAMAS
Nassau

Kingston
JAMAICA

Belice
BELICE
Belmopan
HONDURAS

MAR CARIBE

Guatemala
GUATEMALA
San Salvador
Tegucigalpa
NICARAGUA
EL SALVADOR
Managua
San José
Colón
Panamá
COSTA RICA
PANAMÁ

COLOMBIA

OCÉANO PACÍFICO

Quito
ECUADOR

PERÚ

0   250   500 kilómetros
0   250   500 millas

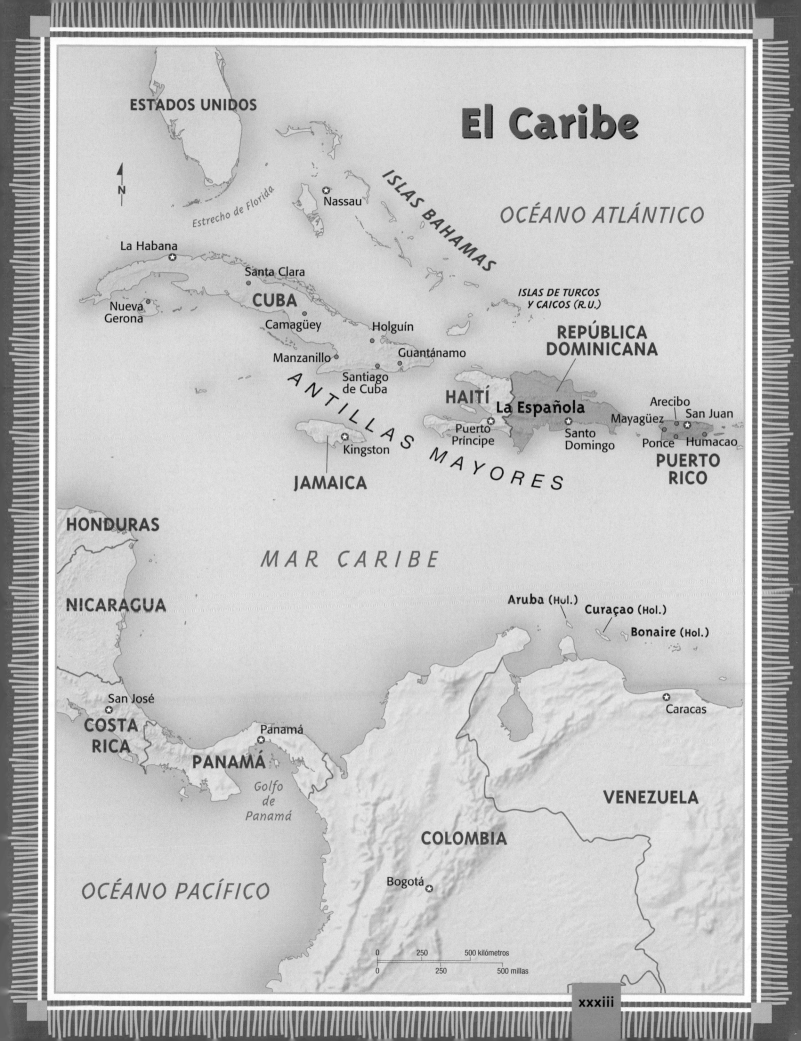

El Caribe

ESTADOS UNIDOS

Estrecho de Florida

Nassau

ISLAS BAHAMAS

OCÉANO ATLÁNTICO

La Habana

Santa Clara

CUBA

Nueva Gerona

Camagüey

Holguín

Manzanillo

Guantánamo

Santiago de Cuba

ISLAS DE TURCOS Y CAICOS (R.U.)

REPÚBLICA DOMINICANA

HAITÍ

La Española

Arecibo

Mayagüez

San Juan

Puerto Príncipe

Santo Domingo

Ponce

Humacao

PUERTO RICO

ANTILLAS MAYORES

Kingston

JAMAICA

HONDURAS

MAR CARIBE

NICARAGUA

Aruba (Hol.)

Curaçao (Hol.)

Bonaire (Hol.)

San José

COSTA RICA

Panamá

PANAMÁ

Golfo de Panamá

Caracas

VENEZUELA

COLOMBIA

Bogotá

OCÉANO PACÍFICO

| 0 | 250 | 500 kilómetros |

| 0 | 250 | 500 millas |

Sudamérica

España

OCÉANO ATLÁNTICO

FRANCIA

MAR CANTÁBRICO

La Coruña

ASTURIAS CANTABRIA Bilbao
GALICIA
CORDILLERA CANTÁBRICA PAÍS VASCO
León NAVARRA LOS PIRINEOS ANDORRA
Pamplona
CASTILLA-LEÓN Río Ebro CATALUÑA
Valladolid Río Duero
Zaragoza Barcelona
E S P A Ñ A ARAGÓN
Salamanca
Río Tajo
SIERRA DE GUADARRAMA MADRID
Madrid
PORTUGAL COMUNIDAD Islas Baleares Menorca
VALENCIANA Palma
CASTILLA-LA MANCHA Valencia Mallorca

Río Guadiana Ibiza
Lisboa
EXTREMADURA MAR MEDITERRÁNEO

Córdoba MURCIA
Sevilla Río Guadalquivir
Granada
ANDALUCÍA SIERRA NEVADA
Málaga

Gibraltar (R.U.)
Estrecho de Gibraltar Ceuta (España)

N

Melilla (España)

OCÉANO
ATLÁNTICO

MARRUECOS

África

CAMERÚN

Malabo

GUINEA
ECUATORIAL

Golfo de
Guinea Bata

GABÓN

Islas Canarias (España)

OCÉANO ATLÁNTICO

La Palma
Santa Cruz
de Tenerife

Tenerife Las Palmas
Gran Canaria

ÁFRICA

0   50 kilómetros

0   50 millas

0   50   100 kilómetros

0   50   100 millas

0   200 kilómetros

0   200 millas

ETAPA **PRELIMINAR**

¡Hola, bienvenidos!

OBJECTIVES

- Greet people

- Introduce yourself

- Say where you are from

- Exchange phone numbers

- Say which day it is

¿Qué ves?

Look at the photo of the first day of school.

1. How might the students be greeting one another?
2. What are they carrying?
3. Where should new students go? At what time?

¡Bienvenidos estudiantes nuevos!

Reunión: 8:30
Auditorio Colón

¡Hola!

NOTA CULTURAL

When greeting, it is customary to shake hands. Many people also exchange a kiss on the cheek or a hug. The greeting changes with the time of day. **Hola** can be used anytime. **Buenos días** is used in the morning, **Buenas tardes** in the afternoon and early evening, and **Buenas noches** at night.

Hola.

Buenos días.

Buenas tardes.

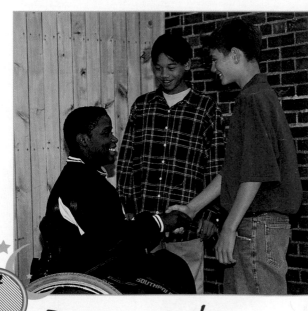

Buenas noches.

Adiós

Adiós.

Hasta luego.

Hasta mañana.

Nos vemos.

ACTIVIDAD 1 · Buenos días

How would you greet a friend at these times?

modelo

5:00 P.M.	*Buenas tardes.*

1. 8:00 P.M.   3. 2:00 P.M.   5. anytime
2. 10:45 A.M.   4. 8:30 A.M.   6. 9:00 P.M.

ACTIVIDAD 2 · Hasta mañana

Use different expressions to say good-bye to these people.

1. Ana   3. Señora Díaz
2. Señor Ruiz   4. Alfredo

ACTIVIDAD 3

¿Saludo o despedida?

Imagine that you are in a Spanish-speaking community. Identify what you hear as a greeting (**saludo**) or a farewell (**despedida**) for these eight phrases.

ACTIVIDAD 4 · Nos vemos

Greet and say good-bye to your partner, according to these situations.

1. Greet each other in the afternoon. You will see each other tomorrow.
2. Greet each other in the evening. You don't expect to see each other anytime soon.
3. Greet each other in the morning. You will see each other later today.

▪ **MÁS PRÁCTICA** *cuaderno* p. 1
▪ **PARA HISPANOHABLANTES** *cuaderno* p. 1

¿Cómo te llamas?

Me llamo Tomás.

Chicos

Adán	Fernando	Marcos
Alejandro	Francisco	Mateo
Álvaro	Gerardo	Miguel
Andrés	Gilberto	Nicolás
Arturo	Gregorio	Pablo
Benjamín	Guillermo	Patricio
Carlos	Ignacio	Pedro
Cristóbal	Iván	Rafael
Daniel	Jaime	Ramón
David	Javier	Raúl
Diego	Jorge	Ricardo
Eduardo	José	Roberto
Enrique	Juan	Teodoro
Esteban	Julio	Timoteo
Federico	Leonardo	Tomás
Felipe	Luis	Vicente

Me llamo Alma.

Chicas

Alejandra	Elena	Mercedes
Alicia	Emilia	Micaela
Alma	Estefanía	Mónica
Ana	Estela	Natalia
Andrea	Eva	Patricia
Anita	Francisca	Raquel
Bárbara	Graciela	Rosa
Beatriz	Isabel	Rosalinda
Carlota	Juana	Rosana
Carmen	Julia	Sofía
Carolina	Luisa	Susana
Claudia	Margarita	Teresa
Consuelo	María	Verónica
Cristina	Mariana	Victoria
Diana	Marta	Yolanda

Francisco: Hola. ¿Cómo te llamas?

Alma: Me llamo Alma.

Francisco: Encantado, Alma.
Me llamo Francisco.

Alma: Es un placer, Francisco.

el apellido   el nombre

APOYO PARA ESTUDIAR

Chico, chica

In Spanish, all nouns have either a masculine or feminine gender. Masculine nouns usually end in **-o** and feminine nouns usually end in **-a**.

Raquel: Hola.
Me llamo Raquel.

Susana: Me llamo
Susana. Encantada.

Raquel: Igualmente.

Susana: ¿Cómo se
llama el chico?

Raquel: Se llama Jorge.

Jorge: ¿Cómo se
llama la chica?

Enrique: Se llama
Ana.

Rosa: Buenos días. Me llamo Rosa. ¿Cómo te llamas?

Carlos: Mucho gusto, Rosa. Me llamo Carlos.

Rosa: El gusto es mío.

5 Me llamo…

How do these people introduce themselves?

modelo

Marcos García	*Me llamo **Marcos García.***

1. Marta Blanco
2. Raúl Morales
3. Rosa Vivas
4. Felipe Estrada
5. Ana Martínez
6. Ricardo Herrera
7. Arturo Cruz
8. Sofía Ponce

6 ¿Cómo te llamas en español?

Find out the Spanish names of five classmates.

modelo

You: *¿Cómo te llamas?*   **Classmate:** *Me llamo Ana.*

7 ¿Cómo se llama?

- Greet and introduce yourself to a classmate.
- Point to others and find out their names.
- Say good-bye.

modelo

You: *Buenos días. Me llamo… ¿Cómo te llamas?*
Classmate: *Me llamo Mónica. Encantada.*

You: *Es un placer. ¿Cómo se llama la chica?*
Classmate: *Se llama Mariana.*

You: *Adiós. Hasta luego.*
Classmate: *Nos vemos.*

Nota

Boys say **encantado.** Girls say **encantada.**

MÁS PRÁCTICA *cuaderno* p. 2

PARA HISPANOHABLANTES *cuaderno* p. 2

¿De dónde es?

Es de México.

Es de Estados Unidos.

Es de Ecuador.

Es de Perú.

NOTA CULTURAL

Spanish speakers sometimes use the articles **el, la, las,** or **los** before these country names. Their use is optional.

(la) Argentina

(el) Ecuador

(los) Estados Unidos

(las) Filipinas

(el) Paraguay

(el) Perú

(la) República Dominicana

(el) Uruguay

Es de España.

Es de Puerto Rico.

Es de Costa Rica.

Es de Argentina.

22

23

Color Key

Spanish is the official language.

Much Spanish is spoken.

LOS PAÍSES DEL MUNDO HISPANOHABLANTE

Argentina 21

Belice 4

Bolivia 17

Chile 18

Colombia 14

Costa Rica 8

Cuba 10

Ecuador 15

El Salvador 5

España 22

Estados Unidos 1

Filipinas 24

Guam 25

Guatemala 3

Guinea Ecuatorial 23

Honduras 6

México 2

Nicaragua 7

Panamá 9

Paraguay 19

Perú 16

Puerto Rico 12

República Dominicana 11

Uruguay 20

Venezuela 13

Soy de...

Raquel: ¿De dónde es?
Susana: Es de Uruguay.

Ricardo: ¿De dónde eres?
Manuel: Soy de Guatemala.

8

ACTIVIDAD 8  ¿De dónde es?

You and your partner have made some new friends. Tell where they are from. Change roles.

modelo

Tomás: España

You: ¿De dónde es **Tomás**?

Partner: Es de **España**.

1. Estefanía: Panamá
2. Graciela: Cuba
3. Vicente: Costa Rica
4. Ignacio: Honduras
5. Mercedes: México
6. Alejandro: Nicaragua
7. Iván: Puerto Rico
8. Claudia: El Salvador

ACTIVIDAD 9  ¿De dónde eres?

You meet several South Americans. Role-play the situation with a partner, following the model.

modelo

1

You: ¿De dónde eres?   **Partner:** Soy de Ecuador.

ACTIVIDAD 10  Nuevos amigos

Listen as several people introduce themselves to you. Say their country of origin.

modelo

Álvaro: ¿Cuba o Colombia?

Álvaro es de **Colombia**.

1. Alma: ¿Puerto Rico o Costa Rica?
2. Guillermo: ¿Honduras o Estados Unidos?
3. Carmen: ¿Uruguay o Paraguay?
4. Eduardo: ¿México o España?
5. Yolanda: ¿Venezuela o Guatemala?
6. Adán: ¿Argentina o Nicaragua?

ACTIVIDAD 11  ¿Eres de...?

Imagine that everyone in your class is from different Spanish-speaking countries. Choose a country. Ask other students questions to find out which country each person is from. Follow the model.

modelo

Student 1: ¿Eres de Honduras?

You: No.

Student 2: ¿Eres de Guatemala?

You: Sí, soy de Guatemala.

Nota

To say yes, use **sí**. **No** is the same as in English.

■ **MÁS PRÁCTICA** cuaderno pp. 3–4

■ **PARA HISPANOHABLANTES** cuaderno pp. 3–4

El abecedario (El alfabeto)

avión

bota

cerdo

dinero

escalera

flor

gafas

huevo

imán

jarra

kiwi

lápiz

maleta

nieve

ñu

oso

paraguas

queso

reloj

guitarra

sombrero

tijeras

unicornio

video

wafle

xilófono

yogur

zanahoria

ACTIVIDAD **12** 🎧 **Información**

Listen to two people introduce themselves. Complete the information, writing down their first and last names as they are spelled.

1. a. nombre
   b. apellido

2. a. nombre
   b. apellido

ACTIVIDAD **13** 👥 **¿Cómo te llamas?**

Find out the Spanish names of five classmates. Write the names down as they spell them.

modelo

You: _¿Cómo te llamas?_

Classmate: _Me llamo Esteban, E - S - T - E - B - A - N._

(e, ese, te, e, be, a, ene)

Pronunciación

Here is how to say the name of each letter of the Spanish alphabet.

a = a	k = ka	rr = erre
b = be, be larga	l = ele	s = ese
c = ce	m = eme	t = te
d = de	n = ene	u = u
e = e	ñ = eñe	v = ve, uve, ve corta
f = efe	o = o	w = doble ve, doble uve
g = ge	p = pe	x = equis
h = hache	q = cu	y = i griega, ye
i = i	r = ere	z = zeta
j = jota		

■ **MÁS PRÁCTICA** _cuaderno_ p. 5

■ **PARA HISPANOHABLANTES** _cuaderno_ p. 5

Los números de cero a diez

cero

uno

dos

tres

cuatro

cinco

seis

siete

ocho

nueve

diez

Roberto: ¿Cuál es tu teléfono?

Ignacio: 8–9–7–3–1–4–2.

¿Qué día es hoy?

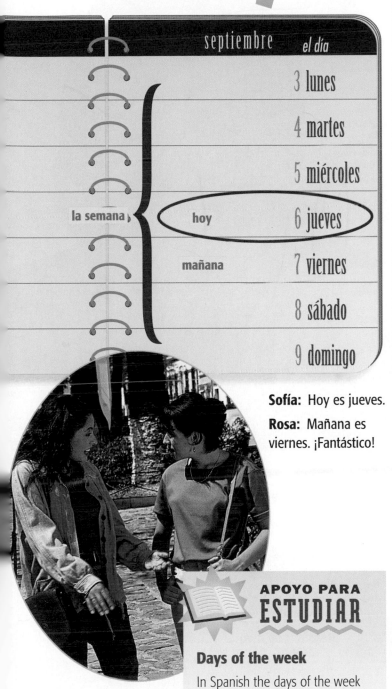

septiembre	el día
	3 lunes
	4 martes
	5 miércoles
hoy	6 jueves
mañana	7 viernes
	8 sábado
	9 domingo

la semana

Sofía: Hoy es jueves.

Rosa: Mañana es viernes. ¡Fantástico!

APOYO PARA ESTUDIAR

Days of the week

In Spanish the days of the week are not capitalized.

ACTIVIDAD **14**  **¿Cuál es tu teléfono?**

Ask for and write down the telephone numbers of five classmates.

modelo

You: *Carolina, ¿cuál es tu teléfono?*

Classmate: *Seis - seis - tres - seis - nueve - cinco - siete.*

ACTIVIDAD **15** ◆ **El día**

Tell what day it is today and tomorrow.

modelo

jueves	*Hoy es **jueves**. Mañana es viernes.*

1. lunes
2. sábado
3. miércoles
4. martes
5. domingo
6. viernes

ACTIVIDAD **16**  **¿Qué día?**

You often forget what day it is. Ask your partner for help. Change roles.

modelo

lunes

You: *¿Qué día es hoy?*

Partner: *Hoy es **lunes**.*

You: *¡Sí! Mañana es martes.*

1. sábado
2. miércoles
3. viernes
4. domingo
5. jueves
6. martes

MÁS PRÁCTICA *cuaderno* p. 6

PARA HISPANOHABLANTES *cuaderno* p. 6

Frases útiles

In the Classroom

Abran los libros.	Open your books.
Cierren los libros.	Close your books.
Escriban…	Write…
Escuchen…	Listen (to)…
Lean…	Read…
Levanten la mano.	Raise your hand.
Miren el pizarrón.	Look at the chalkboard.
la foto.	the photo.
Pásenme la tarea.	Pass in the homework.
Repitan.	Repeat.
Saquen un lápiz.	Take out a pencil.
Siéntense.	Sit down.

Skills

Escuchar

Hablar

Leer

Escribir

Helpful Spanish Phrases

¿Cómo se dice…?	How do you say…?
Más despacio, por favor.	More slowly, please.
No sé.	I don't know.
¿Qué quiere decir…?	What does… mean?
Repita, por favor.	Repeat, please.

In the Text

Cambien de papel.
Change roles.

Completa la conversación.
Complete the conversation.

Contesta las preguntas.
Answer the questions.

Di quién habla.
Say who is speaking.

¿Es cierto o falso?
True or false?

Escoge la respuesta correcta.
Choose the correct response.

    la palabra
     word
    la frase
     phrase
    la oración
     sentence

Escucha…
Listen to…

Explica…
Explain…

Lee…
Read…

Pregúntale a otro(a) estudiante…
Ask another student…

Trabaja con otro(a) estudiante…
Work with another student…

Trabaja en un grupo de…
Work in a group of…

ACTIVIDAD
17 Instrucciones

Repond to your teacher's classroom instructions.

ACTIVIDAD
18 En la clase

What is the teacher telling the students? Match the picture with the instructions below.

a. Abran los libros.   **c.** Miren el pizarrón.
b. Pásenme la tarea.   **d.** Levanten la mano.

ACTIVIDAD
19 ¡Atención, clase!

Take turns giving classroom instructions to partners, who respond appropriately.

ACTIVIDAD
20 ¡Abran los libros!

In groups, look through your book to find examples of the instructions you have learned. Write down the page number for each one.

MÁS PRÁCTICA *cuaderno* p. 7
PARA HISPANOHABLANTES *cuaderno* p. /

Onda Internacional

VIDEO   DVD

El concurso

In this book you will get to know teens from different parts of the Spanish-speaking world. Many of these young people are interested in a contest sponsored by a Spanish magazine for teens called *Onda Internacional.* Why are they interested? Read on!

U.S.A.

Hi! I've got the new edition of Onda Internacional magazine. It has many different articles. There are articles about Spanish-speaking countries, sports, fashion, food, school, leisure activities, and much more. And look! There's a contest. Write an article or prepare a photo essay about what it means to you to be latino or latina. The two winners will travel to parts of the Spanish-speaking world and work for the magazine. Well, get out your cameras, pencils, paper, and ideas, and take part in the contest!

Puerto Rico

Spain

Ecuador

APOYO PARA ESTUDIAR

Reading a poster

When you read a poster, look at the size of lettering, kinds of words, colors, visuals, and any other items it contains. Based on what you already know about *Onda Internacional* and what you see on this poster, why might someone use a poster? Give as many reasons as you can.

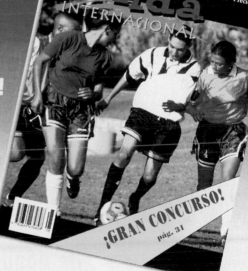

¡Gran concurso!

"¿QUÉ SIGNIFICA SER LATINO DE CORAZÓN?"

¡Lee más información en la revista!

Año 2 No. 1 Precio $2.95

Onda INTERNACIONAL

¡GRAN CONCURSO!
pág. 31

Mexico: Monte Albán

¿Comprendiste?

1. Although you may know little Spanish, are there words whose meaning you can guess? Which ones? What do you think they mean? What helps you guess their meaning?
2. What do you notice different about punctuation? What does that tell you about the meaning of the phrases?

¿Qué piensas?

What about this poster catches your attention or stimulates your interest?

En uso

REPASO Y MÁS COMUNICACIÓN

OBJECTIVES
- Greet people
- Introduce yourself
- Say where you are from
- Exchange phone numbers
- Say which day it is

 ACTIVIDAD 1 En la clase

Marta speaks with two people. Complete the conversations with the words given.

> adiós   hasta   llamo   se   placer   llama
> encantada   llamas   mañana   tardes
> hola   mucho   me
> vemos   mío

Marta: ¡___1___! Me llamo Marta. ¿Cómo te ___2___?

Andrea: ___3___ llamo Andrea. ___4___.

Marta: Igualmente. ¿Cómo se ___5___ el chico?

Andrea: ___6___ llama Mateo.

Marta: Es un ___7___, Andrea. Nos ___8___.

Andrea: ___9___, Marta. ___10___ luego.

Marta: Buenas ___11___, Mateo. Me ___12___ Marta.

Mateo: ___13___ gusto, Marta.

Marta: El gusto es ___14___. Hasta ___15___.

ACTIVIDAD 2 ¿De dónde eres?

You are talking to some international students who say where they and their friends are from. Where are they from?

modelo

Luisa (Chile) / Jorge (Puerto Rico)

*Me llamo **Luisa**. Soy de **Chile**. **Jorge** es de **Puerto Rico**.*

1. Julio (Panamá) / Mónica (Bolivia)
2. Diana (Estados Unidos) / Rafael (Uruguay)
3. Patricio (España) / Alejandra (Guatemala)
4. Natalia (Argentina) / Benjamín (México)
5. Gregorio (Cuba) / Verónica (El Salvador)

Now you can...
- greet people.
- introduce yourself.

To review
- greetings and introductions, see pp. 2–5.

Now you can...
- say where you are from.

To review
- saying where you are from, see pp. 6–8.

Now you can...
• exchange phone numbers.

To review
• numbers, see p. 12.

ACTIVIDAD **3** **Teléfonos**

You need some phone numbers. With a partner, role-play conversations asking for friends' numbers. Follow the model.

Rosana
530-4401

modelo

Rosana: 530-4401

You: *Rosana, ¿cuál es tu teléfono?*

Rosana: *Cinco - tres - cero - cuatro - cuatro - cero - uno.*

1. Timoteo: 927-2296
2. Mariana: 820-3981
3. Cristóbal: 450-5649
4. Emilia: 392-4100
5. Leonardo: 758-3141
6. otro(a) estudiante: ¿?

Now you can...
• say which day it is.

To review
• days of the week, see p. 13.

ACTIVIDAD **4** **¿Qué día es hoy?**

Tell what day it is today, based on what tomorrow is.

modelo

Mañana es viernes.

Hoy es jueves.

1. Mañana es domingo.
2. Mañana es miércoles.
3. Mañana es lunes.
4. Mañana es jueves.
5. Mañana es martes.
6. Mañana es sábado.

Hola

Greet a partner and introduce yourself. Talk about which day it is today and tomorrow. Say good-bye.

modelo

You: *Hola. Me llamo…
¿Cómo te llamas?*

Partner: *Mucho gusto. Me llamo…*

You: *¿Qué día es…?*

Mucha información

Imagine that everyone has a new identity. Ask three classmates for the information needed to complete the chart.

modelo

You: *Hola. Me llamo… ¿Cómo te llamas?*

Student 1: *Es un placer. Me llamo Carolina. Soy de Perú. ¿De dónde eres?*

You: *Soy de Honduras. ¿Cuál es tu teléfono?*

Student 1: *Siete - tres - cero - siete - seis - seis - dos. ¿Cuál es tu…?*

Nombre	País	Teléfono
1. Carolina	Perú	730-7662
2.		
3.		

En tu propia voz

Escritura Write to your new pen pal. Include the following information.

- Write a greeting.
- Introduce yourself.
- Say where you are from.
- Write three questions for your new pen pal to answer.

En resumen

REPASO DE VOCABULARIO

GREETINGS

Greeting People

Buenos días.	Good morning.
Buenas tardes.	Good afternoon.
Buenas noches.	Good evening.
Hola.	Hello.

Responding

El gusto es mío.	The pleasure is mine.
Encantado(a).	Delighted/Pleased to meet you.
Es un placer.	It's a pleasure.
Igualmente.	Same here.
Mucho gusto.	Nice to meet you.

Saying Good-bye

Adiós.	Good-bye.
Hasta luego.	See you later.
Hasta mañana.	See you tomorrow.
Nos vemos.	See you later.

INTRODUCING YOURSELF

el apellido	last name, surname
el nombre	name, first name
¿Cómo te llamas?	What is your name?
¿Cómo se llama?	What is his/her name?
Me llamo…	My name is…
Se llama…	His/Her name is…

SAYING WHERE YOU ARE FROM

¿De dónde eres?	Where are you from?
¿De dónde es?	Where is he/she from?
Soy de…	I am from…
Es de…	He/She is from…

EXCHANGING PHONE NUMBERS

¿Cuál es tu teléfono?	What is your phone number?

Numbers from Zero to Ten

cero	zero
uno	one
dos	two
tres	three
cuatro	four
cinco	five
seis	six
siete	seven
ocho	eight
nueve	nine
diez	ten

SAYING WHICH DAY IT IS

¿Qué día es hoy?	What day is today?
Hoy es…	Today is…
Mañana es…	Tomorrow is…
el día	day
hoy	today
mañana	tomorrow
la semana	week

Days of the Week

lunes	Monday
martes	Tuesday
miércoles	Wednesday
jueves	Thursday
viernes	Friday
sábado	Saturday
domingo	Sunday

OTHER WORDS AND PHRASES

no	no
sí	yes

Skills

escribir	to write
escuchar	to listen
hablar	to talk, to speak
leer	to read

SPANISH IS THE OFFICIAL LANGUAGE OF THESE COUNTRIES:

Argentina	Argentina
Bolivia	Bolivia
Chile	Chile
Colombia	Colombia
Costa Rica	Costa Rica
Cuba	Cuba
Ecuador	Ecuador
El Salvador	El Salvador
España	Spain
Guatemala	Guatemala
Guinea Ecuatorial	Equatorial Guinea
Honduras	Honduras
México	Mexico
Nicaragua	Nicaragua
Panamá	Panama
Paraguay	Paraguay
Perú	Peru
Puerto Rico	Puerto Rico
República Dominicana	Dominican Republic
Uruguay	Uruguay
Venezuela	Venezuela

ESTADOS UNIDOS

MI MUNDO

ALASKA

CANADÁ

NUEVA YORK

SAN JOSÉ ESTADOS UNIDOS CHICAGO

LOS ÁNGELES
SAN DIEGO

DALLAS

ISLAS HAWAI EL PASO HOUSTON

SAN ANTONIO MIAMI

MÉXICO

STANDARDS

Communication
- Greeting and introducing others
- Saying where people live and are from
- Expressing likes and dislikes
- Describing people and their clothing
- Identifying family members, their ages, and their birthdays
- Expressing possession

Cultures
- The influence of Spanish speakers in the United States
- Tejano music
- A traditional birthday celebration
- Traditional holidays

Connections
- Social Studies: Hispanic traditions and events and those of other communities in the U.S.
- Social Studies: Hispanic celebrations and those of other communities in the U.S.

Comparisons
- Unique music forms
- Events marking transition from childhood to adulthood
- Important holidays

Communities
- Using Spanish in Spanish-speaking communities for personal enjoyment
- Using Spanish in the workplace

MURALES are popular art sometimes found on the sides of buildings in L.A. Often their artists are Chicano, or Mexican American. What street art have you seen?

INTERNET Preview
CLASSZONE.COM

- More About Latinos
- Webquest
- Self-Check Quizzes
- Flashcards
- Writing Center
- Online Workbook
- eEdition Plus Online

POBLACIÓN: 281,421,906

POBLACIÓN DE DESCENDENCIA HISPANA:
35,305,818

CIUDAD CON MÁS LATINOS: Nueva York

**CIUDAD CON MAYOR PORCENTAJE (%)
DE LATINOS:** El Paso

EN ESTADOS UNIDOS

Las ciudades que ves en el mapa tienen un gran número de latinos. En esta unidad vas a visitar Miami, San Antonio y Los Ángeles. ¡Vamos!

> **i More About Latinos**
> CLASSZONE.COM

FAJITAS reflect the Mexican influence on Los Angeles cuisine. What Mexican dishes have you tried?

EL ÁLAMO, a former Spanish mission from 1718, reminds us how long Spanish influences have been in San Antonio. In what parts of the U.S. might someone be able to visit a former Spanish mission?

EL SÁNDWICH CUBANO, filled with ham, pork, and cheese, is a popular meal in Miami. Can you guess which ethnic group brought this food to Miami?

CASCARONES, eggshells filled with confetti, are used to celebrate the April **Fiesta.** People break them on each other's heads for good luck. What do you do to celebrate events in your community?

JON SECADA, Cuban American singer and songwriter, performs in English and Spanish. He has won Grammy awards for his work. What other Latino musicians do you know?

- Comunicación

- Culturas

- Conexiones

- Comparaciones

- Comunidades

MI MUNDO

¡En español! helps you become
a competent learner of Spanish in these five ways:

Communication

**Communicate in
another language!**

How do we get acquainted
with others? We converse,
ask, explain, describe; we
talk. In what other ways do
we give and receive information
that develops relationships?

Comparisons

Compare your culture and language to other ones.

Studying and learning Spanish give you a fresh understanding of
your own language and culture. You discover comfortable similarities
and interesting differences. For example, word order in Spanish and
English sentences
sometimes differs.
What other differences
in language have you
found? The photo
offers a clue.

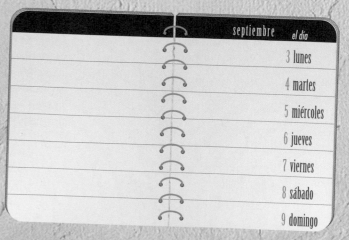

septiembre	el día
	3 lunes
	4 martes
	5 miércoles
	6 jueves
	7 viernes
	8 sábado
	9 domingo

Connections

Connect new information to other subjects.

Graphs and charts from mathematics or social studies can be used to report information. And Spanish can help you learn about other subjects. The photo offers a clue to one subject. What is it? Can you think of others?

Cultures

Learn about other cultures.

Daily life is woven into each language and Spanish reflects a way of life. What celebrations might differ between your culture and someone else's culture? The photo offers a clue to one. Can you think of others?

Communities

Use Spanish in your community!
A group of people who share common interests and a common location make a community. Identify different communities in your area. Are there any where you can practice your Spanish?

Fíjate

Each of the following statements relates to one of the areas described (Communication, Comparisons, Connections, Cultures, Communities). Determine which area is best represented by each statement.

1. Writing to pen pals, listening to music with Spanish lyrics, and reading information in Spanish on the Internet are ways to use Spanish language skills.

2. Calendars printed in Spanish usually end each week with Sunday, not Saturday.

3. Murals painted by chicanos in Los Angeles would be interesting subject matter for an art class.

4. For their 15th birthday, many Hispanic girls celebrate a formal event known as a *quinceañera*.

5. As a student of Spanish, you may be able to help Spanish-speaking clients shopping in stores in your neighborhood.

ETAPA

1

¡Bienvenido a Miami!

OBJECTIVES

- Greet others

- Introduce others

- Say where people are from

- Express likes

¿Qué ves?

Look at the photo of Máximo Gómez Park in Miami.

1. Which people do you think are the main characters in this **Etapa**?

2. Look at their gestures. What are they doing?

3. What do the photos tell you about the community?

CITY OF MIAMI
MAXIMO GOMEZ PARK
DOMINO CLUB   OPEN DAILY 9A.M. TO 8P.M.

En contexto

VIDEO DVD AUDIO

VOCABULARIO

Francisco García Flores has just moved into his new community in Miami. He is getting to know the people there. Look at the illustrations. They will help you understand the meanings of the words in blue and answer the questions on the next page.

un policía

A **La chica** es Alma Cifuentes. **El chico** es Francisco García. Son **amigos.**

Alma: ¿Qué tal?
Francisco: Estoy bien, ¿y tú?
Alma: Regular.

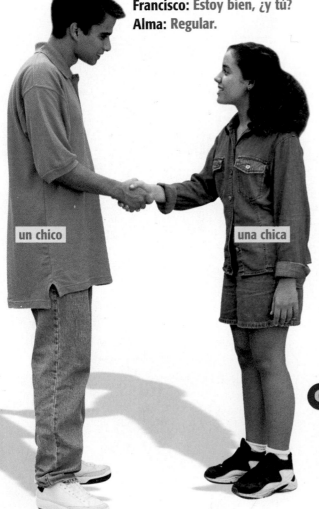

un chico

una chica

B **El policía vive en el apartamento.**

un apartamento

una mujer

C **Mujer:** Gracias.
Francisco: De nada.

una familia

una señorita
una señora
un señor
un muchacho

D La familia García vive en **una**
casa. La señora García es **doctora.**

Francisco: Alma, **te presento a** mi familia.
Señor García: Mucho gusto. ¿Cómo estás?
Alma: Bien, gracias. ¿Cómo está usted?
Señor García: No muy bien hoy.

una maestra

una estudiante

E La mujer es **maestra**
y **la muchacha** es
estudiante.

TENEMOS TAMALES EN HOJA

un hombre

F **El hombre** es **el señor** Estrada.
Alma es **una amiga.**

Alma: **Le presento a** mi amigo, Francisco.
Señor Estrada: Encantado. ¿Cómo estás?
Francisco: Muy bien, gracias, ¿y usted?
Señor Estrada: Si es lunes, **estoy terrible.**

una casa

Preguntas personales

Online Workbook
CLASSZONE.COM

1. ¿Tienes amigos?
2. ¿Eres maestro(a) o estudiante?
3. ¿Vives en un apartamento o en una casa?
4. ¿Cómo se llaman las personas de tu familia?
5. ¿Cómo estás hoy?

En vivo

VIDEO DVD AUDIO

DIÁLOGO

Alma **Francisco** **David** **Arturo** **Sr. Estrada**

PARA ESCUCHAR • STRATEGY: LISTENING

Listen to intonation A rising or falling voice (intonation) helps a listener understand meaning as much as individual words do. The voice often rises at the end of a question and falls at the end of a statement. Listen carefully. Can you tell which sentences are questions? Being a good listener will help you become a good speaker. When you speak, try to imitate the intonation.

¡Bienvenido!

1 ▶ Alma: Hola, me llamo Alma Cifuentes. Soy tu vecina. Ésa es mi casa.
Francisco: Mucho gusto, Alma.

5 ▶ Francisco: ¡Ay, David! Alma, te presento a David. David es el monstruo de Miami.
David: ¡No soy monstruo! ¡Y no soy de Miami!
Alma: Es un placer, señor David.

6 ▶ Alma: Pues, ¿de dónde son ustedes?
Francisco: Nosotros somos de muchos lugares. Mamá es de Puerto Rico. Papá es de México. Yo soy de Puerto Rico y David es de San Antonio.
Alma: Entonces, ¡bienvenido a Miami!

7 ▶ Arturo: ¡Alma, chica! ¿Qué tal?
Alma: Muy bien, gracias, Arturo. Arturo, te presento a Francisco García. Él es mi vecino.
Arturo: Francisco, es un placer.
Francisco: Igualmente, Arturo.

 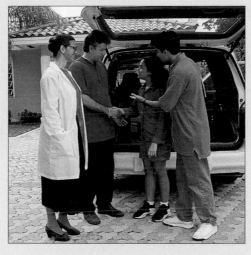 

2 ► **Alma:** Y tú, ¿cómo te llamas?
Francisco: ¿Yo? Yo me llamo Francisco García Flores.
Alma: Encantada, Francisco.

3 ► **Francisco:** Papá, te presento a Alma Cifuentes. Alma, mi papá.
Sr. García: Es un placer, Alma.
Alma: Mucho gusto, señor García.

4 ► **Francisco:** Mamá, Alma Cifuentes. Alma, mi mamá.
Sra. García: Mucho gusto, Alma.
Alma: El gusto es mío, señora.

8 ► **Alma:** A Arturo le gusta mucho correr. A mí me gusta también. ¿Te gusta correr, Francisco?
Francisco: No, no me gusta mucho correr.

9 ► **Sr. Estrada:** ¡Alma! ¿Cómo estás hoy?
Alma: Muy bien, señor Estrada, ¿y usted?
Sr. Estrada: Hoy es lunes, ¿no? Si es lunes, estoy terrible.
Alma: Le presento a mi amigo Francisco.
Francisco: Es un placer, señor Estrada.

10 ► **Francisco:** Este concurso es muy interesante.

En acción

VOCABULARIO Y GRAMÁTICA

OBJECTIVES

- Greet others
- Introduce others
- Say where people are from
- Express likes
- *Use familiar and formal greetings*
- *Use subject pronouns and the verb* **ser**
- *Use* **ser de** *to express origin*
- *Use verbs to talk about what you like to do*

ACTIVIDAD 1

La conversación

Escuchar Decide whether each statement about the dialog is true or false. Say **sí** or **no**.

modelo

Alma introduces herself.

Sí.

---

1. Francisco is glad to meet Alma.
2. Francisco's last name is García Flores.
3. Señora García meets Alma.
4. David is from Miami.
5. Francisco likes to run.
6. Alma is not very well.

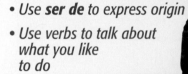

ACTIVIDAD 2

¿Quién habla?

Escuchar Who is speaking in each case: **Alma,
Francisco,** or **el señor Estrada**?

modelo

«Papá es de México.»
Francisco

1. «Hola, me llamo Alma Cifuentes.»
2. «Yo soy de Puerto Rico.»
3. «A Arturo le gusta mucho correr.»
4. «Si es lunes, estoy terrible.»
5. «¡Bienvenido a Miami!»
6. «Encantada, Francisco.»
7. «El gusto es mío, señora.»
8. «No me gusta mucho correr.»
9. «Este concurso es muy interesante.»

ACTIVIDAD 3

¡Hola!

Hablar Introduce yourself to the classmate that
sits next to you. Then change roles.

modelo

Estudiante A: *Hola, me llamo David Cisneros.*

Estudiante B: *Mucho gusto, David.*

También se dice

There are different ways to say *boy* and *girl* in Spanish.

- **chaval(a):** Spain
- **chavo(a):** Mexico
- **pibe(a):** Argentina
- **muchacho(a):** many countries
- **joven:** "teenager" in many countries
- **niño(a):** used for younger boys and
  girls in many countries
- **chico(a):** many countries

ACTIVIDAD 4

¿Quién es?

Hablar Tell who each person of the community is: **una chica, un chico, un hombre,** or **una mujer.**

modelo
Es **una mujer**.

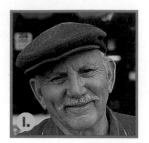
1.

2.

3.

4.

5.

Conexiones

Los estudios sociales Every March the Cuban community of Miami celebrates its heritage at the **Festival de Calle Ocho,** the most popular street in "Little Havana" and Miami's center of Cuban culture. The festival began in 1978 and offers music, dance, visual arts, and food.

PARA HACER:

• Where do you think the name Festival de Calle Ocho comes from?

• Find out the names of some foods available in the Cuban community in Miami.

• Find out how another Latin American community celebrates its heritage, and report on it.

En la comunidad

Hablar Identify people in Alma's community. Complete the sentences with the words below.

doctora

chica   **señora**

policía

maestro   **estudiante**

modelo

La muchacha es ___estudiante___ .

(maestro / estudiante)

1. El señor Nieves es ___ .
   (policía / señora)

2. La mujer es la ___ Vidal.
   (doctora / maestro)

3. Ernesto es ___ .
   (chica / estudiante)

4. El hombre es ___ .
   (doctora / maestro)

5. La ___ Guzmán es una vecina de Alma.
   (señora / estudiante)

6. El chico y la ___ son amigos.
   (maestro / chica)

7. El ___ es un vecino.
   (estudiante / doctora)

8. El señor Gómez es ___ .
   (chica / policía)

9. Arturo y la ___ Morales son amigos. (estudiante / señora)

10. La ___ vive en una casa.
    (chica / maestro)

¿Quiénes son?

Escribir Write who each person is and where he or she lives.

modelo

la señorita Álvarez:

***La señorita Álvarez** es maestra. Vive en **un apartamento**.*

1. el señor Gómez:

2. Alma:

3. la señora García:

4. Arturo:

Familiar and Formal Greetings

▶ There are different ways to say *How are you?* in Spanish.

Familiar:

Mr. Estrada greets Alma by saying:

—¡Alma!
¿Cómo estás hoy?
*Alma! **How are you** today?*

¿Cómo estás? is a familiar greeting.

Use with: • a friend
• a family member
• someone younger

Another familiar greeting: **¿Qué tal?**

....

Tú is a familiar way to say *you*.

Formal:

If Alma had spoken first, she might have said:

—¡Señor Estrada!
¿Cómo está usted?
*Mr. Estrada! **How are you?***

¿Cómo está usted? is a formal greeting.

Use with: • a person you don't know
• someone older
• someone for whom you want to show respect

Usted is a formal way to say *you*.

7 Gramática

¿Quién?

Hablar/Leer To whom is Arturo speaking in each case?

1. ¡Hola! ¿Cómo estás? (Francisco / el señor Estrada)
2. Buenas tardes. ¿Cómo está usted? (la señora García / Alma)
3. ¡Hola, chica! ¿Qué tal? (David / Alma)
4. Muy bien, gracias. ¿Y usted? (el señor García / David)
5. ¡Hola! ¿Qué tal? (la señora García / Francisco)
6. Buenos días. ¿Cómo estás? (el señor Gómez / Alma)

MÁS PRÁCTICA *cuaderno* p. 13
PARA HISPANOHABLANTES *cuaderno* p. 11

Online Workbook
CLASSZONE.COM

¿Formal o familiar?

Hablar/Escribir Ask each person how he or she is.

modelo

Juan

¿Cómo estás, **Juan**?

1. Antonio
2. señorita Díaz
3. Felipe
4. señor Castro
5. Luisa
6. señora Ramos
7. Paquita
8. doctora Flores
9. otro(a) estudiante
10. tu maestro(a)

¿Qué tal?

Escribir Write what you think each pair says to greet one another.

Conexiones

La geografía The United States is a nation of great ethnic diversity. The Spanish-speaking population is the fastest growing ethnic segment. There are Spanish-speaking people of every nationality in the U.S. Some of the largest groups come from Mexico, Puerto Rico, Cuba, and the Dominican Republic.

PARA HACER:
- Identify the listed countries on a map.
- Categorize them by region: Norteamérica, Sudamérica, Centroamérica, or el Caribe.
- List their capitals.

El Salvador	Guatemala
México	Colombia
Puerto Rico	Argentina
Cuba	Panamá
la República Dominicana	Venezuela
	Perú

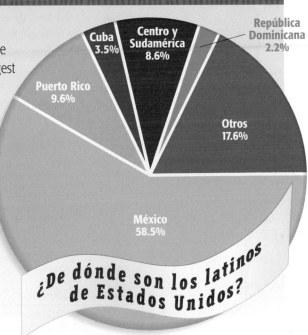

¿De dónde son los latinos de Estados Unidos?

Hablar Role-play the greetings with another student. Change roles.

modelo

Juan–señor Álvarez

Juan: *¿Cómo está usted, señor Álvarez?*

Sr. Álvarez: *Bien, gracias, ¿y tú, Juan?*

Juan: *Regular.*

1. Pablo–Felipe
2. señora Ruiz–señor Muñoz
3. Francisco–señor Fernández
4. Juan–Julia
5. señora Campos–Susana
6. doctor García–Raúl
7. Javier–Miguel
8. señor Guzman–Anita

GRAMÁTICA

Describing People: Subject Pronouns and the Verb ser

To discuss people in Spanish, you will often use **subject pronouns**. When you want to describe a person or explain who he or she is, use the verb **ser**.

When Alma introduces Francisco to Arturo, she uses a **subject pronoun** with **ser**.

—**Él es** mi vecino.
He is my neighbor.

Francisco uses other examples.

—**Nosotros somos** de muchos lugares.
We are from many places.

—**Yo soy** de Puerto Rico.
I am from Puerto Rico.

Singular	Plural
yo soy *I am*	**nosotros(as) somos** *we are*
tú eres *familiar* *you are*	**vosotros(as) sois** *you are*
usted es *formal* *you are*	**ustedes son** *you are*
él, ella es *he, she is*	**ellos(as) son** *they are*

Vosotros(as) is only used in Spain.
Ustedes is formal in Spain; formal and familiar in Latin America.

If Alma were to say that someone is a neighbor, she would say:

—**Él es un** vecino.

However, if she were to say that someone is a policeman, she would say:

—**Él es** policía.

The word **un** or **una** does not appear before a profession.

¡Descríbelos!

Leer Use a pronoun to explain who each person from the community is. Use each pronoun only once.

> <u>Ella</u> *es una amiga.*

1. _____ eres doctora.
2. _____ somos amigas.
3. _____ es doctor.
4. _____ son amigas.
5. _____ somos estudiantes.
6. _____ son amigos.
7. _____ es maestra.

a. ellos
b. tú
c. ustedes
d. él
e. ella
f. nosotros
g. nosotras

¡Escucha! ¿Quién es?

Escuchar Choose the correct sentence to indicate who the person is.

1. a. Ella se llama Francisca.
   b. Él se llama Francisco.
2. a. Ellas son policías.
   b. Ellos son policías.
3. a. A él le gusta correr.
   b. A ella le gusta correr.
4. a. Ella no está bien.
   b. Él no está bien.
5. a. Ellos son estudiantes.
   b. Ellas son estudiantes.

MÁS PRÁCTICA *cuaderno* p. 14

PARA HISPANOHABLANTES *cuaderno* p. 12

¡A dibujar!

Hablar Choose a person from the list. On a piece of paper, draw an item to represent this person. Take turns with other students guessing the people represented in the drawings.

> modelo
>
> **Estudiante A:** *¿Eres maestra?*
> **Estudiante B:** *No, no soy maestra.*
> **Estudiante C:** *¿Eres policía?*
> **Estudiante B:** *Sí, soy policía.*

estudiante
doctor/doctora
maestro/maestra
policía

APOYO PARA ESTUDIAR

Cracking the language code

Spanish is not translated English. Spanish has its own way of expressing ideas. Grammar is the rules for putting words together in order to make sense. How many expressions can you find where Spanish and English express the same idea differently? Think about these when practicing so you prepare yourself for real communication. Read Spanish examples carefully. Read English equivalents when you need help.

Yo soy...

Escribir Think of words or names of professions you would use to describe various people in your community. Write five sentences using elements from the first two columns. You can decide what profession or description to write for the green column.

modelo

Ella es doctora.

Nota

To make a noun plural, add **-s** if it ends in a vowel, **-es** if it ends in a consonant: amiga**s**, doctor**es**.

■ **MÁS COMUNICACIÓN** p. R1

1
yo
él
nosotros
ellas
tú
ella
ellos
ustedes

2
eres
soy
somos
es
son

3
¿?

NOTA CULTURAL

Spanish is the native language of about half the residents of Miami. Cubans are the majority group within Spanish-speaking Miami, but there are people from all over the Spanish-speaking world here. When in Miami, you can use your Spanish to make new friends.

GRAMÁTICA

Using ser de to Express Origin

▶ To say where a person is from use: **ser** + **de** + **place**

San Antonio, Texas

—David **es de** San Antonio.

—Papá **es de** México.

MÉXICO

Francisco says:
—Nosotros **somos de muchos lugares**.
*We **are from** many places.*

—Mamá **es de** Puerto Rico.
—Yo **soy de** Puerto Rico.

PUERTO RICO

ACTIVIDAD 15 Gramática

¿De dónde son?

Hablar/Escribir Where are the exchange students from?

modelo

Elena / Argentina
Elena es de Argentina.

1. Carlos / España
2. tú / Panamá
3. nosotros / México
4. Ana y Felipe / Bolivia
5. ellos / Chile
6. Carmen y yo / Costa Rica
7. ella / Miami
8. ellas / Puerto Rico
9. él / Cuba
10. yo / ¿?

ACTIVIDAD 16 Gramática

¡Son de muchos lugares!

Hablar You are in a new community. Take turns with another student asking and answering questions about where the people are from.

modelo

Ana: México

Estudiante A: ¿De dónde es **Ana**?

Estudiante B: Ella es de **México**.

los policías: Chile

Estudiante B: ¿De dónde son **los policías**?

Estudiante A: Ellos son de **Chile**.

1. los muchachos: Guatemala
2. la muchacha: Perú
3. Luisa: Ecuador
4. Ramón: Venezuela
5. las mujeres: El Salvador
6. Paco: Uruguay
7. Inés: Colombia
8. los hombres: Argentina
9. David: México
10. Ana: Honduras

MÁS PRÁCTICA *cuaderno* p. 15

PARA HISPANOHABLANTES *cuaderno* p. 13

Online Workbook
CLASSZONE.COM

Es de...

Hablar Take turns with two other students telling where these people are from.

modelo

*Yo soy de California. Mamá es de Nebraska. Linda es de Chicago. Pablo es de Washington. (**o:** Jorge y María son de Nueva York.)*

I. you

2. a family member

3. two friends

4. a neighbor

5. a teacher

¡Somos de lugares diferentes!

Hablar/Escribir Imagine that you are from another place. Circulate around the class and ask other students where they are from. Make a list and then report back to the class what you find out.

modelo

Tú: *¿De dónde eres, Juan?*

Juan: *Soy de San Francisco.*

Nombre	Es de...
1. Juan	San Francisco
2.	
3.	
4.	
5.	

NOTA CULTURAL

Much of Florida's architecture reflects Spanish influences. The private Vizcaya mansion (left) in Miami and buildings at Flagler College (right) in St. Augustine are especially good examples.

Using Verbs to Talk About What You Like to Do

When you want to talk about what you like to do, use the phrase:

Me gusta + *infinitive*

> The *infinitive* is the basic form of a verb.

Other helpful phrases to talk about what people like:

Te gusta correr.	*You like **to run**.*
Le gusta correr.	*He/She likes **to run**.*
¿Te gusta correr?	*Do you like **to run**?*
¿Le gusta correr?	*Does he/she like **to run**?*

Arturo would say: —**Me gusta correr.**
*I like **to run**.*

To say someone doesn't like to do something, use **no** before the phrase.

—**No** me gusta **correr**.
*I **don't like** to run.*

Vocabulario

Infinitives

bailar

cantar

comer

escribir

leer

nadar

patinar

trabajar

¿Qué te gusta?

ACTIVIDAD 19 Gramática

Me gusta...

Leer/Hablar Respond **sí** or **no** to the following statements.

1. Me gusta bailar.

2. Me gusta cantar.

3. Me gusta trabajar.

4. Me gusta escribir correo electrónico *(e-mail)*.

5. Me gusta patinar sobre hielo *(on ice)*.

6. Me gusta leer novelas.

7. Me gusta comer tacos.

8. Me gusta nadar.

9. Me gusta patinar.

10. Me gusta hablar por teléfono.

MÁS PRÁCTICA *cuaderno* p. 16

PARA HISPANOHABLANTES *cuaderno* p. 14

Online Workbook
CLASSZONE.COM

ACTIVIDAD 20

Preferencias

Hablar Ask another student what he or she likes to do. Change roles.

modelo

Estudiante A: *¿Te gusta patinar?*

Estudiante B: *Sí, me gusta patinar.*

Estudiante A
PREGUNTAS

¿Te gusta...?

 1.

 2.

 3.

 4.

 5.

 6.

Estudiante B
RESPUESTAS

Sí, me gusta...   No, no me gusta...

ACTIVIDAD 21

Presentaciones

Hablar Work in groups of three. Your friends don't know each other. Introduce them.

modelo

señor Estrada–David

Estudiante A: *Señor Estrada, le presento a mi amigo, David.*

Señor Estrada: *Mucho gusto, David.*

David: *Igualmente, señor Estrada.*

Nota

To make a formal introduction, use **Le presento a…** To make a familiar introduction, use **Te presento a…**

1. Alma–Jorge
2. señor Gómez–Carlos
3. Arturo–David
4. señorita Álvarez–Manuel
5. señora Delgado–Emilio
6. señor Montenegro–Magdalena

ACTIVIDAD 22

¡Un nuevo amigo!

Escuchar Listen to what your new friend says. Answer the questions.

1. ¿Cómo se llama el chico?
   a. Ángel
   b. Enrique
2. ¿De dónde es?
   a. Los Ángeles
   b. Miami
3. ¿Cómo está hoy?
   a. Muy bien
   b. Bien
4. ¿Qué le gusta hacer?
   a. bailar y patinar
   b. bailar y cantar
5. ¿Le gusta trabajar?
   a. sí
   b. no

ACTIVIDAD 23

¿Quién eres tú?

Escribir/Hablar Write about yourself. Then talk with another student.

modelo

¡Hola! Me llamo Elena. Yo soy de Miami. Vivo en un apartamento. Me gusta leer, bailar y cantar.

Nota

To say what kind of home you live in, use the phrase **Vivo en…**

■ **MÁS COMUNICACIÓN** p. R1

Online Workbook
CLASSZONE.COM

Pronunciación

Refrán

Pronunciación de las vocales The vowels a, e, i, o, u are always pronounced the same way. One word in Spanish that uses all the vowels is the word for the animal known as a bat. It is **murciélago.** Try to pronounce it.

Here is a popular nonsense rhyme that children use when playing games. It is the Spanish version of "Eeny, meeny, miney, moe." Use it to practice vowels.

Tin, marín
de dos pingües
cúcara, mácara
títere, fue.

SOY UN MURCIÉLAGO.

Una estudiante de Nicaragua

Una chica viaja sola[1] en avión[2] a Miami. Se llama Eva. Eva es de Nicaragua, pero este año estudia en Estados Unidos. Eva es estudiante del programa del Intercambio Académico Internacional. A Eva le gusta viajar y le gusta practicar el inglés. Pero ahora Eva está un poco tímida.

En el aeropuerto internacional de Miami los letreros[3] están en inglés ¡y español! Eva se siente[4] más contenta. Los oficiales de la aduana[5] también son bilingües y muy simpáticos. Eva ya tiene confianza[6] y va

---

[1] travels alone
[2] airplane
[3] signs
[4] feels
[5] customs
[6] has confidence

AeroÁguila

billete de pasajero

Emitido por
Transportes AeroÁguila, S.A.
Managua/Aeropuerto de Managua
Miembro del Grupo Internacional
de Transportes Aéreos

El pasajero debe examinar
cuidadosamente este billete,
especialmente el aviso de las
condiciones del contrato.

MÉNDEZ E

MANAGUA

047:4411:611:136:2

64490402 23SEP
TAP AEROAGUILA
MANAGUA

a la sala de espera[7]. Una simpática familia norteamericana la espera con un letrero que dice, «¡Bienvenida Eva! Welcome Eva!»

Eva llora[8] de gusto y de emoción.

«Sí, voy a estar contenta. ¡Voy a pasar un buen año aquí en Miami!»

---

[7] waiting room
[8] cries

Online Workbook
CLASSZONE.COM

¿Comprendiste?

1. ¿Quién es Eva?
2. ¿De dónde es ella?
3. ¿Adónde viaja?
4. ¿Qué le gusta?

¿Qué piensas?

1. How do you think it would feel to live in another country for a year?
2. What would you have to do to prepare for such a trip?
3. What do you think you would learn, besides a new language?

En uso
REPASO Y MÁS COMUNICACIÓN

OBJECTIVES
- Greet others
- Introduce others
- Say where people are from
- Express likes

ACTIVIDAD 1 ¡Hola!

You hear this conversation in your community.
Complete the conversation with the appropriate words.

bien   gusto   usted   cómo   gracias
está   estás   tal   tú   presento

Carlos: Hola, Sara. ¿Qué __1__?

Sara: Muy bien, gracias, ¿y __2__?

Carlos: No muy __3__. Hoy es lunes.

Sara: Carlos, te __4__ a mi maestro de español, el señor Sánchez.

Sr. Sánchez: Mucho __5__, Carlos. ¿__6__ estás?

Carlos: Estoy terrible. ¿Y __7__? ¿Cómo __8__ hoy?

Sr. Sánchez: Regular. ¿Cómo __9__ tú, Sara?

Sara: Estoy muy bien, __10__.

ACTIVIDAD 2 Te presento a...

Introduce the following people.

modelo

Daniela–Antonio

Daniela, te presento a **Antonio.**

1. doctora Cruz–Miguel
2. Jorge–Gabriel
3. señora Ramos–Eva
4. señor Orozco–Víctor
5. Celia–Yolanda
6. Pablo–Juan
7. señorita Quintana–Ana
8. Mónica–Octavio

Now you can...
- greet others.

To review
- vocabulary for greetings, see p. 28.
- familiar and formal greetings, see p. 36.

Now you can...
- introduce others.

To review
- making introductions, see p. 29 and p. 45.

ACTIVIDAD 3 ¿Quiénes son?

Who are these people at a party and where are they from?

modelo

la señora Moreno: policía (Bolivia)

*Ella es **policía**. Es de **Bolivia**.*

1. el señor Ortiz: maestro (Venezuela)
2. Julia: mi amiga (Paraguay)
3. tú: estudiante (Miami)
4. María y Rosa: amigas (Colombia)
5. Roberto y yo: vecinos (Chile)
6. usted: doctor (Puerto Rico)
7. la señora Romero: mi vecina (Los Ángeles)
8. José y yo: amigos (Guatemala)
9. yo: estudiante (Estados Unidos)
10. las mujeres: doctoras (Costa Rica)

ACTIVIDAD 4 Preferencias

What does the person like or not like to do?

modelo

Marta: sí

Le gusta correr.

tú: no

No te gusta patinar.

1. Adriana: sí
2. la maestra: sí
3. tú: sí
4. ella: no

5. Raúl: no
6. yo: sí
7. yo: no
8. tú: sí

Now you can...
- say where people are from.

To review
- subject pronouns and the verb **ser**, see p. 38.
- **ser de** to express origin, see p. 41.

Now you can...
- express likes.

To review
- verbs to talk about what you like to do, see p. 43.

 **Nuevos amigos**

PARA CONVERSAR
STRATEGY: SPEAKING

Understand, then speak Make sure you understand what your partner says. If you don't, say **Repite, por favor** (*Please repeat*). Once you understand, speaking clearly helps make you understood.

Imagine you are a new student. Answer the questions of another student. Change roles.

1. ¿Cómo te llamas?
2. ¿Cómo estás hoy?
3. ¿De dónde eres?
4. ¿Te gusta…?

 **¡Mucho gusto!**

Using the information from Activity 5, introduce your new friend to another student or to your teacher.

 *En tu propia voz*

Escritura You are talking to a friend. Explain who the people in your community are and where they are from. Use your imagination!

¿Quién?

¿Qué le gusta?   ¿De dónde es?

Conexiones

Los estudios sociales
Compare Francisco's community with your own. Draw two intersecting circles. In one circle, write about the people in Francisco's new community. For example, Arturo is a student. Who are the people in your community? What do they do and where are they from originally? If they were all born in the U.S., do you know what country their families were originally from? Write about them in the second circle. What things does your circle have in common with Francisco's? List them where the two circles overlap.

LA COMUNIDAD DE FRANCISCO   MI COMUNIDAD

Arturo Francisco   estudiante vive en una casa   mi amiga yo

Venn diagram

En resumen

REPASO DE VOCABULARIO

SAYING WHERE PEOPLE ARE FROM

¿De dónde + ser...?	Where is... from?
ser de...	to be from...

People

el (la) amigo(a)	friend
la chica	girl
el chico	boy
la familia	family
el hombre	man
la muchacha	girl
el muchacho	boy
la mujer	woman
el señor	Mr.
la señora	Mrs.
la señorita	Miss

Professions

el (la) doctor(a)	doctor
el (la) estudiante	student
el (la) maestro(a)	teacher
el (la) policía	police officer

Subject Pronouns

yo	I
tú	you (familiar singular)
él	he
ella	she
usted	you (formal singular)
ustedes	you (plural)
nosotros(as)	we
vosotros(as)	you (familiar plural)
ellos(as)	they

Places

la comunidad	community
el mundo	world
el país	country

GREETING OTHERS

¿Cómo está usted?	How are you? (formal)
¿Cómo estás?	How are you? (familiar)
¿Qué tal?	How is it going?
Estoy...	I am...
(No muy) Bien, ¿y tú/usted?	(Not very) Well, and you (familiar/formal)?
Regular.	So-so.
Terrible.	Terrible./Awful.
Gracias.	Thank you.
De nada.	You're welcome.

INTRODUCING OTHERS

Te/Le presento a...	Let me introduce you (familiar/formal) to...

SAYING WHERE YOU LIVE

Vivo en...	I live in...
Vive en...	He/She lives in
el apartamento	apartment
la casa	house

EXPRESSING LIKES

¿Te gusta...?	Do you like...?
¿Le gusta...?	Does he/she like...?
Me gusta...	I like...
Te gusta...	You like...
Le gusta...	He/She likes...

Activities

bailar	to dance
cantar	to sing
comer	to eat
correr	to run
escribir	to write
leer	to read
nadar	to swim
patinar	to skate
trabajar	to work

OTHER WORDS AND PHRASES

bienvenido(a)	welcome
el concurso	contest
el lugar	place
mucho/s(a/s)	much, many
no	not
o	or
pero	but
también	also, too
y	and

Juego

Le gusta bailar pero no le gusta correr. Le gusta leer pero no le gusta cantar. Le gusta nadar pero no le gusta comer mucho. ¿Qué actividades no le gusta hacer a Marisol?

Marisol

correr **cantar** **comer**

ETAPA

2

Mis buenos amigos

OBJECTIVES

- Describe others

- Give others' likes and dislikes

- Describe clothing

¿Qué ves?

Look at the photo of the River Walk in San Antonio.

1. What do the teenagers look like?

2. What have they been buying?

3. What handicrafts do you see in the photo?

4. Which street name do you think comes from Spanish?

PASEO DEL RÍO, SAN ANTONIO

TRAVIS

COLLEGE

El Álamo

Plaza del Álamo

COMMERCE

MARKET

Paseo del Río

PASEO DE LA VILLITA

Parque HemisFeria

La Villita

En contexto
VOCABULARIO

Francisco's friends back in San Antonio are waiting to go to a Tejano music concert. Look at the illustrations. They will help you understand the meanings of the words in blue and answer the questions on the next page.

A Raúl, Rosalinda, Bill y Graciela son los amigos de Francisco.

castaño
el pelo
alto
morena
rubio
el pelo largo
el pelo corto
delgado
pelirroja
la blusa blanca
la falda morada
el perro
gordo
la bolsa
baja

Raúl es **cómico**.

Rosalinda es **bonita** y muy **inteligente**.

Bill (o Guillermo en español) es muy **simpático**. Tiene **un perro** que se llama Bud. Bud es **gordo**.

Graciela es **guapa**.

los zapatos   los pantalones

B Los mariachis llevan chaquetas y **pantalones negros.** Los sombreros son **grandes.**

trabajador

los ojos

la camiseta

el gato

C El hombre trabaja en el bote. Es muy **trabajador.** No es **perezoso.**

D El sombrero es grande. Los cascarones son **pequeños.** ¡Hay cascarones **azules y verdes!**

verde

azul

La chica es **paciente** y **seria. El gato es feo.**

Preguntas personales

1. ¿Eres alto(a)?
2. ¿Tu pelo es largo o corto?
3. ¿Eres trabajador(a) o perezoso(a)?
4. ¿Eres rubio(a), moreno(a), castaño(a) o pelirrojo(a)?
5. ¿Cómo eres tú?

En vivo

VIDEO DVD AUDIO

DIÁLOGO

Raúl   Rosalinda   Graciela   Guillermo

PARA ESCUCHAR • STRATEGY: LISTENING

Listen to stress Voice emphasis (stress) helps you understand sentences with extra emotion. Listen for greater emphasis on the first word of the sentence. Can you hear that emphasis? When these stressed sentences are written, they have exclamation points. Don't look at the written words. Can you guess which sentences are being written with exclamation points as you listen?

Con los amigos...

1 ▶ **Alma:** ¡Paco! ¡Cuántas fotos!
  Francisco: Son fotos de mis amigos y de mi familia. Son para el concurso.

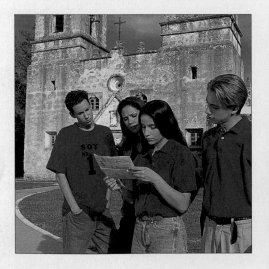  

5 ▶ **Alma:** Y la chica que lleva la blusa morada, ¿cómo se llama?
  Francisco: Ella es mi amiga Rosalinda.
  Alma: ¡Tiene el pelo largo!

6 ▶ **Alma:** Es muy bonita.
  Francisco: También es muy inteligente. En el colegio, es seria y trabajadora. Le gusta mucho estudiar.

7 ▶ **Alma:** Y tu amiga pelirroja, ¿cómo se llama?
  Francisco: Es Graciela. Graciela es muy simpática. Es mi mejor amiga.

2 ▶ Francisco: Tengo un video de mis amigos. ¿Te interesa?

Alma: ¡Claro que sí, cómo no!

3 ▶ Alma: ¡Qué divertidos son!

Francisco: Es verdad. Raúl es muy cómico. Raúl lleva jeans y una camiseta roja.

4 ▶ Raúl: Paco, ¿te gusta mi camiseta?

Alma: Raúl es muy guapo.

Francisco: ¡Por favor! ¡No digas eso! Es muy egoísta.

8 ▶ Francisco: Guillermo es rubio. Y su perro Bud, ¡es gordo! A Guillermo le gusta caminar con el perro.

9 ▶ Francisco: ¡Guillermo es fuerte! Pero es un poco perezoso.

10 ▶ Alma: ¡Qué buen amigo eres! ¡Y qué buenos amigos tienes! Pues, ahora tienes una nueva amiga…

Francisco: ¡Sí! ¡A los nuevos amigos!

En acción
VOCABULARIO Y GRAMÁTICA

OBJECTIVES

- Describe others
- Give others' likes and dislikes
- Describe clothing
- *Use definite articles*
- *Use indefinite articles*
- *Use adjectives with correct gender*
- *Use adjectives with correct number*

¿Quién es?

Escuchar Based on the dialog, tap the face or say the name of the person who is being described.

1. Es cómico y guapo.
2. Es seria y trabajadora.
3. Es pelirroja y simpática.
4. Es fuerte, pero un poco perezoso.

Raúl · Rosalinda · Guillermo · Graciela

¿Sí o no?

Escuchar Based on the dialog, tell whether each statement is correct or not. Say **sí** or **no**.

modelo

Raúl es feo.

No.

1. Francisco tiene un video de sus amigos.

2. Rosalinda es cómica.

3. Alma dice: «Ahora tienes una nueva amiga.»

4. Para Francisco, los nuevos amigos son importantes.

5. Bud es delgado.

También se dice

Did you notice that Alma calls Francisco **Paco? Paco** is a nickname for **Francisco,** just like *Frank* is a nickname for *Francis* or *Franklin*.

¿Te gusta?

Hablar/Escribir What do you like to do?

1 On a sheet of paper, make a chart like the one below.

2 Ask five classmates if they like to do the activities listed in the chart.

3 Record their names and answers (**sí** or **no**) in the chart.

4 Calculate how many students like to do each activity.

modelo

Estudiante A: *Juan, ¿te gusta correr?*

Estudiante B: *No, no me gusta correr.*

Actividad/Persona	patinar	leer	correr	nadar	cantar	bailar
Juan	sí	sí	no	sí	sí	sí

ACTIVIDAD 4

Personas famosas

Hablar Choose a word to complete each statement about the following well-known Spanish speakers.

1. El popular cantante español, Enrique Iglesias, es _____. (gordo, delgado)

2. Felipe López es _____. (alto, bajo)

3. La cantante mexicana, Lucero, tiene el pelo _____. (largo, corto)

4. La actriz puertorriqueña, Rosie Pérez, es _____. (seria, cómica)

5. El cantante puertorriqueño, Ricky Martin, es _____. (feo, guapo)

6. La astronauta Ellen Ochoa es _____. (perezosa, trabajadora)

N O T A CULTURAL

While many Spanish speakers wear jeans on certain occasions, they tend to dress up more than usual, even for casual occasions such as taking a walk.

Las diez diferencias

Leer/Escribir Can you find all the differences between the two pictures? First, decide whether each sentence describes Picture A or Picture B. Then, summarize your findings on a separate sheet of paper and be prepared to share them with the class!

modelo

El muchacho es perezoso.

*En B, **el muchacho es perezoso.** En A, **el muchacho** no **es perezoso.**
Es trabajador.*

1. El gato es gordo.
2. Marta es baja.
3. El hombre es rubio.
4. La mujer es rubia.
5. Raúl es serio.
6. Marta es alta.
7. El gato es delgado.
8. Raúl es cómico.
9. El hombre es castaño.
10. El muchacho es trabajador.

Using Definite Articles with Specific Things

▶ Nouns name people, animals, places, or things.

• All Spanish nouns have **masculine** or **feminine** gender.

el chico   **la chica**

• When nouns identify one item, they are **singular**.

el amigo   **la amiga**

• When they identify more than one item, they are **plural**.

los amigos

▶ In Spanish, the **definite article** that accompanies a noun will match its gender and number.

		Definite Article	**Noun**
Masculine	Singular	**el** *the*	chic**o** *boy*
	Plural	**los** *the*	chic**os** *boys*
Feminine	Singular	**la** *the*	chic**a** *girl*
	Plural	**las** *the*	chic**as** *girls*

matches gender *matches number*

Vocabulario

La ropa

los calcetines   el sombrero

la camisa   el suéter

la chaqueta

el vestido

los jeans

¿Cuál es tu ropa favorita?

Alma says:

matches

—¡Tiene **el** pel**o** largo!
She has long hair!

Francisco says: *matches*

—¡A **los** nuevos amig**os**!
To new friends!

▶ The gender of a noun must be learned. Usually

• nouns ending with **-o** are **masculine.**

• nouns ending with **-a** are **feminine.**

To help you learn the gender of a noun, each **noun** is given with its definite article.

ACTIVIDAD 6 Gramática

Los vecinos de Raúl

Hablar/Escribir Raúl is describing his neighbors. Complete his sentences with **el, la, los,** or **las.**

1. ____ chicas son Ana y Luisa.

2. ____ señorita Madrigal es maestra.

3. ____ señor Robles es policía.

4. ____ señor y ____ señora son doctores.

5. ____ muchachos son estudiantes.

MÁS PRÁCTICA *cuaderno* p. 21

PARA HISPANOHABLANTES
cuaderno p. 19

Online Workbook
CLASSZONE.COM

APOYO PARA ESTUDIAR

Gender Knowing the gender of nouns that refer to people is easy. But how do you learn the gender of things? When learning a new word, such as **camiseta,** say it with the definite article: **la camiseta.** Say it to yourself and say it aloud several times. That will help you remember its gender.

ACTIVIDAD 7

¿Qué llevan?

Hablar/Escribir Make a list of the clothes Graciela is packing for her trip. Use the definite articles **el, la, los,** or **las.**

modelo

1. *el vestido* 2. *las blusas*

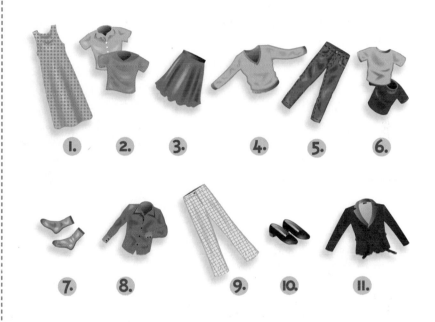

ACTIVIDAD 8

La ropa

Hablar Tell a classmate which items of the clothing you are wearing are your favorites.

modelo

los pantalones y la camiseta

Using Indefinite Articles with Unspecified Things

A noun may sometimes appear with an indefinite article. The **indefinite article** that accompanies a noun will also match its gender and number.

		Indefinite Article	Noun
Masculine	Singular	**un** *a*	*matches gender* chic**o** boy
Masculine	Plural	**unos** *some*	*matches number* chic**os** boys
Feminine	Singular	**una** *a*	chic**a** girl
Feminine	Plural	**unas** *some*	chic**as** girls

Francisco says:

matches gender

—Raúl lleva **una** camiseta…

*Raúl wears **a** T-shirt…*

ACTIVIDAD 9 Gramática

¿Qué es?

Hablar/Escribir Take turns with another student asking and answering questions about clothing.

modelo

Estudiante A: ¿Es un zapato?

Estudiante B: ¿Un zapato? ¡No, es **un sombrero**!

zapato

MÁS PRÁCTICA *cuaderno* p. 22

PARA HISPANOHABLANTES *cuaderno* p. 20

Online Workbook
CLASSZONE.COM

I. vestido

2. blusa

chaqueta

3.

4. zapatos

5. camiseta

6.

sombrero

¿Qué llevas tú?

Hablar/Escribir Say what you wear to each place.

modelo

un partido de fútbol americano
Llevo unos jeans y un suéter.

Nota

To say what you wear, use **llevo**.

1. la clase de español
2. un baile
3. una fiesta en julio
4. una fiesta en noviembre
5. un restaurante elegante

♻ Categorías

Escribir Work with a classmate. List as many words as possible under the following categories.

modelo

Personas: un chico, una madre, una señorita...

profesiones   ropa

animales   personas

Using Adjectives to Describe: Gender

Adjectives describe nouns. Like articles, they match the gender of the nouns they describe. In Spanish, adjectives usually follow the noun.

Masculine adjectives often end in **-o**.	Feminine adjectives often end in **-a**.

▸*agrees*◂	▸*agrees*◂
el chic**o guapo**	la chic**a guapa**
the good-looking boy	*the good-looking girl*

Most adjectives that end with **-e** match both genders.

el chic**o paciente** ◂— *same word* —▸ la chic**a paciente**

Many adjectives that end with a **consonant** match both genders.

el chic**o fenomenal** ◂— *same word* —▸ la chic**a fenomenal**

Some add **-a** to become feminine. These adjectives must be learned.

becomes

el chic**o trabajador** ⟶ la chic**a trabajadora**
the hard-working boy   *the hard-working girl*

Vocabulario

Adjectives

aburrido(a) *boring*	**fuerte** *strong*
bueno(a) *good*	**interesante** *interesting*
divertido(a) *fun*	**malo(a)** *bad*

¿Cómo eres?

Descripciones

Hablar Describe each student using **es** and one of the words provided.

1. Ángela
¿guapo(a)?
¿trabajador(a)?

2. Pedro
¿trabajador(a)?
¿cómico(a)?

3. Marta
¿trabajador(a)?
¿aburrido(a)?

4. Laura
¿simpático(a)?
¿malo(a)?

5. Tomás
¿cómico(a)?
¿fuerte?

Los amigos de Francisco

Leer Your friend is curious. Describe Francisco's friends to him or her.

1. Graciela es una amiga _____ [simpático(a)].
2. Mónica es _____ [malo(a)].
3. Javier no es un chico muy _____ [interesante].
4. Rosalinda es una chica _____ [bonito(a)].
5. Felipe es un amigo _____ [aburrido(a)].
6. ¡Qué _____ [cómico(a)] es Raúl!
7. Linda es _____ [divertido(a)].
8. Es un perro muy _____ [inteligente].
9. ¡Qué _____ [fuerte] es Guillermo!
10. Alma es _____ [bueno(a)].

MÁS PRÁCTICA *cuaderno* p. 23
PARA HISPANOHABLANTES *cuaderno* p. 21

Online Workbook
CLASSZONE.COM

¡Todos somos diferentes!

Escribir Write the descriptions of the following students.

modelo

Ana: interesante y guapo(a)
*Ella es **interesante y guapa.***

1. Graciela: interesante y divertido(a)
2. Guillermo: fuerte y trabajador(a)
3. Raúl: delgado(a) y simpático(a)
4. Rosalinda: moreno(a) y bonito(a)

ACTIVIDAD 15

¿Cómo es?

Hablar Your friend doesn't know these people. Choose appropriate descriptive words to explain what they're like.

modelo

tu vecino

Estudiante A: *¿Cómo es **tu vecino**?*

Estudiante B: *Él es trabajador.*

Nota

To ask what someone is like, use:

¿Cómo + ser + noun?

¿Cómo es Guillermo?

What is Guillermo like?

1. tu amigo
2. tu amiga
3. tu vecina
4. el (la) maestro(a) de matemáticas
5. tu papá
6. tu maestro(a) de español

■ **MÁS COMUNICACIÓN** p. R2

GRAMÁTICA

Using Adjectives to Describe: Number

▶ Adjectives must also match the number of the nouns they describe. To make an adjective plural, add **-s** if it ends with a vowel, **-es** if it ends with a consonant.

los chico**s**:

    guapo s, divertido s

    fenomenal es

las chica**s**:

    guapa s, divertida s

    fenomenal es

▶ When an adjective describes a group with both genders, the **masculine** form of the adjective is used.

    El chic**o** y la chic**a** son **guap o s**.

¿Cómo son?

Hablar/Escribir Describe what these people are like. Use an adjective of your own, or choose one from the list.

modelo

los abuelos

Los abuelos son simpáticos.

---

paciente/s
fenomenal/es
cómico(a)/s
importante/s
simpático(a)/s
serio(a)/s
perezoso(a)/s
aburrido(a)/s

---

1. los padres
2. el amigo
3. los tíos
4. la vecina
5. los maestros
6. las hermanas
7. el primo
8. las tías
9. los vecinos
10. las primas

¡Muchos colores!

Escuchar/Escribir Raúl wears colorful clothing. Listen and write the color of the clothing.

1. los pantalones
2. la camisa
3. la chaqueta
4. los calcetines
5. los zapatos

MÁS PRÁCTICA *cuaderno* p. 24

PARA HISPANOHABLANTES *cuaderno* p. 22

Online Workbook
CLASSZONE.COM

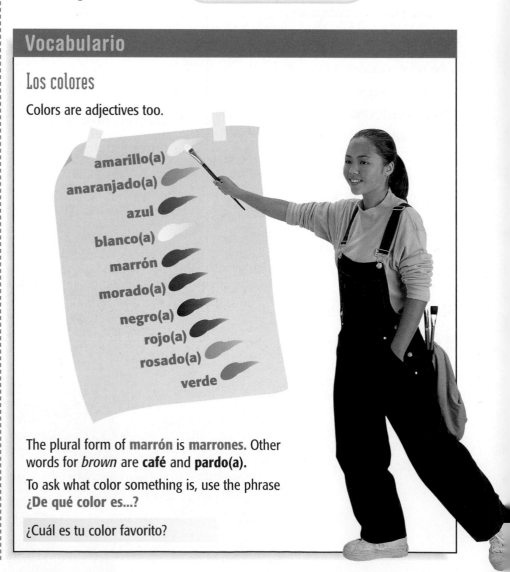

Vocabulario

Los colores

Colors are adjectives too.

amarillo(a)
anaranjado(a)
azul
blanco(a)
marrón
morado(a)
negro(a)
rojo(a)
rosado(a)
verde

The plural form of **marrón** is **marrones**. Other words for *brown* are **café** and **pardo(a)**.

To ask what color something is, use the phrase **¿De qué color es...?**

¿Cuál es tu color favorito?

ACTIVIDAD 18

Los ojos y el pelo

Hablar/Escribir Take turns with a classmate describing the hair and the color of the eyes of Francisco and his friends.

modelo

Francisco tiene los ojos marrones y el pelo corto. Es moreno.

Nota

Tener means *to have*. Use **tiene** to talk about the features a person has.

1.

2.

3.

4.

Conexiones

La lengua: Origen de las palabras Have you ever wondered why many names of cities, towns, mountains, rivers, and states in the United States are Spanish? It is because the Spanish were the first Europeans to explore the American continent. You have learned the word **amarillo.** Have you heard of Amarillo, Texas? Why do you think that city was given that name? *(Hint: Think of the color of the land in that part of the country.)*

PARA HACER:
Identify three places in the U.S. with Spanish names. Then, use a dictionary to try to determine why they were given those names. For example, Montana means "mountainous place" and Sierra Nevada means "snowy peaks."

¿Cómo es Teresa?

Escuchar Listen to the paragraph. Are the sentences true (**sí**) or false (**no**)?

1. Teresa es baja y rubia.
2. Ella tiene los ojos azules y el pelo largo.
3. En el colegio, es cómica y divertida.
4. Es una chica muy inteligente.
5. Le gusta bailar, pero no le gusta patinar.

También se dice

Different Spanish words can be used to talk about jeans. Sometimes the word **jeans** is used, just as in English. This is called a loan word. Other words are:

- **bluyines:** many countries
- **pantalón de mezclillas:** Mexico
- **vaqueros:** Argentina, Spain
- **tejanos:** Spain
- **mahones:** Puerto Rico

♻ ¿Qué lleva y qué le gusta?

Hablar Describe to your partner what each person is wearing and what he or she likes to do.

modelo

Yolanda: trabajar

Tú: *¿Qué lleva **Yolanda**?*

Otro(a) estudiante: ***Yolanda** lleva pantalones marrones y una camiseta amarilla. Le gusta **trabajar**.*

Nota

To ask what a person is wearing, say **¿Qué lleva?**

To answer, use **lleva.**

1. la señorita Vidal: leer

2. Felipe: nadar

3. Ana María: correr

4. Juan Carlos: bailar

ACTIVIDAD 21 ¿Cómo son?

PARA CONVERSAR
STRATEGY: SPEAKING

Trust your first impulse When speaking, your first impulse will usually be right. Go ahead and speak! Making mistakes is natural, and you will make more when speaking than when writing. We all make mistakes, so don't worry if you make a few! When you make a mistake, pause and correct yourself.

Hablar Give your opinion of each person. Change roles.

modelo

el señor Álvarez: el maestro / bueno

Estudiante A: ¿Cómo es **el señor Álvarez**?

Estudiante B: No es un **buen maestro**.
　　　　　　　o: Es un **buen maestro**.

Nota

Sometimes an adjective may precede a noun. When the words **bueno** or **malo** precede a masculine singular noun, they are shortened to **buen** and **mal**. When **grande** precedes any singular noun, it becomes **gran** and its meaning changes to *great*.

1. Francisco: el estudiante / malo
2. la señorita Álvarez: la maestra / grande
3. Raúl: el amigo / grande
4. el señor Gómez: el policía / bueno
5. Alma: la vecina / malo
6. Rosalinda: la estudiante / bueno
7. Graciela: la amiga / grande
8. Guillermo: el estudiante / bueno

ACTIVIDAD 22 ¿Cómo es?

Hablar/Escribir What is the person like?

1. With a partner, describe in writing a fellow classmate both in terms of what he or she looks like as well as what he or she is wearing.

2. Read your description to the class. Can the class guess whom you are describing?

modelo

La persona es una chica alta. Ella tiene el pelo corto. Es rubia. Ella lleva unos jeans y un suéter rosado.

■ **MÁS COMUNICACIÓN** p. R2

Online Workbook
CLASSZONE.COM

Pronunciación

Trabalenguas

Pronunciación de la f, la s y la ch The letter **f** and **s**, and the combination **ch**, are pronounced the same in Spanish as they are in English. To practice the sounds, repeat these tongue twisters.

—¡Qué falda
fantástica!
—dice Sara
Sánchez.

¿Con cuántas
planchas plancha
Pancha?

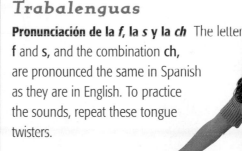

En colores

VIDEO   DVD

CULTURA Y COMPARACIONES

EL CONJUNTO

PARA CONOCERNOS
STRATEGY: CONNECTING CULTURES

When learning about another language, you also learn about the people who speak it—their way of life, traditions, and contributions to the world. In addition, you learn to think about your own culture.

Recognize regional music Is there a kind of music unique to your area or that you like a lot? What people or events influenced its development? What instruments are used? (See p. R11 for the names of instruments in Spanish.) Compare this music to Tejano music, using a Venn diagram.

JAZZ   TEJANO

saxofón (guitarra) acordeón

Un instrumento
típico es el bajo
sexto. Es una
guitarra española
grande. Tiene
doce cuerdas³.

———————
³ twelve strings

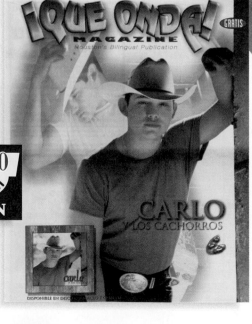

Hay mucha música
tejana en las estaciones
de radio de San Antonio.
También hay información
en revistas¹ y periódicos².

———————
¹ magazines   ² newspapers

72 setenta y dos
Unidad 1

Selena: una artista famosa de la música tejana

TEJANO

Los músicos de la foto llevan camisas negras, chaquetas y sombreros.

En San Antonio hay muchos grupos de música tejana. Un grupo de música tejana se llama «un conjunto tejano».

La música tejana tiene influencias de la música de Europa y de México. También tiene influencias de la música de Estados Unidos.

Otro instrumento típico es el acordeón. Tiene teclas[4] blancas y negras y un sonido[5] divertido.

---

[4] keys
[5] sound

More About Latinos
CLASSZONE.COM

¿Comprendiste?

1. ¿Cómo se llama un grupo de música tejana?
2. ¿De dónde tiene influencias la música tejana?
3. ¿Cuáles son los instrumentos típicos?
4. ¿Qué es un bajo sexto?

¿Qué piensas?

1. ¿Cuál es tu música favorita?
2. ¿Cómo se llama tu grupo favorito? Compara el grupo con un conjunto tejano.

En uso
REPASO Y MÁS COMUNICACIÓN

OBJECTIVES
- Describe others
- Give others' likes and dislikes
- Describe clothing

ACTIVIDAD 1 La comunidad

Describe the people of the community.

modelo

ella: *bueno(a) / amigo(a)*   muchachos: *estudiante / inteligente / trabajador(a)*

Ella** es una **buena amiga.   **Los *muchachos* son *estudiantes inteligentes* y *trabajadores*.**

1. señora: maestro(a) / paciente / cómico(a)
2. muchacho: bueno(a) / amigo(a)
3. señores: policía / fuerte / simpático(a)
4. yo: estudiante / trabajador(a)
5. él: grande / maestro(a)
6. nosotros: estudiante / interesante / serio(a)
7. chico: malo(a) / estudiante
8. señoras: vecino(a) / aburrido(a) / perezoso(a)
9. tú: estudiante / inteligente
10. señor: bueno(a) / doctor(a)

ACTIVIDAD 2 ¡Muy diferentes!

Mr. and Mrs. García are very different. Read what he likes to do and then tell what she likes to do.

modelo

Le gusta leer. (cantar)

*No **le gusta leer**. Le gusta **cantar**.*

1. Le gusta trabajar. (escuchar música)
2. Le gusta correr. (nadar)
3. Le gusta patinar. (bailar)
4. Le gusta llevar jeans. (llevar pantalones)
5. Le gusta comer pizza. (comer un sándwich)
6. Le gusta hablar. (escuchar)
7. Le gusta leer. (escribir)
8. Le gusta llevar una camiseta. (llevar una blusa)

Now you can...
- describe others.

To review
- definite and indefinite articles, see p. 62 and p. 64.
- adjectives, see p. 65 and p. 67.

Now you can...
- give others' likes and dislikes.

To review
- verbs to talk about what others like to do, see p. 59.

Now you can...

• describe clothing.

To review

• vocabulary for clothing, see p. 62.

• definite and indefinite articles, see p. 62 and p. 64.

• colors, see p. 68.

ACTIVIDAD 3 **¿Qué llevan?**

Tell what the people at the party are wearing.

modelo

chico

El *chico* lleva *una camiseta amarilla* y *unos pantalones blancos*.

1. mujer   **2.** hombre   **3.** muchacho

4. chica   **5.** señorita   **6.** señor

Now you can...

• describe others.

• describe clothing.

To review

• vocabulary for clothing, see p. 62.

• adjectives, see p. 65 and p. 67.

• colors, see p. 68.

ACTIVIDAD 4 **Mis amigos**

Tell which friend Alma describes.

1. Es alto y tiene el pelo corto y negro.

2. Es bajo, feo y anaranjado.

3. Lleva una blusa blanca, una falda anaranjada y calcetines blancos.

4. Es pelirrojo y tiene una camisa blanca.

5. Tiene el pelo largo y rubio.

6. Lleva una chaqueta azul y pantalones negros.

7. Lleva una camiseta roja, jeans y zapatos blancos.

Nico   Anita   Horacio   Conchita   Gustavo

8. Es gordo y perezoso.

9. Lleva un suéter morado, pantalones amarillos y zapatos marrones.

10. Es alta y rubia.

ACTIVIDAD 5 — Amigos

PARA CONVERSAR

STRATEGY: SPEAKING

Think, plan, then speak Think about what you want to say. Rely on what you have practiced and memorized. Plan, then speak, using what you know.

Describe one of Francisco's friends, including characteristics and clothing. Another student will guess who it is.

Raúl   Arturo   Guillermo

Alma   Rosalinda   Graciela

ACTIVIDAD 6 — Los estudiantes de la clase

Describe a student in the class, including characteristics and clothing. Say what he or she likes. The class will guess who it is.

ACTIVIDAD 7 — En tu propia voz

Escritura Write a description of a famous or popular person. Include characteristics, clothing, and what he or she likes to do. Read your description while other students draw the person and guess who it is.

modelo

Es gordo. Lleva una chaqueta roja y unos pantalones rojos. Tiene el pelo blanco. Es un hombre simpático. Le gusta comer.

Es Santa Claus.

Conexiones

La música   Research music of the Spanish-speaking country of your choice. Report to the class. Your presentation may use writing, drawing, and/or music recordings. To learn the names of common instruments, see p. R11. Use **ser** and **tiene** to describe the music. For example, **Es música interesante y divertida.** As you hear your classmates' reports, write down the characteristics of the different types of music. Which ones are similar?

	Música tejana
Influencias	Europa, México, Estados Unidos
¿Cómo es?	divertida
Los músicos llevan...	jeans
Instrumentos	acordeón, bajo sexto

En resumen
REPASO DE VOCABULARIO

DESCRIBING OTHERS

¿Cómo es?	What is he/she like?

Appearance

alto(a)	tall
bajo(a)	short (height)
bonito(a)	pretty
castaño(a)	brown (hair)
corto(a)	short (length)
delgado(a)	thin
feo(a)	ugly
fuerte	strong
gordo(a)	fat
grande	big, large; great
guapo(a)	good-looking
largo(a)	long
moreno(a)	dark hair and skin
pelirrojo(a)	redhead
pequeño(a)	small
rubio(a)	blond

Features

Tiene...	He/She has...
los ojos (verdes, azules)	(green, blue) eyes
el pelo (rubio, castaño)	(blond, brown) hair

Personality

aburrido(a)	boring
bueno(a)	good
cómico(a)	funny, comical
divertido(a)	enjoyable, fun
inteligente	intelligent
interesante	interesting
malo(a)	bad
paciente	patient
perezoso(a)	lazy
serio(a)	serious
simpático(a)	nice
trabajador(a)	hard-working

DESCRIBING CLOTHING

What one is wearing

¿De qué color...?	What color...?
Llevo.../Lleva...	I wear...He/She wears...
¿Qué lleva?	What is he/she wearing?

Clothing

la blusa	blouse
el calcetín	sock
la camisa	shirt
la camiseta	T-shirt
la chaqueta	jacket
la falda	skirt
los jeans	jeans
los pantalones	pants
la ropa	clothing
el sombrero	hat
el suéter	sweater
el vestido	dress
el zapato	shoe

Colors

amarillo(a)	yellow
anaranjado(a)	orange
azul	blue
blanco(a)	white
marrón	brown
morado(a)	purple
negro(a)	black
rojo(a)	red
rosado(a)	pink
verde	green

OTHER WORDS AND PHRASES

la bolsa	bag
el (la) gato(a)	cat
el (la) perro(a)	dog
nuevo(a)	new
otro(a)	other, another
pues	well
¡No digas eso!	Don't say that!
¡Qué (divertido)!	How (fun)!
Es verdad.	It's true.

Juego

La mujer alta tiene el pelo corto y negro. Lleva una chaqueta azul y una falda larga. ¿Quién es?

a.

b.

c.

Te presento a mi familia

OBJECTIVES

- Describe family

- Ask and tell ages

- Talk about birthdays

- Give dates

- Express possession

¿Qué ves?

Look at the photo of a home in Los Angeles.

1. Describe the people.

2. What do you think their relationships are?

3. What is each person doing?

4. Where in the United States might you see houses like this one?

En contexto

VIDEO DVD AUDIO

VOCABULARIO

Francisco's cousin Verónica is having a party for her fifteenth birthday. Look at the illustrations. They will help you understand the meanings of the words in blue and answer the questions on the next page.

¡FELICIDADES!

el abuelo   la abuela

A Hoy es **una fecha** muy especial. Es **el cumpleaños** de Verónica. Ella está **feliz. ¿Cuántos años tiene** ella? Tiene **quince años de edad.** ¡Tiene una **fiesta quinceañera!**

[handwritten annotations: date, happy, birthday, birthday, party, years, age]

B Los señores García son los más **viejos** de la familia. Son **los abuelos** de Verónica. Javier y Juan García son **los hijos** de ellos.

[handwritten annotations: old, grandparents, How old is she/he, children]

La familia

```
        Abuelo — Abuela
          ┌──────┴──────┐
Yolanda — Javier    Juan — Anita
    ┌──────┴──────┐   ┌──────┴──────┐
Verónica      Andrés  Francisco   David
```

Feliz Quince Años

C Los **padres** de Verónica tienen una familia simpática. Verónica y Andrés son **hermanos**. Andrés es **joven**. Es **el hermano menor** de Verónica. Verónica es **la hija** y Andrés es **el hijo** de Javier y Yolanda. Verónica es la hija **mayor**.

Parents (handwritten)
brothers (handwritten)
young (handwritten)

Javier García — el padre
la madre
la hermana — el hermano
Yolanda
Verónica — Andrés

Juan García — Anita
el tío
la tía
el primo
el primo
David — Francisco

Otras palabras para hablar de la familia:

el (la) esposo(a) husband (wife)
el (la) hermanastro(a) stepbrother (stepsister)
la madrastra stepmother
el (la) medio(a) hermano(a) half-brother (half-sister)
el (la) nieto(a) grandson (granddaughter)
el padrastro stepfather

D Los padres de Francisco son **los tíos** de Verónica. Verónica es **la prima** de Francisco y de David.

Online Workbook
CLASSZONE.COM

Preguntas personales

1. ¿Tienes primos? ¿Tíos? ¿Abuelos?
2. ¿Tu familia es grande o pequeña?
3. ¿Tienes hermanos mayores o menores?
4. ¿Cuántos hermanos tienes?
5. ¿Cómo se llaman tus padres? ¿Tus hermanos?

En vivo

VIDEO   DVD   AUDIO

DIÁLOGO

| Javier | Verónica | Yolanda | Andrés |

Con la familia...

PARA ESCUCHAR • STRATEGIES: LISTENING

Visualize As you listen, point to the images that you hear named. Link the image and the name. This helps you learn and remember.

Get the main idea In order to understand, listen first to try to get the general idea of what is happening. What is the general topic of conversation between Francisco and Alma here?

1 ▶ Alma: ¿Y quién es este señor?
Francisco: Es mi tío Javier. La foto es de su cumpleaños. Tiene ahora 39 años. Es el hermano menor de mi papá.

 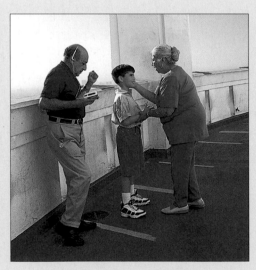 

5 ▶ Alma: Y esta familia, ¿quién es?
Francisco: Bueno, éstos son mis abuelos.

6 ▶ Alma: ¡Qué simpáticos son tus abuelos!
Francisco: Son muy activos. Mi abuelo siempre dice: «Soy viejo por fuera pero soy joven por dentro.»

7 ▶ Alma: Y tu abuela, ¿cómo es?
Francisco: Mi abuela es muy paciente, especialmente con sus queridos nietos. Ella adora a sus nietos.

2▶ Francisco: Es artista. Le gusta pintar murales. Hay muchos murales en la ciudad de Los Ángeles.

Alma: ¡Ay! ¡Qué chévere! ~cool

3▶ Alma: Y esta chica, ¿quién es?

Francisco: ¡Oh!, ¿esa chica? Esa chica es mi prima Verónica. Verónica es muy divertida.

4▶ Alma: ¿Qué edad tiene Verónica?

Francisco: Pues, su cumpleaños es en octubre. Así que ahora tiene quince años. Verónica es muy atlética.

8▶ Alma: ¿Quién es la mujer que está con tu tío Javier?

Francisco: Ella es su esposa. Es mi tía Yolanda.

9▶ Francisco: Ellos son los hijos de mi tío Javier y mi tía Yolanda.

Alma: ¡Ah, sí!, ésa es tu prima.

Francisco: Sí, y él es Andrés, mi primo.

Alma: ¿Cuántos años tiene Andrés?

Francisco: Andrés tiene siete años.

10▶ Alma: Tu familia es muy fotogénica.

Francisco: Gracias, Alma. Oye, ¿cuál es la fecha de hoy?

Alma: El once de noviembre. ¿Por qué?

Francisco: ¡Ay! Sólo tengo diez días más para el concurso.

En acción
VOCABULARIO Y GRAMÁTICA

- Describe family
- Ask and tell ages
- Talk about birthdays
- Give dates
- Express possession
- *Use the verb* **tener**
- *Express possession using* **de**
- *Use possessive adjectives*
- *Use dates and months*

ACTIVIDAD
1

¿Quién es?

Escuchar Based on the dialog, say the name of the person who is being described.

1. Tiene siete años.
2. Es la tía de Francisco.
3. Es artista.
4. Es muy atlética.

Verónica

Javier

Yolanda

Andrés

¿Sí o no?

Escuchar Based on the dialog, tell whether the statements below are true or false. Say **sí** or **no.** If the statement is false, correct it.

modelo

Yolanda es la abuela de Verónica.

No. Yolanda es la madre de Verónica.

1. Javier es el tío de Andrés.
2. Verónica es la prima de Francisco.
3. Andrés es el hermano mayor de Verónica.
4. Yolanda es la abuela de Javier.
5. Verónica y Andrés son los hijos de Javier y Yolanda.

La familia

Leer Explain who the members of Francisco's family are. Use the correct word: **abuelos, primo, prima, hermano, tía, tío, tíos, madre, padre, padres.**

1. Verónica es la _____ de Francisco.
2. Yolanda y Javier son los _____ de él.
3. David es su _____.
4. Andrés es su _____.
5. Juan y Anita son sus _____.
6. Los señores García mayores son sus _____.
7. Anita es su _____.
8. Yolanda es su _____.
9. Javier es su _____.
10. Juan es su _____.

También se dice

There are many ways to say *How awesome!* in Spanish. Alma says **¡Qué chévere!** in the dialog.

- **¡Qué bárbaro!** Argentina
- **¡Qué buena nota!** Ecuador
- **¡Qué guay!** Spain
- **¡Qué padre!** Mexico

¡QUÉ CHÉVERE!

¡Una familia simpática!

Hablar Describe Verónica's family, using the following words:

los padres   el cumpleaños   **la hermana**

los hijos   el hermano   mayor

quince   **los abuelos**   menor

1. Los señores García son _____ de Verónica.

2. Verónica es _____ de Andrés.

3. Ella es la hermana _____.

4. Yolanda y Javier son _____ de Andrés.

5. Andrés es _____ de Verónica.

6. Él es el hermano _____ de ella.

7. Verónica y Andrés son _____ de Yolanda y Javier.

8. Hoy es _____ de Verónica.

9. Ella tiene _____ años.

Yo ♥ a mis abuelos

ACTIVIDAD 5

♻ Descripciones

Hablar/Escribir Choose one of the people below. Describe that person to your partner. Your partner will guess who it is. Take turns.

modelo

Estudiante A: *Es delgado, bajo y moreno. Es joven y simpático. Tiene el pelo corto.*

Estudiante B: *Es Andrés.*

1. Francisco

2. Verónica

3. Rafael

4. el abuelo 5. la abuela

6. Yolanda 7. Javier

Conexiones

El arte Fernando Botero is a famous artist from Colombia. His style is to always make people and animals look enormous. This painting is called **Los músicos** (*The Musicians*).

PARA HACER: Describe the people in this painting, or create a portrait or collage of your family and describe its members. Share your descriptions with the class! Remember the adjectives you have learned as you write your descriptions.

GRAMÁTICA

Saying What You Have: The Verb tener

When you want to talk about what you have, use the verb **tener**.

yo	tengo	nosotros(as)	tenemos
tú	tienes	vosotros(as)	tenéis
usted, él, ella	tiene	ustedes, ellos(as)	tienen

Francisco says:

—¡Sólo **tengo** diez días más!
I have only ten more days!

Tener is also used to talk about how old a person is.

—¿**Cuántos años** tiene Verónica?
How old is Verónica?

—**Tiene** quince **años.**
She is fifteen years old.

NOTA CULTURAL

The oldest house currently standing in Los Angeles is the Avila Adobe, located on Olvera Street, in the city's historic center. It was built as a home for the rancher Francisco Abela in 1818, a time when California was part of Mexico, not the United States!

ACTIVIDAD 6 Gramática

¿Qué tienen?

Leer/Escribir Complete the sentences about what Francisco says people have by using the correct form of the verb **tener**.

1. Yo _____ cuatro buenos amigos.
2. Mis amigas Graciela y Rosalinda _____ el pelo largo.
3. Mi amigo Raúl _____ vecinos simpáticos.
4. Mis amigos y yo _____ muchas fotos de amigos.
5. ¿Y tú? ¿_____ muchas fotos?
6. Yo _____ padres divertidos.
7. Mi prima Verónica _____ un hermano menor.
8. Mis padres _____ una casa bonita.
9. Nosotros _____ una familia simpática.

MÁS PRÁCTICA *cuaderno* p. 29
PARA HISPANOHABLANTES *cuaderno* p. 27

Online Workbook
CLASSZONE.COM

La familia de Antonio

Escuchar Listen to what Antonio says about his family. Then answer the questions.

1. ¿Cómo se llama el hermano menor de Antonio?
   a. Alberto   **b.** Andrés

2. ¿Cuántos años tiene Andrés?
   a. 8   **b.** 17

3. ¿Quién es Luisa?
   a. su madre   **b.** su hermana

4. ¿Quiénes son Rosa y Alberto?
   a. sus abuelos   **b.** sus padres

5. ¿Cómo son Marta y Rafael?
   a. viejos y divertidos   **b.** jóvenes y divertidos

¿Cuántos años tienen?

Escribir Write a sentence telling how old each person is. When the age is not given, invent the age of a relative who fits the description.

modelo

la abuela: 70

La abuela tiene **setenta años.**

1. los padres: 38
2. los hermanos mayores: 22
3. el abuelo: ¿?
4. la prima: ¿?
5. la tía: ¿?

Vocabulario

Los números de 11 a 100

11 once	18 dieciocho	25 veinticinco	40 cuarenta
12 doce	19 diecinueve	26 veintiséis	50 cincuenta
13 trece	20 veinte	27 veintisiete	60 sesenta
14 catorce	21 veintiuno	28 veintiocho	70 setenta
15 quince	22 veintidós	29 veintinueve	80 ochenta
16 dieciséis	23 veintitrés	30 treinta	90 noventa
17 diecisiete	24 veinticuatro	31 treinta y uno	100 cien

For 21, 31, and so on, use **veintiún, treinta y un,** and so on before a masculine noun and **veintiuna, treinta y una,** and so on before a feminine noun.

Tengo **veintiún** años. Tienes **treinta y una** camisetas.

¿Cuántos años tienes?

ACTIVIDAD 9

♻ En la clase

Hablar/Escribir Explain how many of each type of person there are in the class.

modelo

chicos altos

*Hay cinco **chicos altos** en la clase.*

Nota

The word **hay** is used to mean *there is* or *there are*.

Hay muchos murales en la ciudad de Los Ángeles.

There are *many murals in the city of Los Angeles.*

Hay un concurso muy interesante.

There is *a very interesting contest.*

To say there are none, use **No hay**...

1. chicas castañas
2. chicos castaños
3. chicos rubios
4. chicas rubias
5. chicos morenos
6. chicas morenas
7. chicos ¿?
8. chicas ¿?
9. chicos bajos
10. chicas atléticas

GRAMÁTICA

Expressing Possession Using de

In English, you express possession by adding **'s** to the **noun** that refers to the possessor. In Spanish, you use the preposition **de** to refer to the **possessor**.

el hermano **de** papá
Dad's brother

los hijos **de** Javier
Javier's children

ACTIVIDAD 10 Gramática

La ropa de...

Hablar After a pool party, everyone is packing up their clothes. Tell to whom each item belongs.

modelo

Andrés / camisa

*Es **la camisa** de **Andrés**.*

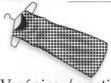

1. Verónica / vestido
2. Raúl / chaqueta
3. Juan / zapato

4. Anita / blusa
5. David / camiseta
6. Yolanda / falda

MÁS PRÁCTICA *cuaderno* p. 30

PARA HISPANOHABLANTES *cuaderno* p. 28

Online Workbook
CLASSZONE.COM

¿De quién es?

PARA CONVERSAR

STRATEGY: SPEAKING

Rehearse Practicing with a partner is a rehearsal for real conversation, so make the most of it. Think of real situations where you can use what you are practicing, such as asking about what people in the class are wearing.

Hablar Work with another person to explain whose clothing it is. Change roles.

modelo

chaqueta: Francisco

Estudiante A: *¿De quién es la* ***chaqueta****?*

Estudiante B: *Es de* ***Francisco.***

Nota

Use the expression **¿De quién es...?** to ask who owns something. To answer, use **Es de...**

1. falda: Verónica
2. vestido: Anita
3. suéter: Andrés
4. camiseta: Javier
5. blusa: la abuela
6. ¿?

La familia de Rafael Ramos

Hablar/Escribir Explain who each member of Rafael's family is.

modelo

Teresa

Teresa *es la abuela de Rafael.*

Lucía

Lucía *es la hermana de Rafael.*

■ **MÁS COMUNICACIÓN** p. R3

Expressing Possession: Possessive Adjectives

Possessive adjectives tell you who owns something or describe a relationship between people or things. In Spanish, possessive adjectives agree in number with the nouns they describe.

Singular Possessive Adjectives

mi *my*	**nuestro(a)** *our*
tu *your (familiar)*	**vuestro(a)** *your (familiar)*
su *your*	**su** *your*
su *his, her, its*	**su** *their*

Plural Possessive Adjectives

mis *my*	**nuestros(as)** *our*
tus *your (familiar)*	**vuestros(as)** *your (familiar)*
sus *your*	**sus** *your*
sus *his, her, its*	**sus** *their*

Francisco would say:

—Es **mi** tío.
*He is **my** uncle.*

—Son **mis** abuelo**s**.
*They are **my** grandparents.*

▶ The adjectives **nuestro(a)** and **vuestro(a)** must also agree in gender with the nouns they describe.

agrees
nuestr**o** abuel**o**

agrees
nuestr**o**s abuel**o**s

agrees
nuestr**a** abuel**a**

agrees
nuestr**a**s abuel**a**s

▶ If you need to emphasize, substitute the adjective with:

de + **pronoun** or the person's name

This also helps to clarify the meaning of **su** and **sus.**

becomes
Es **su** tío. → Es el tío **de él**.

	de nosotros(as)
	de vosotros(as)
de usted, él, ella	**de** ustedes, ellos(as)

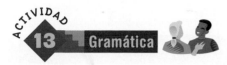

♻ ¿De quién es la ropa?

Hablar You are helping the secretary find out who owns the clothing in the Lost and Found at your school. Ask another student if an article of clothing is his or hers. Change roles.

modelo

(no)

Estudiante A: ¿Es tu chaqueta?

Estudiante B: *No, no* es mi **chaqueta.**

1. (sí)

2. (no)

3. (no)

4. (sí)

5. (no)

6. (sí)

Juego

Marco tiene un hermano. José tiene un año. El hermano de Marco se llama José. ¿Cuántos años tiene el hermano de Marco?

¿Quiénes son?

Hablar You are at a party at two friends' house. They are brother and sister. Ask one of them who everyone is. Change roles.

modelo

abuela

Estudiante A: ¿Quién es?

Estudiante B: *Es nuestra abuela.*

Nota

To ask who a person is, use *¿Quién es?* To ask who several people are, use *¿Quiénes son?*

1. tía
2. vecina
3. primo
4. tío
5. padres
6. hermanas

MÁS PRÁCTICA *cuaderno* p. 31

PARA HISPANOHABLANTES *cuaderno* p. 29

Online Workbook CLASSZONE.COM

15

¿De quién es?

Hablar/Escribir Tell to whom the following belong. Follow the clues.

modelo

el gato (de él)   *Es su gato.*

1. el perro (de nosotras)
2. la bolsa (de ella)
3. el apartamento (de ellos)
4. las camisetas (de nosotros)
5. la casa (de ustedes)
6. los hijos (de él)

ACTIVIDAD
16

¿De quién es la camisa?

Hablar Take turns asking and telling whose clothes these are. Don't hesitate to be creative in your answers.

modelo

camisa / tu hermano

Estudiante A: ¿*La camisa es de tu hermano?*

Estudiante B: *Sí, es su camisa.*

pantalones / tu padre

Estudiante B: ¿*Los pantalones son de tu padre?*

Estudiante A: *No, los pantalones son de mi madre.*

1. vestido / tu tía
2. calcetines / tu padre
3. blusas / ellas
4. chaquetas / tus abuelos
5. falda / tu abuela
6. camisetas / Rafael
7. zapatos / tu hermana
8. camisa / Gloria
9. pantalones / tu hermano
10. sombrero / Graciela

GRAMÁTICA

Giving Dates: Day and Month

When you want to give the date, use the following phrase:

Es el + number + de + month.

—Cuál es la fecha de hoy?
What is the date today?

—Hoy **es el once** de noviembre.
*Today **is the eleventh of** November.*

In Spanish, the only date that does not follow this pattern is the first of the month.

Es el primero de noviembre.
It is** November **first.

Notice that the names of months are not capitalized in Spanish.

NOTA CULTURAL

In Spanish-speaking countries, the date is written with the number of the day first, then the number of the month: el dos de mayo = 2/5 = May 2nd.

Vocabulario

Los meses del año

enero	febrero	marzo	abril

mayo	**junio**	**julio**	**agosto**
septiembre	**octubre**	**noviembre**	**diciembre**

¿Cuál es tu mes favorito?

Los cumpleaños

Hablar/Escribir Explain when their birthdays are.

1. Verónica: 22/10
2. Alma: 4/1
3. la abuela: 23/7
4. yo: ¿?
5. mi madre: ¿?
6. mi amigo: ¿?

MÁS PRÁCTICA *cuaderno* p. 32

PARA HISPANOHABLANTES
cuaderno p. 30

Online Workbook
CLASSZONE.COM

Los días de fiesta

Escribir Write the date for each of the holidays.

modelo

Es el veinticinco de diciembre.

 1.

 2.

 3.

 4.

 5.

ACTIVIDAD 19

¿Cuál es la fecha de tu cumpleaños?

Hablar/Escribir Ask other students when their birthdays are. How many birthdays are there in each month? Make a chart like the chart you see here.

Nombre	Su cumpleaños es
Ramón	el 13 de junio

ACTIVIDAD 20

¿En qué mes llevas...?

Hablar/Escribir Tell which article of clothing you wear during each of the months on the list. Use a different article of clothing for each month.

modelo

enero

En **enero** llevo un suéter.

1. julio
2. diciembre
3. abril
4. agosto
5. octubre
6. febrero

Conexiones

La geografía

Latin American countries celebrate their independence from Spain in the nineteenth century, just as we celebrate our independence on July 4th. Here along the map you see the flags chosen by some countries to represent them as independent nations.

PARA HACER:
- Identify each country represented by its flag.
- Say and write out its date of independence. For example, el 16 de septiembre, México.

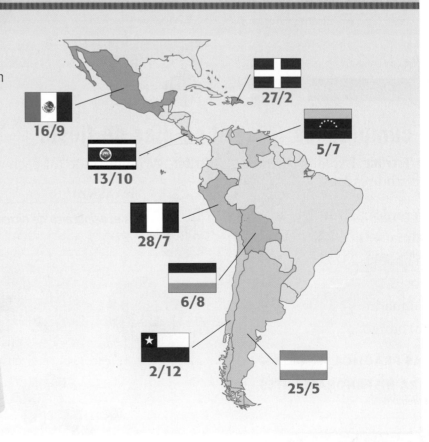

¿Cuál es la respuesta?

Escuchar Listen and choose the correct answer.

1. **a.** Tiene cinco años.
   b. Tiene setenta años.
   c. Tiene veinte años.

2. **a.** Son viejas.
   b. Son grandes.
   c. Son jóvenes.

3. **a.** Soy policía.
   b. Soy estudiante.
   c. Soy maestro.

4. **a** Llevo un suéter.
   b. Llevo una camiseta.
   c. Llevo una chaqueta.

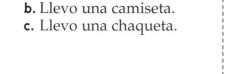

NOTA CULTURAL

When you speak to your grandfather, do you call him "grandfather"? Or do you say "grandpa"? To express affection for family members and other acquaintances, most Spanish speakers add the suffix **-ito** or **-ita** to a word. For example, **hermanita**, **abuelito**, **hijito**.

Mi madre

Escribir Describe a family member using as many details as possible.

modelo

Mi madre se llama Elena.
Es alta y castaña.
Tiene los ojos verdes.
Le gusta cantar y leer.
Es muy inteligente.
Tiene cuarenta años.
Su cumpleaños es el cuatro de mayo.

■ **MÁS COMUNICACIÓN** p. R3

Online Workbook
CLASSZONE.COM

Pronunciación

Trabalenguas

Pronunciación de la *m* y la *n* The letters m and n are pronounced in Spanish just as they are in English. Try the following tongue twisters.

Mi mamá me mima.

Nueve nenes nadan.

En voces

LECTURA

PARA LEER

STRATEGY: READING

Picture clues Looking at the pictures that accompany a reading can help you understand the reading better. Look at the illustrations on these pages. What do you think the reading will be about?

Los Ángeles:
Una carta¹ del pasado²

Aquí tienes un fragmento de una carta de Miguel José Guerra, un chico español, que vivía³ en Los Ángeles en ¡1784!

> 2 de agosto de 1784
>
> Querido⁴ primo:
>
> ¿Cómo estás? ¿Cómo está toda la familia allá en Málaga⁵? Aquí en el Pueblo de Nuestra Señora de Los Ángeles estamos contentos. ¡Hoy mi familia y yo no trabajamos!
>
> Generalmente, mi hermana y yo trabajamos en el campo⁶ con mamá y papá. (Mi hermana ya tiene 15 años y yo tengo 13, pero mi papá es muy viejo —¡él tiene 36 años!) Papá es fuerte y

---

¹ letter
² past
³ lived

⁴ Dear
⁵ city in the south of Spain
⁶ fields

muy moreno por el sol⁷ del campo.
Mamá es muy fuerte también y siempre
muy bonita.

Hoy es el día de Nuestra Señora de Los
Ángeles, la patrona de mi pueblo.
Hay celebración y fiesta. Llevo mi ropa
elegante y mi hermana también.
Vamos a la capilla⁸ con mamá y papá
y con los tíos y los primos de aquí.
Hay música y danzas tradicionales y
¡mucha buena comida⁹!

Un abrazo¹⁰ de tu primo,
Miguel José

Online Workbook
CLASSZONE.COM

¿Comprendiste?

1. ¿Quién escribe la carta?
2. ¿A quién le escribe? ¿Dónde vive esa persona?
3. ¿Por qué está contento?
4. ¿Cuántos miembros de la familia hay? ¿Quiénes son?
5. ¿Cómo celebran el día?

¿Qué piensas?

1. Why do you think Miguel has family in Spain?
2. Why do you think Miguel's whole family had to work?
3. What do you think it would be like to work with your family?

⁷ sun
⁸ Vamos…capilla
  We go to chapel.
⁹ food
¹⁰ hug

En colores

CULTURA Y COMPARACIONES

PARA CONOCERNOS
STRATEGY: CONNECTING CULTURES
Compare rites of passage In your community what are some events, formal or informal, that mark a young person's transition from childhood to adulthood? What are they called and when do they occur? How are they celebrated? If you could design your own event, how would it be celebrated? Use a word web to record your thoughts. Think of its components as you read **«La quinceañera»**.

La palabra *quinceañera* se refiere a[1] dos conceptos. Una quinceañera es una chica de quince años. Una quinceañera también es una fiesta en que se celebra el cumpleaños de una chica de quince años.

La quinceañera lleva un vestido especial. Es tradicional llevar un vestido rosado.

Hay mucha preparación para la quinceañera. Hay muchas decoraciones.

La quinceañera

¡FELICIDADES!

La tradición más importante es que la familia acompaña a la quinceañera en su día especial.

La quinceañera es una tradición especial de la cultura latina. Representa el momento en que una chica llega a ser[2] una mujer. Las tradiciones son diferentes en cada región. Una tradición es tener una ceremonia religiosa. Algunas fiestas se celebran en la casa de la familia. Otras se celebran en un hotel o un restaurante. La familia de la quinceañera invita a todos sus primos, sus tíos, sus abuelos y sus buenos amigos.

More About Latinos
CLASSZONE.COM

¿Comprendiste?

1. ¿Qué es una quinceañera?
2. ¿Cuál es una tradición de la quinceañera?
3. ¿Dónde se celebran las fiestas?
4. ¿Qué lleva la quinceañera?

¿Qué piensas?

1. ¿Qué fiestas hay en tu comunidad?
2. ¿Hay otras fiestas similares para una chica en tu comunidad? ¿Para un chico?

---

[1] refers to
[2] becomes

En uso

REPASO Y MÁS COMUNICACIÓN

OBJECTIVES

- Describe family
- Ask and tell ages
- Talk about birthdays
- Give dates
- Express possession

Now you can...

- describe family.

To review

- vocabulary for family, see p. 80.

ACTIVIDAD 1 Una familia feliz

Complete Mónica's description of her family.

modelo

Tengo tres _primos_ . Lucas es mi primo _mayor_ .

Mi familia es muy interesante. Mis ___1___ son Gregorio y Berta. Tengo una ___2___ que se llama Rosita. Ella es mi hermana ___3___. Mi padre tiene un hermano. Es mi ___4___ Carlos. Es muy cómico. Sus tres ___5___ son Paquita, Lucas y Pepe. Ellos son mis ___6___. La ___7___ de ellos es mi tía Amalia. Mis primos y yo tenemos unos ___8___ muy simpáticos: Rafael y Esperanza Santana.

Rafael

Esperanza

Gregorio | **Berta**

Carlos | **Amalia**

Mónica **Rosita** **Paquita**

Lucas **Pepe**

Now you can...

- tell ages.

To review

- the verb **tener**, see p. 88.
- vocabulary for numbers, see p. 89.

ACTIVIDAD 2 ¿Cuántos años tienen?

Tell the ages of the people Verónica knows.

modelo

Yolanda: 44   **Yolanda** tiene **cuarenta y cuatro años.**

1. Juan y Anita: 42
2. el señor Uribe: 100
3. su prima: 28
4. yo: 15
5. los amigos de los García: 70
6. tú: 13
7. la señora Quiroga: 91
8. su tío: 67
9. nosotros: 38
10. usted: 83
11. Rafael: 17
12. Carlota: 21

Now you can...

• talk about birthdays.

To review

• possession using **de,** see p. 90.

• dates and months, see p. 94.

ACTIVIDAD 3 ¿Cuándo cumplen años?

Tell the date of each person's birthday.

modelo

Antonio: 19/7

*El cumpleaños de **Antonio** es **el diecinueve de julio.***

I. Rafael: 23/12

2. Francisco: 15/3

3. Rosalinda: 6/2

4. la señora García: 1/10

5. David: 30/6

6. Yolanda: 25/11

Un pastel para la quinceañera

Now you can...

• give dates.

To review

• dates and months, see p. 94.

ACTIVIDAD 4 Las fiestas

What are the dates of these holidays?

modelo

17/3

el diecisiete de marzo

I. 25/12	**4.** 11/11	**7.** 5/5	**10.** 14/2
2. 4/7	**5.** 14/6	**8.** 6/1	**II.** 17/3
3. 1/1	**6.** 12/10	**9.** 2/2	**12.** 31/10

Now you can...

• express possession.

To review

• the verb **tener,** see p. 88.

• possessive adjectives, see p. 92.

ACTIVIDAD 5 Amigos internacionales

Describe people's international friends and family members.

modelo

Inés: amiga de México (bonito)

Inés** tiene **una amiga de México.** Su amiga es **bonita.

I. Víctor: vecinos de Cuba (viejo)

2. yo: doctor de Guatemala (joven)

3. ustedes: amigos de Argentina (simpático)

4. nosotras: maestra de la República Dominicana (cómico)

5. tú: tíos de Chile (trabajador)

6. Raquel y Mario: prima de Puerto Rico (moreno)

7. Lisa y yo: amigo de España (guapo)

 **ACTIVIDAD 6** ¡Tenemos unas preguntas!

PARA CONVERSAR
STRATEGY: SPEAKING
Practice speaking smoothly Speaking smoothly without starts and stops helps others understand you. So first think about what you want to say, then practice saying it smoothly and naturally.

Work together to write questions for your teacher. Include questions about his or her family and birthday.

modelo

¿Quién es su madre?

¿Tiene usted...? ¿Cuántos años...?

¿Cuál es la fecha de...? ¿De dónde...?

¿Cómo es...? ¿Cómo se llama...?

 **ACTIVIDAD 7** Su familia

Draw your family tree. Include names and ages. Using another student's family tree, describe his or her family to a group from the class.

modelo

La familia de Julio es pequeña. Él tiene un hermano mayor. No tiene hermanas. Su padre se llama Víctor y su madre se llama Lisa…

 **ACTIVIDAD 8** *En tu propia voz*

Escritura Escribe un poema de cinco líneas describiendo a un miembro de tu familia.
(Hint: Write a five-line poem (cinquain) describing a family member.)

modelo

Abuelo

Delgado, moreno

Muy inteligente

Le gusta leer

Persona divertida

En la comunidad

Theresa is a student in Massachusetts. Spanish comes in handy when she and a friend help two fifth-grade Guatemalan girls learn English. At home, she practices speaking Spanish with her brother, who also studies it in school. She also writes letters in Spanish to a little girl in Guatemala, and she is able to read the letters the girl writes back. Do you correspond with anyone in Spanish?

En resumen
REPASO DE VOCABULARIO

DESCRIBING FAMILY

Family Members

la abuela	grandmother
el abuelo	grandfather
los abuelos	grandparents
la hermana	sister
el hermano	brother
los hermanos	brother(s) and sister(s)
la hija	daughter
el hijo	son
los hijos	son(s) and daughter(s), children
la madre	mother
el padre	father
los padres	parents
el (la) primo(a)	cousin
la tía	aunt
el tío	uncle
los tíos	uncle(s) and aunt(s)

Descriptions

joven	young
mayor	older
menor	younger
viejo(a)	old

EXPRESSING POSSESSION

¿De quién es...?	Whose is...?
el (la)... de...	(someone)'s...
Es de...	It's...
mi	my
tu	your (familiar)
su	your, his, her, its, their
nuestro(a)	our
vuestro(a)	your (plural familiar)

ASKING AND TELLING AGES

Asking About Age

la edad	age
¿Cuántos años tiene...?	How old is...?
Tiene... años.	He/She is...years old.

Numbers from 11 to 100

once	eleven
doce	twelve
trece	thirteen
catorce	fourteen
quince	fifteen
dieciséis	sixteen
diecisiete	seventeen
dieciocho	eighteen
diecinueve	nineteen
veinte	twenty
veintiuno	twenty-one
treinta	thirty
cuarenta	forty
cincuenta	fifty
sesenta	sixty
setenta	seventy
ochenta	eighty
noventa	ninety
cien	one hundred

Juego

El abuelo tiene 24 años más que su hijo Carlos. Carlos tiene 35 años más que su hijo Antonio. Los tres combinados tienen 100 años. ¿Cuántos años tiene...

1. el abuelo?
2. Carlos?
3. Antonio?

GIVING DATES

Asking the Date

el año	year
la fecha	date
¿Cuál es la fecha?	What is the date?
Es el... de...	It's the...of...

Months

el mes	month
enero	January
febrero	February
marzo	March
abril	April
mayo	May
junio	June
julio	July
agosto	August
septiembre	September
octubre	October
noviembre	November
diciembre	December

TALKING ABOUT BIRTHDAYS

el cumpleaños	birthday
felicidades	congratulations
feliz	happy

OTHER WORDS AND PHRASES

ahora	now
la ciudad	city
con	with
dentro	inside
fuera	outside
hay	there is, there are
más	more
muy	very
¡Qué chévere!	How awesome!
¿Quién es?	Who is it?
¿Quiénes son?	Who are they?
sólo	only
tener	to have
todo(a)	all

Conexiones
OTRAS DISCIPLINAS Y PROYECTOS

La historia

Did you know that in Spanish **florida** is used to describe a place with many flowers? Spanish explorers named the land that later became the state of Florida when they reached it in 1513 while searching for the "fountain of youth." They also founded St. Augustine, the oldest European-established city in the United States.

More than two centuries later, Spanish colonists (**colonizadores**) and missionaries (**misioneros**) traveled northward from **Nueva España** (present-day Mexico) to Texas and California, establishing settlements and mission churches (**misiones**), many of which can still be visited today.

Find out what mission churches survive in California today. Choose one and investigate its history.

The Mission of San Xavier del Bac was founded in 1700 near Tucson, Arizona, by Father Eusebio Kino.

El arte

Muralists (**pintores muralistas**) in Los Angeles have created folk murals in public places expressing the Spanish-speaking community's interests and concerns. These murals echo the works of the great Mexican muralists Diego Rivera and José Clemente Orozco, as well as the traditions of wall painting of the ancient Aztecs and Mayas.

Find out about the history of your own town, city, or region. Who were the original settlers? How have things changed over the years? Use what you find out to plan a mural depicting your town's history.

Wall painting from the ancient city of **Teotihuacán**. It shows a jaguar with a plumed headdress blowing a conch instrument.

Proyecto cultural

As a class project, find cities in the American Southwest that probably were settled by Spanish explorers or Mexican colonists.

1. In groups of three or four, look at this map of the Southwest.

2. Discuss the clues that will help you find these cities. Do the names begin with **el** or **la, los** or **las**? What other clues can you find? (For example, **Santa** or **San**, which means "Saint.")

3. With your group, draw a map of the American Southwest today. Name and highlight cities with Spanish names. If you need help, your teacher will give you clues.

4. Share your work with the class by hanging the maps on the bulletin board.

Padre Junípero Serra was born in Spain. He traveled to Mexico and then was sent north to start missions. He founded several missions in California.

2

 STANDARDS

Communication
- Describing classes, classroom objects, and schedules
- Saying how often you do something
- Asking and telling time
- Requesting snack and lunch food
- Discussing after-school plans
- Talking about places and people you know

Cultures
- School in Mexico City
- The history of Mexico City
- Regional vocabulary
- The importance of parks to life in Mexico

Connections
- Mathematics: Using pie charts to summarize survey results in Spanish
- Health: Researching the nutritional value of Mexican foods

Comparisons
- Daily schedules of young people in Mexico City and the U.S.
- Snack foods of Mexico City and the U.S.
- Historical areas in Mexico City and the U.S.

Communities
- Using Spanish beyond the school experience
- Using Spanish for personal enjoyment

INTERNET Preview
CLASSZONE.COM

- More About Mexico
- Webquest
- Self-Check Quizzes
- Flashcards
- Writing Center
- eEdition Plus Online

DIEGO RIVERA (1886–1957) painted *La vendedora de flores* (1942) as well as many other paintings and murals. What paintings by Mexican artists have you seen?

ALMANAQUE CULTURAL

POBLACIÓN: 8.591.309

ALTURA: 2.309 metros (7.575 pies)

CLIMA: 19° C (66° F)

COMIDA TÍPICA: tortillas, frijoles, tacos

GENTE FAMOSA DE MÉXICO: Lázaro Cárdenas (político), Carlos Fuentes (escritor), Amalia Hernández (bailarina), Frida Kahlo (pintora), Diego Rivera (pintor)

¿VAS A MÉXICO, D.F.? Generalmente los mexicanos usan la palabra *México* para hablar del país. Para hablar de la Ciudad de México, usan las frases *la capital, el distrito federal* o simplemente *el D.F.* El distrito federal está en el centro de la ciudad.

More About Mexico
CLASSZONE.COM

EL PALACIO DE BELLAS ARTES, begun in 1904 by an Italian architect, was finished 30 years later by a Mexican one. The Ballet Folklórico performs here. What do you think its name means?

EL BALLET FOLKLÓRICO has communicated the spirit of Mexico through dance since 1959. It was founded by Amalia Hernández. What traditional dances of the United States do you know?

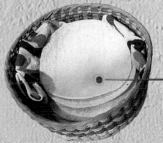

TORTILLAS are traditionally made by hand. The price of tortillas is set by the government. What Mexican dishes made with tortillas have you tried?

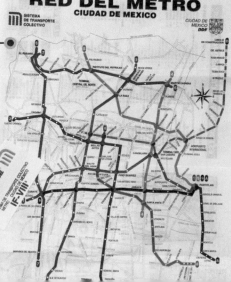

SISTEMA DE TRANSPORTE COLECTIVO
RED DEL METRO
CIUDAD DE MEXICO

EL METRO opened in 1969 to combat pollution. It serves over 4 million people a day. To ride it, ask for a **billete!** Why might you ride a subway?

LÁZARO CÁRDENAS (1895–1970), president 1934–1940, made great improvements in Mexico. The Department of Tourism was created during his presidency, and Mexico became internationally influential. Who is the current president of Mexico?

UNIDAD 2

UNA SEMANA TÍPICA

- Comunicación

- Culturas

- Conexiones

- Comparaciones

- Comunidades

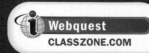
Webquest
CLASSZONE.COM

Explore communication in
Mexico City through guided
Web activities.

Comunicación

As a student of Spanish, you will have
the opportunity to communicate in
another language. This means engaging
in new kinds of conversations, giving
and finding out new information, and
expressing your ideas in new ways.

Comunicación en acción Describe a las
personas de la foto. ¿Es el chico rubio o
moreno? ¿Qué lleva? ¿Tiene la chica el pelo
largo o corto? ¿Qué lleva ella? ¿Son estudiantes?

Comunidades

In this unit you will
learn how one student
uses Spanish in his
own community. He
helps Spanish-speaking
children with their
homework and uses
Spanish in his
part-time job.

Conexiones

You will be able to understand spoken
and written Spanish that informs you
about many school subjects. You will also
be able to present information and talk
about your own ideas as well as write
different types of reports.

Este mural es de la Universidad Autónoma de México. Es de Orozco, un artista mexicano famoso.

Culturas

By learning to read Spanish and to understand spoken Spanish, you will have the opportunity to learn about different aspects of culture. In this unit you will learn about places in Mexico . . .

. . . and Mexican food.

A muchos mexicanos les gusta comer tacos al pastor. Es una comida típica de México.

Comparaciones

You will also learn what Mexican teens do in a typical week. Do you think they enjoy some of the same activities you do?

A algunos adolescentes les gusta jugar al básquetbol, cantar con los amigos o leer.

Fíjate

Look closely at the photo captions. You probably don't understand every word, but by looking at the pictures and at the words you do know, you probably understand the information they convey.

1. Where are the two students eating?
2. Who created the design on the university building?
3. Name the food shown that is typical of Mexico.
4. Name an activity that Mexican teens do that you also do.

ETAPA

1

Un día de clases

OBJECTIVES

- Describe classes and classroom objects

- Say how often you do something

- Discuss obligations

¿Qué ves?

Mira la foto del centro de la Ciudad de México.

1. ¿Tiene pelo corto la chica?

2. ¿Son rubios o morenos los chicos?

3. ¿Es roja o rosada la chaqueta del chico?

4. ¿Isabel tiene clases el sábado?

Horario: Isabel Palacios

Hora	lunes	martes	miércoles	jueves	viernes
12:30	computación	inglés	computación	inglés	computación
1:30	literatura	matemáticas	literatura	matemáticas	literatura
2:30	arte	educación física	arte	educación física	arte
3:30	receso	receso	receso	receso	receso
4:00	historia	música	historia	música	historia
5:00		ciencias naturales		ciencias naturales	

En contexto

VIDEO   DVD   AUDIO

VOCABULARIO

Isabel spends most of the week in school. Here Isabel describes the things she uses there.

A

Bienvenidos a mi **escuela. En la clase,** el maestro **habla** mucho. Los estudiantes **escuchan** al maestro. Las lecciones son interesantes.

el diccionario   el lápiz

el papel

el escritorio   el cuaderno

B Para **estudiar,** tengo **un escritorio.** En mi escritorio, tengo **un cuaderno, un diccionario, un lápiz** y **papel.**

una buena nota

la mochila

la pluma   la calculadora

el libro

C En mi **mochila,** tengo mi **libro** de **ciencias,** mi **calculadora** y mi **pluma.** También tengo mi tarea. ¡Siempre **saco una buena nota** en la tarea!

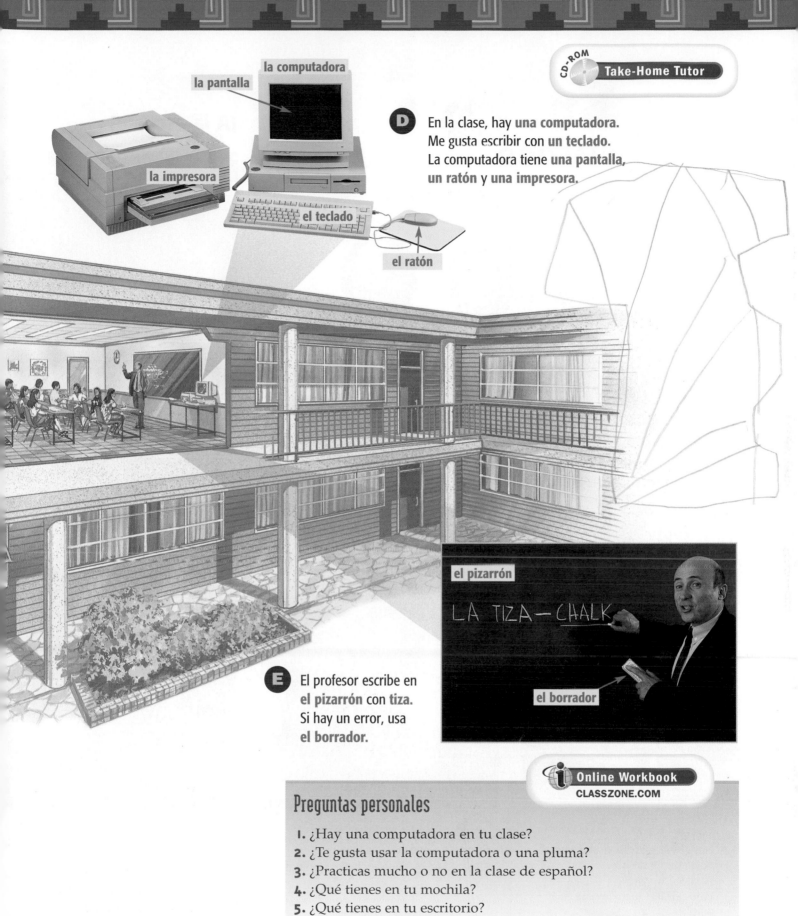

la computadora

la pantalla

la impresora

el teclado

el ratón

D En la clase, hay **una computadora.**
Me gusta escribir con **un teclado.**
La computadora tiene **una pantalla,**
un ratón y **una impresora.**

el pizarrón

LA TIZA—CHALK

el borrador

E El profesor escribe en
el pizarrón con **tiza.**
Si hay un error, usa
el borrador.

Online Workbook
CLASSZONE.COM

Preguntas personales

1. ¿Hay una computadora en tu clase?
2. ¿Te gusta usar la computadora o una pluma?
3. ¿Practicas mucho o no en la clase de español?
4. ¿Qué tienes en tu mochila?
5. ¿Qué tienes en tu escritorio?

En vivo

VIDEO DVD AUDIO

DIÁLOGO

¡A la escuela!

 **Isabel**

 Mamá

 Ricardo

 **Prof. Martínez**

PARA ESCUCHAR • STRATEGY: LISTENING

Listen for feelings Many things happen to Isabel in this scene. How does she feel? What do you hear that makes you think she feels that way?

1 ▶ Isabel: ¿Qué pasa con la computadora? ¡Y la pantalla! ¿Qué pasa con el ratón? Con razón. Hay que conectar el ratón al teclado.

5 ▶ Isabel: Necesito sacar una buena nota en esta clase.
Ricardo: Yo también. Estudio todos los días, pero la clase es difícil.

6 ▶ Profesor: Good morning, class.
Clase: Good morning, Professor Martínez.

7 ▶ Isabel: Tengo que sacar una buena nota. ¡Es muy importante!
Profesor: Miss, would you like to share your ideas with the class?

2 ▶ Isabel: ¡Papel! ¡La impresora no tiene papel!

Mamá: ¡Pronto! ¡Siempre llegas tarde a la escuela!

3 ▶ Mamá: ¿Necesitas tu cuaderno? ¿Y tus libros? ¿Y la calculadora?

Isabel: Sí, mamá, claro.

4 ▶ Mamá: ¿Y tu tarea, Isabel? ¿Tu tarea para la clase de ciencias naturales?

8 ▶ Isabel: Lo siento. No hablo más.

Profesor: This is English class.

Isabel: I'm sorry, teacher. I won't talk anymore.

9 ▶ Isabel: ¡Qué vergüenza! Siempre escucho con atención en la clase de inglés.

Ricardo: Cálmate, Isabel. ¿Qué clases tienes hoy?

Isabel: Tengo matemáticas y ciencias naturales.

10 ▶ Isabel: ¡Qué horror!

Ricardo: ¿Qué?

Isabel: ¡Mi tarea para la clase de ciencias naturales! ¡Está en la impresora, en mi casa! ¡Tengo que hablar con la profesora Díaz! ¡Ahora mismo!

En acción

VOCABULARIO Y GRAMÁTICA

ACTIVIDAD 1

Todo para la escuela

Escuchar/Escribir Complete each sentence based on the dialog. Use each answer only once.

1. ¿Qué pasa con _____ ?
2. Hay que conectar _____ .
3. _____ no tiene papel.
4. ¿Necesitas tu _____ ?
5. Necesito sacar _____ .
6. Siempre escucho con atención en _____ de inglés.
7. Tengo que hablar con _____ .

a. la impresora
b. la profesora Díaz
c. la computadora
d. una buena nota
e. el ratón
f. cuaderno
g. la clase

También se dice

Mexico has a lot of distinctive regional vocabulary. Many Mexicans would say **calificaciones** instead of **notas, gis** instead of **tiza,** and **libreta** instead of **cuaderno.** In many countries you may hear the word **pizarra** instead of **pizarrón** and **mouse** instead of **ratón. Mouse** is a loan word from English.

Un día de clases

Escuchar Are the statements about the dialog true or false? Respond to each one with **sí** or **no**. If the statement is false, correct it.

modelo

Isabel siempre llega tarde a la escuela.

Sí. Isabel siempre llega tarde a la escuela.

1. Isabel usa la computadora.
2. Isabel necesita la tiza y un borrador.
3. En la clase de inglés es importante hablar en español.
4. Ricardo estudia mucho.
5. Isabel tiene clases de matemáticas y ciencias naturales.
6. La tarea de Isabel para la clase de ciencias naturales está en su mochila.
7. Ricardo tiene que hablar con la profesora Díaz.
8. Para Isabel, ¡todo es muy fácil de preparar!

Conexiones

Las ciencias Calendars based on the movements of the sun and/or the moon have been used since ancient times. **La Piedra del Sol,** or Sun Stone, shows the Aztec calendar. In an Aztec year there were 18 months. Each month had 20 days.

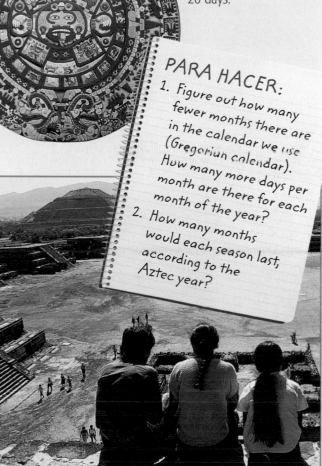

PARA HACER:

1. Figure out how many fewer months there are in the calendar we use (Gregorian calendar). How many more days per month are there for each month of the year?

2. How many months would each season last, according to the Aztec year?

Among the ruins at Teotihuacán, just northeast of Mexico City, are the Pyramid of the Sun and the Pyramid of the Moon.

♻ ¿Qué hay en la clase?

Hablar Work with another student. Say whether you see the following items in the photograph.

modelo

una mochila azul

Estudiante A: *¿Hay **una mochila azul**?*

Estudiante B: *No, no hay **una mochila azul**. Hay una mochila **roja**.*

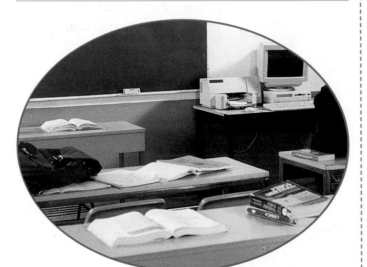

1. un libro
2. un cuaderno
3. un pizarrón
4. una mochila roja
5. un escritorio
6. un borrador
7. dos computadoras
8. dos ratones
9. una impresora
10. ¿?

♻ ¿Qué hay?

Hablar/Escribir Identify the items on Isabel's desk.

modelo

Hay tres libros.

ACTIVIDAD 5

Las materias y tú

Leer/Escribir Read the list of **las materias** below. On a separate sheet of paper, write them in your order of preference. (Use one for the class you like the best.)

Vocabulario

Las materias

el arte

las ciencias

la computación

la educación física

el español (Buenos días.)

los estudios sociales

la historia

el inglés (Good morning.)

la literatura

las matemáticas $x + y = z$

la música

For more class subjects, see p. R11.

Here are other words to talk about classes.

fácil *easy*

difícil *difficult, hard*

el examen *test*

la lección *lesson*

la prueba *quiz*

♻ Remember that you can use these adjectives you've learned, too.

aburrido(a)

interesante

bueno(a)

malo(a)

¿Qué clase tiene mucha tarea?

ACTIVIDAD 6

¿Cómo son las clases?

PARA CONVERSAR

STRATEGY: SPEAKING

Develop more than one way of expressing an idea It adds variety and interest to your speech. For example, in addition to saying what something *is*, you can say what it is *not*.

—¿Cómo es tu clase de historia?

—No es interesante.

Hablar Describe your classes to your partner. He or she will ask you questions about them. Change roles.

modelo

Estudiante A: *¿Qué clases tienes?*

Estudiante B: *Tengo historia, español, inglés...*

Estudiante A: *¿Cómo es la clase de inglés?*

Estudiante B: *Es... No es...*

Estudiante A: *¿Qué te gusta estudiar?*

Saying What You Do: Present of -ar Verbs

To talk about things you do, you use the present tense.
To form the present tense of a regular verb that ends in -ar,

drop the -ar and add the appropriate ending.

estudiar ← o, as, a, amos, áis, or an

The verb estudiar means *to study.*

yo	estudio	nosotros(as)	estudiamos
tú	estudias	vosotros(as)	estudiáis
usted, él, ella	estudia	ustedes, ellos(as)	estudian

Isabel's mother says:
—¿Necesitas tu cuaderno?
Do you need *your notebook?*

¿Qué estudian?

Hablar/Escribir Tell what each person studies.

modelo

Elena:

Elena** estudia **historia.

1. yo: 〔Buenos días.〕

2. mis amigos: x+y=z

3. nosotros: 〔Good morning.〕

4. Federico: ▯▯▯▯

5. tú: 🌎

6. Juana y Miguel: 🎨

7. ella: 🎼

8. Lorenzo y yo: 📚

Vocabulario

Verbs Ending in -ar

ayudar (a) *to help*

buscar *to look for, to search*

contestar *to answer*

enseñar *to teach*

entrar (a, en) *to enter*

esperar *to wait for, to expect*

llegar *to arrive*

llevar *to wear, to carry*

mirar *to look at, to watch*

necesitar *to need*

pasar *to happen, to pass, to pass by*

preparar *to prepare*

usar *to use*

¿Qué pasa cada día?

¿Qué pasa?

Hablar Work with a partner. Take turns asking and answering questions according to the cues and pictures.

modelo

Elena / estudiar / ¿música o arte?

Estudiante A: *¿Elena estudia música o arte?*

Estudiante B: *Estudia arte.*

1. mi hermana / buscar / ¿su libro o su mochila?

2. Miguel / usar / ¿un lápiz o una computadora?

3. las muchachas / llevar / ¿sombreros o calcetines?

4. mis amigos / sacar / ¿buenas notas o malas notas?

MÁS PRÁCTICA *cuaderno pp. 37–38*

PARA HISPANOHABLANTES *cuaderno pp. 35–36*

APOYO PARA ESTUDIAR

Verb Conjugations

Using the right ending on a verb is very important. Often verbs are used without subject pronouns (**yo, tú, él, ella, usted,** and so on). To help remember verb endings, practice each **-ar** verb with a partner in a question/answer exercise:

—¿Estudias…?	—Sí, estudio…
—¿Miran ustedes…?	—Sí, miramos…
—¿Enseña ella…?	—Sí, ella enseña…
—¿Preparan ellos…?	—Sí, ellos preparan…

Online Workbook
CLASSZONE.COM

¿Qué haces?

Hablar Ask a classmate if he or she does these activities.

modelo

sacar buenas notas

Estudiante A: *¿Sacas buenas notas?*

Estudiante B: *Sí, saco buenas notas.*

1. hablar mucho
2. usar un diccionario
3. escuchar en clase
4. preparar la tarea en la computadora
5. llegar tarde a la clase
6. usar una calculadora en la clase de matemáticas
7. mirar el pizarrón
8. estudiar mucho
9. llevar una mochila
10. ayudar en casa

¡Lógicamente!

Escuchar Listen and choose the most logical response to each statement.

1. a. No estudia.
   b. Ayuda a sus padres.
   c. Necesita un lápiz.

2. a. Tiene un examen mañana.
   b. Habla mucho en clase.
   c. No escucha a la maestra.

3. a. Enseña ciencias naturales.
   b. Necesita estudiar.
   c. Espera a su amigo.

4. a. Usa una calculadora.
   b. No estudia mucho.
   c. Ayuda a su abuelo.

5. a. Necesita estudiar mucho.
   b. Estudia en casa.
   c. Busca su diccionario.

Conexiones

La historia In Mexico City there is a place called **La Plaza de las Tres Culturas.** The site contains the ruins of the Aztec marketplace of Tlatelolco. Also there is a church built by the Spaniards. In addition, there are contemporary buildings which represent present-day Mexico.

PARA HACER:

What three cultures does La Plaza de las Tres Culturas refer to?

Find the structures of each culture in the photo.

124 | ciento veinticuatro
Unidad 2

¿Y ustedes?

Hablar Work with a classmate. Ask your partner what activities he or she and a friend do.

bailar
hablar
trabajar
patinar
estudiar
usar
preparar
nadar
cantar

modelo

Tú: *¿Tú y tu amigo(a) **estudian** mucho?*

Otro(a) estudiante: *Si, (No, no) estudiamos…*

■ MÁS COMUNICACIÓN p. R4

GRAMÁTICA — Expressing Frequency with Adverbs

To talk about how often someone does something, you use expressions of frequency. Expressions of frequency are adverbs or adverbial phrases.

siempre	*always*
todos los días	*every day*
mucho	*often*
a veces	*sometimes*
de vez en cuando	*once in a while*
poco	*a little*
rara vez	*rarely*
nunca	*never*

Ricardo and Isabel might say:
—Estudio **todos los días**.
*I study **every day**.*

—Yo **siempre** estudio.
*I **always** study.*

Different adverbs are placed in different parts of a sentence.

These expressions are usually placed **before** the **verb**:

siempre	Isabel **siempre llega** tarde a la escuela.
rara vez	Isabel **rara vez habla** español en la clase de inglés.
nunca	Isabel **nunca usa** un diccionario.

These expressions are usually placed **after** the **verb**:

mucho	Ricardo **estudia mucho**.
poco	Isabel **habla poco** en la clase.

Longer phrases can be placed at the **beginning** or the **end** of the **sentence**:

todos los días	**Todos los días** Isabel llega tarde.
a veces	**A veces**
	De vez en cuando
	Isabel llega tarde **todos los días**.
de vez en cuando	**a veces**.
	de vez en cuando.

Los estudiantes diferentes

Leer María is a good student. Felipe is not. Read the following statements and decide who would probably say each one: María or Felipe.

modelo

Estudio mucho.	María

1. Nunca escucho en clase.
2. Rara vez saco malas notas.
3. Preparo mi tarea todos los días.
4. Estudio poco para los exámenes.
5. A veces entro en la clase tarde.
6. Miro poco el pizarrón.
7. Siempre estudio para las pruebas.
8. Estudio de vez en cuando.

■ **MÁS PRÁCTICA** *cuaderno* p. 39

■ **PARA HISPANOHABLANTES** *cuaderno* p. 37

Online Workbook
CLASSZONE.COM

¿Con qué frecuencia?

Hablar How frequently do you do these things?

1 Work with another student. Take turns asking each other questions about study habits. Use the following words of frequency in your answers.

2 Take notes as you go along.

3 After the survey, report to the class on how much you and your partner have in common.

siempre   todos los días

mucho   de vez en cuando   a veces

rara vez   poco

nunca

modelo

¿Usas la computadora todos los días?

Estudiante A: *¿Usas la computadora todos los días?*

Estudiante B: *No, uso la computadora de vez en cuando.*

Estudiante A (a la clase): *Nora y yo usamos la computadora de vez en cuando.*

1. ¿Estudias español todos los días?
2. Nunca llegas tarde a la escuela, ¿verdad?
3. ¿Siempre escuchas a los maestros?
4. ¿Hablas en clase de vez en cuando?
5. ¿A veces sacas buenas notas? ¿En qué clase(s)?
6. ¿Ayudas a tus amigos de vez en cuando?

ACTIVIDAD 14

El estudiante ideal

Hablar/Escribir Work in a group of three to design a poster. Describe the study habits of the ideal student. Include words of frequency, such as **siempre**, **todos los días**, **mucho**, and **a veces**.

Un estudiante ideal

✓ Prepara su tarea todos los días.
✓ Nunca llega tarde a clase.
✓ Siempre escucha en clase.

GRAMÁTICA

Expressing Obligation with **hay que** and **tener que**

To talk about things someone must do, you can use two different phrases that express obligation.

- Use the impersonal phrase

    hay que + *infinitive*

    if there is **no specific subject**.

    —**Hay que conectar**
    el ratón al teclado.
    *You have to (one must) **connect** the mouse to the keyboard.*

- Use a form of **tener** in the phrase

    tener que + *infinitive*

    if there is a **specific subject**.

    —**Tengo que sacar**
    una buena nota.
    *I have to **get** a good grade.*

¿Qué tienen que hacer?

Hablar/Escribir Tell what Ricardo's friends have to do today. Then say whether you have to do the same things. Choose from the following activities.

estudiar	usar la computadora
correr	ayudar a su abuela
hablar con el maestro	preparar la tarea
esperar a su hermano	

modelo

Juan tiene que estudiar. Yo (no) tengo que estudiar.

Juan

1. Elena

2. Ana y Luis

3. Isabel

4. Felipe y yo

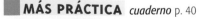 **MÁS PRÁCTICA** *cuaderno* p. 40

 **PARA HISPANOHABLANTES** *cuaderno* p. 38

Online Workbook
CLASSZONE.COM

¿Qué hay que hacer?

Hablar Work with a partner. Tell whether one must do the following to get good grades in math class. Do you and your partner always agree?

modelo

escuchar en clase

*Sí, hay que **escuchar en clase**.*

1. practicar las fórmulas
2. preparar tacos para el maestro
3. llegar tarde
4. usar lápices
5. usar la computadora
6. preparar la tarea todos los días
7. contestar bien las preguntas del maestro
8. ayudar al maestro a borrar el pizarrón
9. estudiar poco
10. leer el libro de matemáticas
11. llevar una camiseta roja
12. trabajar mucho

¿Tienes que hacer esto?

Escribir/Hablar Do you have to do this?

1 Take a moment to jot down five activities you think your classmates might have to do after class today.

2 Circulate around the class asking individuals if they have to do an activity on your list. If so, get each person's signature next to the activity. Collect at least five signatures.

modelo

Tú: *José, ¿tienes que estudiar después de clases hoy?*

José: *Sí, tengo que estudiar.*

Tiene que...	Nombre
estudiar	José

¡Pobre Isabel!

Leer/Hablar Read about Isabel and her science teacher. Explain whether it's necessary to use **el**, **la**, or neither one.

Nota

Use **el** and **la** before titles like **profesor(a)** and **señor(a)** when talking *about* someone.

—¡Tengo que hablar con *la profesora Díaz*!

El señor Martínez es el profesor de inglés.

Do not use articles when talking *to* someone.

—No tengo mi tarea, **profesora Díaz.**

Isabel habla con ___1___ profesora Díaz, su profesora de ciencias naturales.

«Buenos días, ___2___ profesora Díaz. ¿Cómo está usted hoy?»

«Muy bien, Isabel, ¿y tú?»

«Pues, no estoy muy bien, ___3___ profesora. No tengo mi tarea para hoy.»

___4___ profesora Díaz no está muy feliz.

«Isabel, para sacar una buena nota, ¡hay que preparar la tarea todos los días!»

ACTIVIDAD 19

Un día de una maestra de español

Hablar/Escribir Señorita Ramos, the school's most popular Spanish teacher, is having a busy day. Work with a partner to describe what happens during her day.

modelo

Un estudiante llega tarde a la clase de la señorita Ramos.

1.

2.

3.

4.

5.

La clase de tu amiga

Escuchar A friend is describing her Spanish class. Listen to the description. Then answer the questions.

1. La clase de español es _____.
   a. fácil y divertida
   b. difícil pero interesante
   c. fácil pero aburrida

2. La profesora de la clase es de _____.
   a. España
   b. México
   c. Estados Unidos

3. La señorita Casas habla español en clase _____.
   a. rara vez
   b. de vez en cuando
   c. todos los días

4. Tu amiga tiene que _____ cuando la señorita Casas habla.
   a. escribir
   b. escuchar
   c. estudiar

5. Tiene que preparar su tarea todos los días para _____.
   a. practicar mucho
   b. sacar una buena nota
   c. usar la computadora

Mi clase favorita

Escribir Write a paragraph about your favorite class. Include the following details.

1. Identify the class and the teacher.

2. Tell what the teacher does to make the class interesting.

3. Tell what you do in and out of class to be successful.

modelo

Mi clase favorita es historia. La maestra es la señorita Sánchez. Enseña bien. Es muy interesante. Hay que estudiar para sacar una buena nota. Tengo que preparar la tarea todos los días. Siempre preparo la tarea con la computadora.

MÁS COMUNICACIÓN p. R4

Online Workbook
CLASSZONE.COM

Pronunciación

Trabalenguas

Pronunciación de la y y la ll The ll and y have the same sounds in Spanish. At the beginning and middle of words they sound like the y in the English word *yes*. At the end of a word the y sounds like the Spanish i, as in **muy**. Ll does not occur at the end of words. To practice these sounds, say the tongue twisters.

Yolanda ya vive en una casa amarilla.
¿Cómo se llama la llama llorona?

ciento treinta y uno
Ciudad de México Etapa I

131

En voces

LECTURA

PARA LEER

STRATEGY: READING

Look for context clues At first glance, there may appear to be many words in the reading you can't seem to understand. To improve your comprehension, use this strategy: Read each sentence as a whole rather than translating word for word.

Una leyenda azteca

El origen de la Ciudad de México

Los aztecas, una tribu de guerreros[1], deciden dejar[2] su casa en el norte por necesidades económicas. Caminan todos los días por mucho tiempo buscando un lugar nuevo. Pasan por muchos lugares pero no encuentran[3] el lugar perfecto. Esperan ansiosos la señal[4] de su dios[5], Huitzilopochtli.

Pasa mucho tiempo y están los aztecas muy cansados[6]. Llegan a un lago[7] donde miran la señal en medio del lago. Está un águila[8] sobre un cacto, ¡con una serpiente en la boca[9]! Todos miran y hablan.

[1] warriors	[4] sign	[7] lake
[2] leave	[5] god	[8] eagle
[3] find	[6] tired	[9] mouth

—¡Ésta es la señal que esperamos! ¡Ésta es la señal de nuestro dios!

—¡Aquí es donde preparamos nuestra ciudad!

Y así, en el lago de Texcoco, los aztecas empiezan a construir su ciudad. Usan tierra y raíces[10] para crear pequeñas islas[11]. Construyen sus casas en las islas.

Y así fue la creación, en el año 1325, de la gran Tenochtitlán, que ahora es la maravillosa Ciudad de México.

---

[10] earth and roots
[11] islands

Online Workbook
CLASSZONE.COM

¿Comprendiste?

1. ¿Quiénes son los aztecas?
2. ¿Qué buscan?
3. ¿Cuál es la señal que reciben?
4. ¿Qué es Tenochtitlán?

¿Qué piensas?

1. ¿Cómo decide la gente dónde construir una ciudad?
2. ¿Qué es importante para seleccionar el lugar?
3. ¿Sabes la historia de tu ciudad o pueblo? ¿Por qué a la gente le gusta vivir allí?

En uso

REPASO Y MÁS COMUNICACIÓN

Now you can...

- describe classes and classroom objects.

To review

- vocabulary for classroom objects, see pp. 114–115.
- the present tense of regular **-ar** verbs, see p. 122.

ACTIVIDAD 1 En la clase de matemáticas

Correct the statements to match the drawing.

modelo

Hay siete libros en el escritorio de la profesora.

Hay cinco libros en el escritorio de la profesora.

1. Tres muchachas hablan y no escuchan a la profesora.
2. Hay tres cuadernos en el escritorio de la profesora.
3. La profesora usa una calculadora.
4. Hay tres computadoras y dos impresoras.
5. No hay borradores.
6. Las computadoras no tienen ratones.
7. Hay tres pizarrones en la clase.
8. Todos los estudiantes tienen lápices.

ACTIVIDAD 2 ¿Cómo es cada clase?

Choose the option that describes each class.

1. Nosotros siempre escuchamos en la clase de música.
2. Isabel estudia mucho para la clase de inglés.
3. Isabel y Ricardo sacan buenas notas en la clase de arte.
4. Muchos estudiantes llegan tarde a la clase de matemáticas.

a. Es difícil.
b. Es fácil.
c. Es interesante.
d. Es aburrida.

ACTIVIDAD 3 ¡Unos estudiantes excelentes!

All these students are excellent. Tell why, choosing the best option in each case.

modelo

nosotros / preparar la tarea: ¿siempre o nunca?

Nosotros siempre preparamos la tarea.

1. Isabel y Ricardo / llegar tarde: ¿todos los días o rara vez?
2. tú / sacar buenas notas: ¿siempre o nunca?
3. Alma / ayudar a sus amigos: ¿mucho o poco?
4. yo / escuchar al profesor: ¿de vez en cuando o todos los días?
5. Arturo y yo / hablar inglés en la clase de español: ¿a veces o nunca?
6. ellas / mirar el pizarrón: ¿mucho o poco?

ACTIVIDAD 4 Una fiesta pequeña

Tell why these people aren't at Alberto's party.

modelo

Sonia: habla con su madre   **Sonia** *tiene que* **hablar con su madre.**

1. ustedes: estudian
2. yo: preparo la tarea
3. mis amigos y yo: trabajamos
4. tú: esperas a tus padres
5. Samuel: ayuda a su hermano
6. Soledad y Raúl: usan la computadora

ACTIVIDAD 5 ¿Cómo son tus clases?

PARA CONVERSAR

STRATEGY: SPEAKING

Expand the conversation How do you keep a conversation going? Be interested. Find out more about your partner by asking either/or questions to prompt him or her when words don't come. Also, it's hard to keep a conversation going with just **sí** or **no** answers. So, say more rather than less.

¿Te gusta… o…?

¿Cómo es…?

Prepare five questions about classes to discuss with another student.

modelo

Estudiante A: *¿Tienes clase de historia?*

Estudiante B: *Sí, tengo clase de historia.*

Estudiante A: *¿Cómo es la clase?*

Estudiante B: *Es buena. El profesor enseña bien…*

ACTIVIDAD 6 Una visita a la clase

Give new students a "tour" of the class, pointing out items and discussing activities.

modelo

En la clase hay veinte escritorios y un pizarrón…

Los estudiantes estudian y…

ACTIVIDAD 7 En tu propia voz

Escritura Describe your favorite class.

Mi clase favorita es…

En la clase hay…

A veces yo…

El maestro siempre…

Todos los días hay que…

Nosotros nunca…

La maestra se llama…

Los estudiantes siempre…

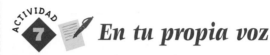

Conexiones

Las matemáticas Interview twenty students who are studying Spanish at your school to find out which class they like best, which class they find hardest, and so on. Summarize your results. Create a pie chart for each question, showing the percentage of students that voted for each class named.

Clase favorita
Resultados de 20 estudiantes

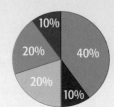

historia	8
literatura	4
español	4
arte	2
música	2

En resumen
REPASO DE VOCABULARIO

DESCRIBING CLASSES

At School

la clase	class, classroom
la escuela	school
el examen	test
la lección	lesson
la prueba	quiz
la tarea	homework

School Subjects

el arte	art
las ciencias	science
la computación	computer science
la educación física	physical education
el español	Spanish
los estudios sociales	social studies
la historia	history
el inglés	English
la literatura	literature
las matemáticas	mathematics
la materia	subject
la música	music

Classroom Activities

enseñar	to teach
escuchar	to listen (to)
estudiar	to study
hablar	to talk, to speak
mirar	to watch, to look at
preparar	to prepare
sacar una buena nota	to get a good grade

DESCRIBING CLASS OBJECTS

el borrador	eraser
la calculadora	calculator
el cuaderno	notebook
el diccionario	dictionary
el escritorio	desk
el lápiz	pencil
el libro	book
la mochila	backpack
el papel	paper
el pizarrón	chalkboard
la pluma	pen
la tiza	chalk

At the Computer

la computadora	computer
la impresora	printer
la pantalla	screen
el ratón	mouse
el teclado	keyboard

SAYING HOW OFTEN

a veces	sometimes
de vez en cuando	once in a while
mucho	often
nunca	never
poco	a little
rara vez	rarely
siempre	always
todos los días	every day

DISCUSSING OBLIGATIONS

hay que	one has to, one must
tener que	to have to

Actions

ayudar (a)	to help
buscar	to look for, to search
contestar	to answer
entrar (a, en)	to enter
esperar	to wait for, to expect
llegar	to arrive
llevar	to wear, to carry
necesitar	to need
pasar	to happen, to pass, to pass by
usar	to use

OTHER WORDS AND PHRASES

¡Ahora mismo!	Right now!
Con razón.	That's why.
difícil	difficult, hard
fácil	easy
mismo(a)	same
pronto	soon
la razón	reason
tarde	late

Juego

Jorge tiene que preparar la tarea de cada clase. ¿En qué materias tiene tarea?

1. Usa una calculadora.
2. Estudia un libro sobre computadoras.
3. Busca una palabra en inglés en su diccionario.
4. Canta.

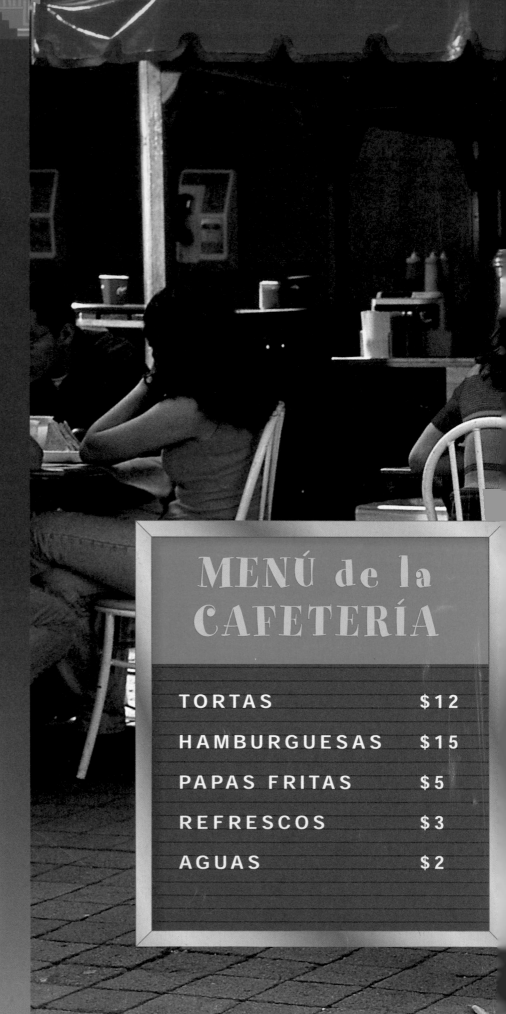

ETAPA

2

¡Un horario difícil!

OBJECTIVES

- Talk about schedules

- Ask and tell time

- Ask questions

- Say where you are going

- Request food

¿Qué ves?

Mira la foto del patio de una escuela mexicana. **¡Ojo!** El símbolo **$** representa pesos mexicanos, **no** dólares.

1. ¿Llevan jeans todos?

2. ¿Hay aguas en el menú?

3. ¿Es verde o azul la mochila de Ricardo?

4. ¿Es roja o rosada la mochila de Isabel?

MENÚ de la CAFETERÍA

TORTAS	$12
HAMBURGUESAS	$15
PAPAS FRITAS	$5
REFRESCOS	$3
AGUAS	$2

En contexto

VIDEO   DVD   AUDIO

VOCABULARIO

Isabel and Ricardo have a lot to do at school today. Let's see where they go at different times during the day.

OFICINA

A

Isabel: Hola, Ricardo. ¿Qué hora es?
Ricardo: Son las once.
Isabel: ¿A qué hora está la maestra en **la oficina**?
Ricardo: A la una.

Horario para hoy

11:00 Oficina
11:30 Biblioteca
2:00 Auditorio
4:00 Gimnasio
5:00 Cafetería

B

Son las once y media. Todos los días Ricardo estudia en **la biblioteca.** Hay muchos libros en la biblioteca.

C

Son las dos. Isabel y Ricardo están en **el auditorio.** ¡Qué bien actúan!

D

Son las cuatro. Ricardo está en **el gimnasio** de la escuela con unos amigos.

la merienda

las papas fritas

la fruta

el refresco

un vaso de agua

la hamburguesa

la torta

E

Son las cinco. Durante **el receso,** Isabel y Ricardo toman **una merienda** en **la cafetería.**

Isabel: Para la merienda siempre **quiero comer una torta** o **fruta.** A veces quiero **tomar un refresco.**

Ricardo: Para la merienda yo quiero comer **una hamburguesa** y **papas fritas. Quiero beber agua.**

Online Workbook
CLASSZONE.COM

Preguntas personales

1. ¿Tu escuela tiene un gimnasio? ¿Un auditorio?
2. ¿Estudias en la biblioteca o en casa?
3. ¿Te gusta comer en la cafetería de la escuela o en casa?
4. ¿Qué te gusta beber: un refresco o agua?
5. Para la merienda, ¿qué te gusta comer?

En vivo

DIÁLOGO

Horas y horarios

Isabel   Maestra   Ricardo

PARA ESCUCHAR • STRATEGY: LISTENING

Listen for the main idea It is important first to understand the main idea without getting lost in the details. Here Isabel is looking for a teacher. What do you hear that tells you that?

1 ▶ Isabel: Busco a la profesora Díaz.
Maestra: No está en este momento.
Isabel: ¿A qué hora llega?
Maestra: A las diez y media.

5 ▶ Ricardo: Quiero comer unas papas fritas, y quiero beber un refresco.
Isabel: Quiero beber un refresco también.

6 ▶ Isabel: ¡Este semestre es horrible! Tengo un horario difícil. Los lunes, miércoles y viernes tengo inglés, historia, matemáticas y literatura. Y los martes y jueves música, geografía, computación y ciencias naturales.

7 ▶ Ricardo: ¿A qué hora es tu clase de computación?
Isabel: A la una de la tarde, con el profesor García.
Ricardo: Mi clase de computación es a las cuatro, con el profesor Anaya.

2▶ Isabel: Profesora, ¿qué hora es?
Maestra: Son las once menos cuarto.

3▶ Maestra: A veces la profesora Díaz está en su oficina durante el almuerzo, y a las tres.
Isabel: Muchas gracias, profesora. Hasta luego.

4▶ Isabel: ¿Adónde vas, Ricardo?
Ricardo: Voy a la cafetería. ¿Me acompañas?
Isabel: Sí, vamos. Tengo tiempo.

8▶ Isabel: Mira, ¿qué es eso?
Ricardo: ¡De verdad es interesante! ¿Te gusta escribir?
Isabel: Sí, me gusta mucho.
Ricardo: ¿Por qué no participamos?

9▶ Isabel: Quiero participar… pero con mi horario…
Ricardo: Isabel, por la noche hay tiempo para trabajar en el concurso…
Isabel: Por la noche tengo que trabajar en mi tarea. ¡Tengo mucha tarea!

10▶ Ricardo: ¿Por qué no vamos a la cafetería para hablar más tranquilos?
Isabel: ¿Cuándo?
Ricardo: A las cinco y veinte.
Isabel: De acuerdo. Voy a las cinco y veinte. ¡Ay! ¡Ya es tarde!

ciento cuarenta y tres
Ciudad de México Etapa 2 143

En acción

VOCABULARIO Y GRAMÁTICA

OBJECTIVES

- Talk about schedules
- Ask and tell time
- Ask questions
- Say where you are going
- Request food
- *Use the verb* ***ir***
- *Use phrases to tell time*
- *Use the verb* ***estar***
- *Use interrogative words*

ACTIVIDAD 1

¿Qué pasa?

Escuchar Based on the dialog, point to the correct photo to complete each statement.

1. La profesora Díaz normalmente llega a su oficina a las ___.

   a.    b.

2. Ricardo quiere beber ___.

   a.   b.

3. Ricardo quiere participar en ___.

   a.   b.

4. Isabel y Ricardo van a la cafetería a ___.

   a.   b.

También se dice

In Latin America, a potato is **una papa,** but in Spain it is **una patata. Papas fritas** are both french fries and potato chips. In Mexico, the verb **tomar** is usually used instead of **beber** to talk about drinking.

El nuevo semestre

Escuchar Are the statements about the dialog true or false? Respond to each one with **sí** or **no**. If the statement is false, correct it.

modelo

Ricardo quiere comer y beber.

Sí. Ricardo quiere comer unas papas fritas y beber un refresco.

1. Son las diez y media.
2. Ricardo e Isabel hablan en el gimnasio.
3. Isabel tiene un horario difícil.
4. Ricardo tiene su clase de computación a la una de la tarde.
5. Ricardo quiere hablar con Isabel sobre el concurso.

¡Una buena merienda!

Hablar You work in the cafeteria. A friend wants to buy something. Help him or her decide. Switch roles.

modelo

Estudiante A: *¿Qué hay para la merienda?*

Estudiante B: *¿Quieres comer **una torta** o **fruta**?*

Estudiante A: ***Una torta,** por favor.*

Nota

To ask what someone wants to eat, say **¿Quieres comer…?**; to ask what someone wants to drink, say **¿Quieres beber…?** Use **por favor** when you want to say *please*.

¿Qué es?

Hablar/Escribir Isabel is showing a new student around school. What does she say?

modelo

*Es **el gimnasio.***

NOTA CULTURAL

In most Spanish-speaking countries, people do not eat at the same time as we do in the United States. For example, many restaurants in Spain are not even open at noon. Likewise, at five o'clock, the restaurant staff would likely be just cleaning up from lunch!

Lunch is usually the main meal of the day. It is eaten from about one o'clock to three. Dinner is lighter. It is eaten anywhere from eight o'clock until ten, or perhaps even later on weekends. The **merienda** bridges the gap between lunch and dinner.

Many people like to have their **merienda** while relaxing in outdoor cafés, which are very common in the Spanish-speaking world.

1.

2.

3.

4.

Conexiones

Las matemáticas In Spanish-speaking countries (and in many other countries), time is often expressed using the 24-hour clock. Hours are counted starting at midnight, so 1:00 A.M. is 0100 and 1:00 P.M. is 1300. "A.M." and "P.M." aren't used at all in this system.

Horario de autobuses			
Salida		**Llegada**	
México, D.F.	8:50	Cuernavaca	9:35
México, D.F.	20:15	Taxco	22:45
México, D.F.	13:30	Acapulco	16:30
México, D.F.	19:00	Guadalajara	3:00

PARA HACER:
Figure out how long each trip takes.
1. Mexico City → Cuernavaca
2. Mexico City → Taxco
3. Mexico City → Acapulco
4. Mexico City → Guadalajara

GRAMÁTICA

Saying Where You Are Going: The Verb ir

When you talk about where someone is going, use the verb **ir**.

The verb **Ir** means *to go*.

yo	**voy**	nosotros(as)	**vamos**
tú	**vas**	vosotros(as)	**vais**
usted, él, ella	**va**	ustedes, ellos(as)	**van**

As a question, **vamos** can mean *Shall we...?* But if stated definitely it means *Let's go!*

Isabel and Ricardo say:

—**¿Adónde vas,** Ricardo?
Where are you going, Ricardo?

—**Voy** a la cafetería.
I'm going to the cafeteria.

Isabel uses the word **adónde** to ask where Ricardo is going. This word means *where.* **Dónde** also means *where.*

- Use **adónde** to mean *where* when there is a verb indicating motion, such as **ir.**

  ¿Adónde va Ricardo?
  (To) Where is Ricardo going?

- Use **dónde** to ask where someone or something is.

  ¿Dónde está Ricardo?
  Where is Ricardo?

Notice how asking *¿a***dónde...?** is similar to asking *to where...?*

Conexiones

La salud As the Spaniards returned from the Americas during the sixteenth and seventeenth centuries, they brought with them plants and animals that were unknown in Europe. Some of these foods eventually became staples of the European diet.

PARA HACER:
Find out how to say the following foods in Spanish. Then classify each as either mainly proteína (protein), carbohidratos (carbohydrates), or grasa (fat). Which has the best nutritional value?

- chocolate
- corn
- potatoes
- turkey

ACTIVIDAD 5 · Gramática

¿Adónde van?

Hablar/Escribir Isabel and Ricardo are talking at school. Complete their conversation with forms of **ir**.

Isabel: ¡Hola, Ricardo! ¿Adónde __1__?

Ricardo: __2__ a la cafetería a tomar un refresco.

Isabel: Yo __3__ a la oficina de la profesora Díaz. Tengo una cita con ella ahora mismo.

Ricardo: Y después, ¿adónde __4__?

Isabel: Después, Andrea y yo __5__ a la biblioteca para estudiar.

Ricardo: Es un semestre difícil, ¿verdad?

Isabel: ¡Sí! ¡Tengo un horario horrible!

MÁS PRÁCTICA *cuaderno* p. 45
PARA HISPANOHABLANTES *cuaderno* p. 43

Online Workbook
CLASSZONE.COM

Vocabulario

La vida diaria

el almuerzo *lunch*

la cita *appointment*

comprar *to buy*

descansar *to rest*

terminar *to finish*

tomar *to take, to eat or drink*

visitar *to visit*

¿Qué te gusta?

El horario de Isabel

Hablar/Escribir Look at Isabel's class schedule. Tell what days she goes to the classes pictured.

$$x + y = z$$

modelo

*Isabel va a **la clase de matemáticas** los martes y jueves.*

Nota

Use **el** with a day of the week to say an event will happen on a specific day. Use **los** with a day of the week to say an event happens every week on that day. Add an **s** to **sábado** and **domingo** when you use **los**.

El lunes voy a la biblioteca.
On Monday I am going to the library.

Los martes y jueves tengo estudios sociales.
On Tuesdays and Thursdays I have social studies.

Los sábado**s** y domingo**s** no tengo clase.
On Saturdays and Sundays I don't have class.

1.
2.
3.
4.
5.
6.  Good morning.
7.
8.

Horario: Isabel Palacios

lunes	martes	miércoles	jueves	viernes
computación	inglés	computación	inglés	computación
literatura	matemáticas	literatura	matemáticas	literatura
arte	educación física	arte	educación física	arte
receso	receso	receso	receso	receso
historia	música	historia	música	historia
	ciencias naturales		ciencias naturales	

Public high schools in Mexico City have two daily schedules. The students attend classes either during the morning, from around 7:30 to 12:30, or during the afternoon, from around 1:00 to 6:00. Are you a "morning person" or an "evening person"? Which schedule would you prefer? Why?

Sara Blanco	lunes	martes	miércoles	jueves	viernes
1:00	inglés		inglés		inglés
1:45		computación		computación	
2:30	literatura	música	literatura	música	literatura
3:15	receso	receso	receso	receso	receso
4:00	educación física	ciencias naturales	educación física	ciencias naturales	educación física
4:45	historia		historia		historia
5:30	matemáticas	arte	matemáticas	arte	matemáticas

ACTIVIDAD 7

Voy a...

Hablar Circulate around the classroom to ask three classmates where they go to do the following. Report your findings to the class.

la biblioteca   la cafetería   el gimnasio

casa   la clase   el auditorio

¿?

modelo

comer

Estudiante A: *¿Adónde vas para comer?*

Estudiante B: *Voy a la cafetería.*

Estudiante C (a la clase): *Tres estudiantes van a la cafetería para comer.*

Nota

When **a** is placed before the definite article **el,** the two words form the contraction **al.**

a + el = **al**   Voy **al** gimnasio.

1. visitar al maestro (a la maestra) de español
2. estudiar
3. correr
4. escuchar un concierto
5. usar la computadora
6. buscar un diccionario

GRAMÁTICA
Telling Time

There are several useful phrases for talking about the current time. Use:

¿Qué hora es?   to ask what time it is.
Son las + *hour*.   to give the time for every hour except one o'clock.
Es la una.   to say it is one o'clock.

Son las doce y *minutes*

Es la una menos *minutes*

Use **y** + *minutes* for the number of minutes **after** the hour.

Son las doce. (12:00)
Son las doce **y diez**. (12:10)
Son las doce **y cuarto**. (12:15)
Son las doce **y media**. (12:30)

Use **menos** + *minutes* for the number of minutes **before** the hour.

Es la una. (1:00)
Es la una **menos diez**. (12:50)
Es la una **menos cuarto**. (12:45)

Use **cuarto** for a quarter of an hour and **media** for half an hour.

To talk about when something will happen, use:

¿A qué hora + *verb* + *event*?

A las + *hour*

A la + *one o'clock*

¿A qué hora es la clase?
What time is the class?

A las (dos, tres).
At (two o'clock, three o'clock).

A la una.
At one o'clock.

ACTIVIDAD 8   Gramática

¿Qué hora es?

Hablar Isabel's father has a collection of clocks. Work with another student to ask and tell the time for each. Change roles.

modelo

Estudiante A: ¿Qué hora es?

Estudiante B: *Son las cinco menos cuarto.*

1.
2.
3.
4.
5.
6.

■ **MÁS PRÁCTICA** *cuaderno* p. 46   ■ **PARA HISPANOHABLANTES** *cuaderno* p. 44

Online Workbook
CLASSZONE.COM

ciento cincuenta y uno
Ciudad de México Etapa 2   **151**

¿A qué hora?

Escuchar/Escribir What time is each class?

1 Listen to the teacher talk about Ana's schedule. Then, on a separate sheet of paper, write down when each of Ana's classes meets.

2 Be prepared to report the time of each class.

modelo

arte: 7:30

Ana tiene la clase de arte a las siete y media de la mañana.

1. matemáticas
2. inglés
3. receso
4. ciencias naturales
5. estudios sociales
6. literatura

 **Tu horario**

PARA CONVERSAR

STRATEGY: SPEAKING

Take risks You learn faster when you are willing to take chances. Don't worry about sounding foolish. Your desire to communicate in Spanish encourages others and helps you.

Hablar Talk with a classmate about your schedule. Use the questions as a guide. Change roles.

1. ¿Qué clases tienes por la mañana?
2. ¿Qué clases tienes por la tarde?
3. ¿A qué hora tienes inglés?
4. ¿A qué hora tienes el almuerzo?
5. ¿A qué hora tienes…?
6. ¿Qué días tienes la clase de…?
7. ¿Qué clase tienes al mediodía?
8. ¿Qué clase tienes a las nueve?

MÁS COMUNICACIÓN p. R5

Vocabulario

Para hablar de la hora

Use these phrases when telling time.

A la una de la mañana/tarde/noche
  At one in the morning/afternoon/night

la medianoche *midnight*

el mediodía *noon*

el reloj *clock, watch*

por la mañana/tarde/noche
  during the morning/afternoon/night

¿Cuándo estudias?

GRAMÁTICA

Describing Location with the Verb estar

To say where people or things are located, use the verb **estar**. Here are its forms in the present tense.

yo	**estoy**	nosotros(as)	**estamos**
tú	**estás**	vosotros(as)	**estáis**
usted, él, ella	**está**	ustedes, ellos(as)	**están**

The teacher says:

—La profesora Díaz **está** en su oficina durante el almuerzo…

*Professor Díaz **is** in her office during lunch…*

ACTIVIDAD 11 Gramática

El sábado a las diez

Hablar/Escribir Complete the sentences to tell where these people are at ten in the morning on Saturday.

1. José ___ en la clase de guitarra.
2. Tú ___ en la biblioteca con tus amigos.
3. La maestra de español y su esposo ___ en el gimnasio.
4. Mis amigos y yo ___ en mi casa.
5. Yo ___ en el apartamento.

MÁS PRÁCTICA *cuaderno* p. 47

PARA HISPANOHABLANTES *cuaderno* p. 45

Online Workbook
CLASSZONE.COM

ACTIVIDAD 12

Están en...

Leer/Hablar Work with a partner. Take turns reading the sentences and guessing where the people are.

modelo

Ellas toman un refresco.

Estudiante A: *Ellas toman un refresco.*

Estudiante B: *Ellas están en la cafetería.*

1. Ella habla con la profesora.
2. Yo escucho música.
3. Nosotros usamos una calculadora.
4. Juan habla inglés.
5. Marta y Tina nadan.
6. La profesora come una fruta.

ACTIVIDAD

13

¿Dónde estás?

Hablar Work with a partner. Take turns asking each other where the following people probably are at the times given.

modelo

tú / a las once y media de la mañana

Estudiante A: *¿Dónde estás a las once y media?*

Estudiante B: *Estoy en la cafetería de la escuela.*

1. tú / a las seis de la tarde
2. tu padre / a las diez de la mañana
3. tu madre / a las tres de la tarde
4. los amigos / a las cuatro y media
5. tu maestro(a) de inglés / a las doce
6. tu hermano(a) / a las seis de la mañana
7. tú y tu amigo(a) / a las dos de la tarde
8. tus abuelos / al mediodía

GRAMÁTICA

Asking Questions: Interrogative Words

There are many ways to ask questions. Here are two ways to create a simple question that has a *yes* or *no* answer.

Statement	Technique	Question
Isabel va a la escuela.	Use rising intonation to imply a question.	¿Isabel va a la escuela?
Isabel va a la escuela.	Switch the position of the **subject** and **verb**.	¿Va Isabel a la escuela?

You've already learned the interrogative words (a)dónde and cuántos(as). Here are more interrogative words.

Some questions are formed by putting a **conjugated verb** after the question word.

*Each interrogative word has an **accent** on the appropriate vowel.*

*All questions are **preceded** by an **inverted question mark** and **followed** by a **question mark.***

cómo	*how*	¿Cómo está Ricardo?
cuál(es)	*which or what*	¿Cuál es el libro?
cuándo	*when*	¿Cuándo estudia Ricardo?
por qué	*why*	¿Por qué va Ricardo a casa?
qué	*what*	¿Qué es?
quién(es)	*who*	¿Quién(es) habla(n) con el profesor?

154   ciento cincuenta y cuatro
Unidad 2

La amiga curiosa

Leer/Escribir Isabel has a curious friend who asks questions about Isabel's science class. Write the appropriate interrogative word to complete each question.

1. ¿A _____ hora tienes la clase? (a las cuatro)
2. ¿ _____ es la clase? (difícil)
3. ¿ _____ enseña la clase? (la profesora Díaz)
4. ¿ _____ es la profesora? (simpática)
5. ¿ _____ tienes que hablar con la profesora? (no tengo mi tarea)
6. ¿ _____ preparas tu tarea? (por la noche)
7. ¿ _____ necesitas para la clase? (un cuaderno)
8. ¿ _____ llegas a clase? (por la mañana)

MÁS PRÁCTICA *cuaderno* p. 48
PARA HISPANOHABLANTES *cuaderno* p. 46

Online Workbook
CLASSZONE.COM

¡Pobre Luis!

Escuchar Listen to the conversation between Ernesto and Luis. Then answer the questions.

1. ¿Por qué no está bien Luis?
   a. Tiene que ayudar a su padre.
   b. Está muy bien.
   c. Tiene un semestre difícil.

2. ¿Qué hora es?
   a. Es la una y veinticinco.
   b. Son las dos y media.
   c. A la una y veinticinco.

3. ¿A qué hora tiene la cita con la señora García?
   a. A las ocho.
   b. A la una y media.
   c. Es la una y media.

4. ¿Cuándo tiene un examen de literatura?
   a. mañana
   b. el lunes
   c. hoy

Different cultures have different ideas about what time to arrive at social gatherings. In Spanish-speaking countries, people tend to have a flexible attitude about the starting and ending times. For example, if you were invited to a party at eight o'clock and you arrived right at eight, you would probably be the only guest there. Guests may arrive an hour or so after a party begins. Likewise, a host would never put an ending time on a party invitation. People are welcome to stay as long as they want.

¡Dime!

Hablar/Leer Work with a partner to play the following roles. A friend of Isabel asks her many questions about her science class. Complete the question and then choose the correct reply according to how the question is asked. Take turns asking and answering questions.

modelo

¿ ___ *tienes la clase? (a las cuatro, en la escuela)*

Estudiante A: *¿A qué hora **tienes la clase**?*

Estudiante B: *a las cuatro*

Estudiante A: *¿Dónde **tienes la clase**?*

Estudiante B: *en la escuela*

1. ¿ ___ es la clase? (a las cuatro, difícil)

2. ¿ ___ enseña la clase? (la señorita Díaz, porque le gusta)

3. ¿ ___ es la profesora? (la señorita Díaz, simpática)

4. ¿ ___ tienes que hablar con la profesora? (a las cuatro, porque no tengo la tarea)

5. ¿ ___ preparas la tarea? (por la noche, en la computadora)

Entrevista

Hablar/Escribir Interview a classmate.

❶ Work with a classmate. Take turns interviewing each other about your various interests.

❷ Write questions for each item on the survey. Then ask your questions.

❸ Make a survey form like the following. Take notes and be ready to report your findings to the class.

La encuesta	
1. clase favorita	
2. maestro(a) favorito(a)	
3. libro favorito	
4. almuerzo favorito	
5. música favorita	

NOTA CULTURAL

In Mexico the word **torta** is used to describe a large sandwich on crusty bread. In Spain **bocadillo** is used. In other countries, **torta** usually means *cake*. In Mexico, the word **pastel** is used to mean *cake*. In Spain, **tarta** is used for *cake*.

torta
bocadillo

torta
pastel
tarta

¿Qué pasa en la fiesta?

Hablar/Escribir Work with a partner. Take turns asking and answering questions about what is going on in each of these party scenes. See which of you can ask the most!

Marisol

modelo

Estudiante A: *¿Qué lleva Marisol?*

Estudiante B: *Lleva una blusa azul y una falda roja.*

Estudiante B: *¿A qué hora llega a la fiesta?*

Estudiante A: *Llega a las ocho y media.*

1. Luis   Eva

2. Marcos   Maribel

3. Tía Antonia

4. Luis   Eva

MÁS COMUNICACIÓN p. R5

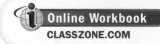
Online Workbook
CLASSZONE.COM

Pronunciación 🎧

Trabalenguas

Pronunciación de la *h* y la *j* The **h** in Spanish is always silent, like the *h* in the English word *honest.* The **j** in Spanish sounds like the English *h* in *Ha, ha!* To practice these sounds, try this tongue twister.

Hoy Juanita hace de jinete.

En colores
CULTURA Y COMPARACIONES

¿Quieres comer una merienda mexicana?

Las meriendas populares

Estados Unidos	México
1.	1.
2.	2.
3.	3.

Aquí tenemos dos tipos de meriendas típicas de México. En México la merienda grande se llama **una torta.** La torta tiene pan redondo[1] y muchos ingredientes. La merienda pequeña se llama **un sándwich.** En Estados Unidos, ¿cómo se llama una torta?

Una merienda típica de México es **el taco al pastor.** Tiene carne asada[2], normalmente puerco[3], en una tortilla de maíz[4]. ¿Es diferente de los tacos que tú comes?

---

[1] round bread
[2] roasted meat
[3] pork
[4] corn

Si te gusta comer fruta para la
merienda, hay una variedad increíble.
O tal vez te interesa[5] un **agua de fruta** en
vez de[6] agua. En México es común beber
aguas de frutas tropicales. Hay aguas de
papaya, piña[7] y muchas otras frutas. ¡Y si
no te gustan las frutas, siempre es posible
comprar **una hamburguesa y papas fritas**!

---

[5] you are interested in
[6] instead of
[7] pineapple

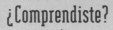

More About Mexico
CLASSZONE.COM

¿Comprendiste?

1. ¿Qué diferencia hay
   entre un sándwich y una torta en México?
2. ¿Cómo es el taco al pastor?
3. ¿Qué hay en un agua de fruta?
4. ¿Cuáles de las meriendas mexicanas comes?

¿Qué piensas?

Estás en México y quieres comer. ¿Qué vas a comprar, una
hamburguesa o una merienda típica de México? ¿Por qué?

159

ETAPA **2**

En uso
REPASO Y
MÁS COMUNICACIÓN

OBJECTIVES

- Talk about schedules
- Ask and tell time
- Ask questions
- Say where you are going
- Request food

Now you can...

- talk about schedules.

To review

- telling time, see p. 151.

ACTIVIDAD 1 ¡Qué horario!

Tell what Sara says about her schedule.

modelo

inglés

Tengo inglés los lunes, miércoles y viernes a las siete y media.

SaraBlanco	lunes	martes	miércoles	jueves	viernes
7:30	inglés	——	inglés	——	inglés
8:15	——	computación	——	computación	——
9:00	literatura	música	literatura	música	literatura
9:45	receso	receso	receso	receso	receso
10:30	educación física	ciencias naturales	educación física	ciencias naturales	educación física
11:15	historia	——	historia	——	historia
12:00	matemáticas	arte	matemáticas	arte	matemáticas

1. arte
2. literatura
3. música
4. ciencias naturales
5. receso
6. historia
7. matemáticas
8. computación

Now you can...

- ask and tell time.

To review

- telling time, see p. 151.
- location with the verb **estar**, see p. 153.

ACTIVIDAD 2 Un día ocupado

You are speaking on the phone with a classmate. You are talking about what time it is and where the following people are. Change roles.

modelo

9:05: Isabel (cafetería)

Estudiante A: *¿Qué hora es?*

Estudiante B: *Son las **nueve y cinco** de la mañana.*

Estudiante A: *¿Dónde está **Isabel**?*

Estudiante B: *Está en **la cafetería**.*

1. 8:15: Gloria (clase de arte)
2. 11:30: Ricardo (gimnasio)
3. 12:50: la profesora (oficina)
4. 1:00: Manuel y Eva (auditorio)
5. 2:40: Isabel (oficina del maestro)
6. 4:25: ustedes (gimnasio)
7. 7:30: René (biblioteca)
8. 9:45: tú (casa)

ACTIVIDAD 3 ¡Muchas preguntas!

Complete Ricardo's friends' questions with the correct interrogative word.

1. ¿ _____ estudias? (En mi casa.)
2. ¿ _____ es tu clase favorita? (La clase de literatura.)
3. ¿ _____ vas al gimnasio? (Por la tarde.)
4. ¿ _____ estás hoy? (Bien.)
5. ¿ _____ es el profesor de computación? (El profesor Anaya.)
6. ¿ _____ vas? (A la cafetería.)
7. ¿ _____ estudias inglés? (Me gusta el inglés.)
8. ¿ _____ están en la biblioteca? (Isabel y Andrea.)
9. ¿ _____ de estos libros necesitas? (El diccionario y el libro de inglés.)

ACTIVIDAD 4 En la escuela

Tell where everyone is going.

modelo

Miguel y Ana tienen que correr.   *Van al gimnasio.*

1. Necesito buscar unos libros.
2. Isabel tiene que hablar con sus profesores.
3. Tú quieres comprar una torta.
4. Mis amigos tienen que cantar en un programa.
5. Nosotros tenemos un examen de español.

ACTIVIDAD 5 En la cafetería

Order each of these snacks.

modelo

Un taco, por favor.

1.   2.   3.   4.   5.   6.

Now you can...
• ask questions.

To review
• interrogative words, see p. 154.

Now you can...
• say where you are going.

To review
• the verb **ir**, see p. 147.

Now you can...
• request food.

To review
• vocabulary for snacks, see p. 141.

ACTIVIDAD 6 · El horario

PARA CONVERSAR

STRATEGY: SPEAKING

Help your partner Make an effort to discover what you have in common. If you think of an activity that you have learned to say but don't remember the word, ask **¿Cómo se dice…?** Help each other out.

Discuss your schedule with a partner.

¿A qué hora…?

estar en la clase de inglés

ir a la cafetería

estar en el gimnasio

preparar la tarea

usar la computadora

descansar

ACTIVIDAD 7 · ¿Dónde estoy?

Describe a situation. Your partners have to guess where you are.

modelo

Estudiante A: *Son las diez. Uso mi calculadora y escucho al profesor.*

Estudiante B: *Estás en la clase de matemáticas.*

ACTIVIDAD 8 · *En tu propia voz*

Escritura List seven questions for a new student.

¿A qué hora…?

¿Cuál es…?

¿Qué…?

¿Dónde estás a las…?

¿Cómo es…?

¿Cuándo…?

¿Por qué…?

¿Adónde vas para…?

¿Quién…?

Conexiones

La salud You can learn about the nutrition in Mexican food from cookbooks, a menu from a Mexican restaurant, or the grocery store. Choose three foods and a beverage and find out about their nutritional value. Read their packaging, request nutritional information from a restaurant, or check a book that lists nutritional values. Create a chart. Which is the most nutritious? Why?

	Calorías	Grasa	Carbohidratos	Vitaminas
1.				
2.				

En resumen

REPASO DE VOCABULARIO

TALKING ABOUT SCHEDULES

el almuerzo	lunch
la cita	appointment
el horario	schedule
el receso	break
el semestre	semester

Activities

comprar	to buy
descansar	to rest
estar	to be
terminar	to finish
tomar	to take, to eat or drink
visitar	to visit

ASKING AND TELLING TIME

¿A qué hora es...?	(At)What time is...?
¿Qué hora es?	What time is it?
A la(s)...	At... o'clock.
Es la.../Son las...	It is... o'clock.
de la mañana	in the morning
de la noche	at night
de la tarde	in the afternoon
la medianoche	midnight
el mediodía	noon
menos	to, before
por la mañana	during the morning
por la noche	during the evening
por la tarde	during the afternoon
el reloj	clock, watch
y cuarto	quarter past
y media	half past

ASKING QUESTIONS

adónde	(to) where
cómo	how
cuál(es)	which (ones), what
cuándo	when
dónde	where
por qué	why
qué	what
quién(es)	who

REQUESTING FOOD

¿Quieres beber...?	Do you want to drink...?
¿Quieres comer...?	Do you want to eat...?
Quiero beber...	I want to drink...
Quiero comer...	I want to eat...

Snacks

el agua (fem.)	water
la fruta	fruit
la hamburguesa	hamburger
la merienda	snack
las papas fritas	french fries
el refresco	soft drink
la torta	sandwich
el vaso de	glass of

SAYING WHERE YOU ARE GOING

ir	to go
al	to the

Places

el auditorio	auditorium
la biblioteca	library
la cafetería	cafeteria, coffee shop
el gimnasio	gymnasium
la oficina	office

OTHER WORDS AND PHRASES

durante	during
por favor	please
la verdad	truth

Juego

¿Adónde van?

Marco: Me gusta escuchar música.

Maricarmen: Necesito buscar unos libros.

Josefina: Voy a hablar con la maestra. Ella no está en clase.

¿Adónde va Marco? ¿Maricarmen? ¿Josefina?

Buenos días.

Good morning.

$x + y = z$

ETAPA 3

Mis actividades

OBJECTIVES

- Discuss plans

- Sequence events

- Talk about places and people you know

¿Qué ves?

Mira la foto del centro de Coyoacán, en la Ciudad de México. *Coyoacán* significa «lugar de los coyotes».

1. ¿Hay muchas personas en el parque?

2. ¿La familia de la foto quiere comer o beber?

3. ¿Hay una universidad en la Ciudad de México?

Ciudad de México

La Villa

Chapultepec Centro Aeropuerto

San Ángel COYOACÁN

Universidad

En contexto

VIDEO DVD AUDIO

VOCABULARIO

Ricardo is taking a walk through a park where he and his friends spend a lot of time after school.

¡**Hola!** Después de clases voy al **parque**. Hay mucho que **hacer**. Me gusta **caminar con el perro**. Mi perro **tiene sed** y quiere **beber** agua. **Voy a** buscar a mis amigos.

la guitarra

A Me gusta **pasar un rato con mis amigos** en el parque. **Tocan la guitarra** y cantan.

la bicicleta

B A veces me gusta **andar en bicicleta**.

166

la tienda

los chicharrones

el parque

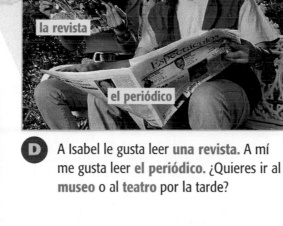

la revista

el periódico

D A Isabel le gusta leer **una revista.** A mí me gusta leer **el periódico.** ¿Quieres ir al **museo** o al **teatro** por la tarde?

E Cuando **tenemos hambre** y sed, compramos una merienda, como fruta y un refresco, en **la tienda.** ¡También me gusta **comer chicharrones!**

C La chica **cuida a su hermano.** Ellos **pasean** por el parque.

Online Workbook
CLASSZONE.COM

Preguntas personales

1. ¿Hay un parque en tu comunidad?
2. ¿Qué te gusta más, andar en bicicleta o correr?
3. ¿Te gusta leer el periódico o una revista?
4. ¿De vez en cuando vas a un museo o al teatro? ¿Vas con tus padres o con amigos?
5. ¿Tocas la guitarra u otro instrumento? ¿Uno(a) de tus amigos(as) toca un instrumento? ¿Cuál?

En vivo

VIDEO DVD AUDIO

DIÁLOGO

Ricardo   Isabel

En el parque

PARA ESCUCHAR • STRATEGY: LISTENING

Listen and observe During a conversation, it is just as important to observe physical actions as it is to listen to the words spoken. Body language supports what is being said and sometimes better expresses meaning. What do you see and hear in this segment that influences Isabel's decision?

1 ▶ **Ricardo:** ¡Hola, Isabel! ¿Qué tal?
Isabel: Bien, no tengo problemas con la clase de ciencias naturales.
Ricardo: ¡Qué bueno!

5 ▶ **Ricardo:** También toco el piano.
Isabel: ¡Mira nada más!
Ricardo: La verdad es que… no toco el piano muy bien.
Isabel: ¡Conozco a alguien muy modesto!

6 ▶ **Ricardo:** ¿Tienes hambre? ¿Comemos unos chicharrones? Esa señora vende unos chicharrones deliciosos.
Isabel: Sí, buena idea. Voy contigo.

7 ▶ **Ricardo:** Vamos a hablar del concurso. ¿Vas a participar?
Isabel: ¿Con mi horario?
Ricardo: Si no haces algo muy complicado, no hay problema.
Isabel: Pero, ¿qué?, ¿qué hago?

2 ▶ **Isabel:** ¿Adónde vamos? Quiero hablar del concurso.
Ricardo: ¿Tienes hambre?
Isabel: No, la verdad, no.

3 ▶ **Ricardo:** ¿Qué haces después de clases?
Isabel: Veo la televisión o paso un rato con mis amigos.
Ricardo: ¿Por qué no vamos al parque?

4 ▶ **Isabel:** Y tú, ¿qué haces después de las clases y antes de cenar?
Ricardo: Si no tengo que cuidar a mi hermano, ando en bicicleta.

8 ▶ **Ricardo:** No te preocupes. Las personas con inspiración no tienen problemas en México.
Isabel: Ricardo, ya es tarde. ¡Es hora de ir a casa!
Ricardo: Sí, es verdad.

9 ▶ **Isabel:** ¡La plaza! ¡La gente! ¡Los animales! ¡Los muchachos! ¡Las actividades! ¡La gente vive en una plaza! ¡Es mi proyecto para el concurso! La plaza es el corazón de la vida mexicana.

10 ▶ **Isabel:** ¡Voy a participar en el concurso! Para conocer a los mexicanos, hay que ir a una plaza. La plaza es un poema.

En acción
VOCABULARIO Y GRAMÁTICA

ACTIVIDAD
1

¿A quién le gusta...?

Escuchar Tell who likes to do the following activities based on what you hear. (Careful! There are some activities that both Ricardo and Isabel like to do!)

 Isabel
 Ricardo

modelo

hablar del concurso

Isabel y Ricardo

1. ver la televisión
2. pasar un rato con los amigos
3. andar en bicicleta
4. tocar el piano
5. comer chicharrones
6. participar en el concurso

También se dice

There are different ways to say *Wow!* when you are amazed by something or someone.

• **¡Anda!:** Spain
• **¡Mira nada más!:** Mexico
• **¡Mirá vos!:** Argentina

170

ACTIVIDAD 2

Ricardo e Isabel

Escuchar Summarize the events of the dialog by completing the following statements.

1. Ricardo e Isabel van _____ .
   a. al parque
   b. a la escuela

2. Ricardo habla de sus _____ .
   a. amigos
   b. actividades

3. Isabel y Ricardo comen _____ .
   a. tacos
   b. chicharrones

4. Isabel va a participar en _____ .
   a. el concurso
   b. la clase de inglés

5. Isabel pasa por _____ .
   a. la plaza
   b. la casa

ACTIVIDAD 3

¿Qué te gusta más?

Hablar/Escribir Which afternoon activity would you prefer to do?

modelo

usar la computadora / andar en bicicleta

Estudiante A: *¿Qué te gusta más, **usar la computadora** o **andar en bicicleta**?*

Estudiante B: *Me gusta más **usar la computadora**.*

1. leer el periódico / leer una revista
2. bailar / cantar
3. tocar el piano / ver la televisión
4. ir al museo / ir al parque
5. patinar / nadar
6. hacer la tarea / cuidar a un(a) hermano(a)
7. pasear con amigos / leer
8. ir a la biblioteca / hablar por teléfono

NOTA CULTURAL

El Museo Nacional de Antropología contains objects from Mexico's native cultures. It is a popular place for school groups to visit.

NOTA CULTURAL

Mexico City has many parks and plazas, but the largest of all is called **el Bosque de Chapultepec**. It is so large (1000 acres) that it is called a **bosque** (*forest*).
El Bosque de Chapultepec contains a zoo, a castle built in 1785, boating lakes, gardens, and playing fields. It is the site for several museums, including **el Museo Nacional de Antropología**. (**Chapultepec** means "place of the grasshoppers" in the native language of the Aztecs.)

¿Qué hacen?

Hablar Work with a partner. What do these people do after class? Do you do the same?

modelo

Estudiante A: *La muchacha cuida a su hermano. ¿Cuidas a tu hermano también?*

Estudiante B: *Sí, yo cuido a mi hermano.* **o:** *No, no cuido a mi hermano.*

1.

2.

3.

4.

5.

ACTIVIDAD 5 ¿Qué haces?

PARA CONVERSAR
STRATEGY: SPEAKING

Use all you know It is easy to rely on what you learned most recently. But it is important to reuse what you've learned before. Try to include activities you learned in Unit 1, such as **cantar** and **nadar,** in your answers.

Hablar/Escribir What do you do?

1 Write two things you do after class.

2 Find out what five classmates do.

3 Write their responses on a separate sheet of paper.

modelo

Estudiante A: *¿Qué haces después de las clases, Marco?*

Estudiante B: *Paso un rato con mis amigos.*

Nombre	Actividad
yo	Ando en bicicleta.
	....
Marco	Pasa un rato con sus amigos.
	....

ACTIVIDAD 6 ¡A comer y beber!

Hablar/Escribir Tell what you will eat or drink when you are hungry or thirsty.

modelo

¡Tengo hambre! Voy a comer una torta.

o: *Voy a comer unas papas fritas.*

Nota

To say that someone is thirsty, use the phrase **tener sed.** To say someone is hungry, use **tener hambre.**

1.

2.

3.

4.

Juego

Paco tiene un vaso de agua.

Pepe tiene sed.

¿Qué tiene el perro?

Gramática

Saying What You Are Going to Do: ir a...

When you talk about things you are planning to do in the future, you say what you are *going to* do. To talk about activities you are going to do, use the phrase:

ir + a + *infinitive*

yo	**voy a**...	nosotros(as)	**vamos a**...
tú	**vas a**...	vosotros(as)	**vais a**...
usted, él, ella	**va a**...	ustedes, ellos(as)	**van a**...

Isabel says:

—¡**Voy a participar** en el concurso!
***I'm going to participate** in the contest!*

ACTIVIDAD 7 Gramática

¿Qué van a hacer?

Hablar Take turns with another student asking and answering questions about what you and your friends are going to do after school.

modelo

tú y tus amigos: hacer ejercicio

Estudiante A: *¿Qué van a hacer?*

Estudiante B: *Vamos a **hacer ejercicio.***

1. tú y tus amigos: leer una novela
2. tú: ver la televisión
3. tú: tocar la guitarra
4. tú y tus amigos: cuidar el perro
5. tú: mandar una carta

Vocabulario

Más para hacer después de clases

cuidar (a) *to take care of*
un animal

el pájaro

el pez

pintar

tocar el piano

ver la televisión

See the words for more pets on p. R11.

mandar una carta

cenar *to have dinner, supper*
hacer ejercicio *to exercise*
preparar *to prepare*
  la cena *supper, dinner*
  (la) comida *food, a meal*
ir al supermercado *to go to the supermarket*

leer *to read*
  una novela *novel*
  un poema *poem*
  (la) poesía *poetry*

¿Qué te gusta hacer?

♻ ¿A qué hora?

Hablar Isabel and Ricardo have a lot to do today. Explain what they are going to do and at what time. What time are *you* going to do these activities?

modelo

Isabel y Ricardo / estudiar en la escuela / 10:00

Isabel y Ricardo *van a* **estudiar en la escuela a las diez.**
Yo voy a **estudiar** *a las seis.*

1. Isabel / usar la computadora / 11:20
2. Ricardo / ir a la biblioteca / 12:45
3. Isabel y Ricardo / tomar un refresco / 1:55
4. Ricardo / hacer ejercicio / 3:00
5. Isabel / pasear con su amiga / 6:30
6. Ricardo / ayudar a su padre / 7:45
7. Ricardo / preparar su tarea / 8:15
8. Isabel y Ricardo / cenar / 9:00
9. Isabel / ver la televisión / 9:35
10. Ricardo / caminar con el perro / 9:45

MÁS PRÁCTICA *cuaderno* p. 53

PARA HISPANOHABLANTES *cuaderno* p. 51

Online Workbook
CLASSZONE.COM

Conexiones

El arte Carmen Lomas Garza is a Mexican American artist who paints many family scenes, such as this birthday party. The blindfolded girl in the center is trying to break the **piñata**. **Piñatas** are hollow papier-mâché figures filled with treats and are usually in the shape of animals.

PARA HACER:
Give as many descriptive phrases about the scene as you can.
For example:
La piñata es un pez azul...
Un señor lleva una camisa blanca...

Birthday Party / Cumpleaños

Primero...

Escuchar Read the sentences. Then listen to the paragraph. In what order is Ricardo going to do these activities?

a. Va a hacer ejercicio en el gimnasio.

b. Va a cenar.

c. Va a pasar un rato con sus amigos.

d. Va a ir a la biblioteca a buscar un libro.

Vocabulario

Sequencing Events

To sequence events, use these words.

primero *first*

entonces *then, so*

luego *later*

por fin *finally*

antes *before*

después *after, afterward*

When a **noun** or an **infinitive** follows **antes** or **después**, use the preposition **de**.

¿Qué haces **después de las clases** y **antes de cenar**?

*What do you do **after** classes and **before** eating dinner?*

Después de las clases, patino.

***After classes,** I skate.*

¿Qué pasa cada día?

♻ Después de las clases...

Escribir Write a paragraph about what you are going to do after school. Sequence your sentences using **primero, antes (de), después (de), entonces, luego.**

modelo

Después de las clases, voy a hacer muchas cosas. Primero, voy a pasar un rato con mis amigos. Luego voy a casa. ¿Y entonces? Siempre tengo que ayudar a mi madre y cuidar a mi hermana. Después de cenar, voy a preparar mi tarea.

■ **MÁS COMUNICACIÓN** p. R6

También se dice

Plaza is a word that refers to any public square in the Spanish-speaking world. The main square in a city or town might be called the **plaza principal** or **plaza mayor.** In Mexico, the main square is called a **zócalo.** The **Zócalo** in Mexico City is where the cathedral and many government buildings are.

Present Tense of Regular -er and -ir Verbs

♻ **¿RECUERDAS?** *p. 122* Remember how to conjugate present tense **-ar** verbs?

estudio	estudiamos
estudias	estudiáis
estudia	estudian

▶ Regular verbs that end in **-er** or **-ir** work similarly. Regular **-er** verbs have the same endings as **-ir** verbs except in the **nosotros(as)** and **vosotros(as)** forms.

The letter change matches the verb ending:
-er verbs = e**mos**, é**is**
-ir verbs = i**mos**, í**s**

com**er** *to eat*

yo	como	nosotros(as)	comemos
tú	comes	vosotros(as)	coméis
usted, él, ella	come	ustedes, ellos(as)	comen

viv**ir** *to live*

yo	vivo	nosotros(as)	vivimos
tú	vives	vosotros(as)	vivís
usted, él, ella	vive	ustedes, ellos(as)	viven

Ricardo says:

—Esa señora **vende** unos chicharrones deliciosos.
*That woman **sells** delicious pork rinds.*

Vocabulario

Verbs Ending in -er and -ir

You have seen the verbs **beber, comer, correr, escribir,** and **leer** before. Here are some others.

Verbs: **-er**

aprender *to learn*
comprender *to understand*
vender *to sell*
ver *to see (**yo: veo**)*

Verbs: **-ir**

abrir *to open*
compartir *to share*
recibir *to receive*
vivir *to live*

¿Qué pasa después de clases?

ACTIVIDAD
11 Gramática

¿Qué pasa?

Hablar/Escribir Choose the best verb and verb form to identify what each person is doing.

modelo

Alberto **vive** en una casa grande. *(vivir / abrir)*

1. Tú _____ el libro. (comer / abrir)
2. Mi padre _____ la televisión. (ver / aprender)
3. Yo _____ el español. (comprender / vender)
4. Mi amiga _____ las matemáticas. (aprender / abrir)
5. La familia _____ muchas cartas. (vivir / recibir)
6. Los chicos _____ en un apartamento. (ver / vivir)

ACTIVIDAD 12 Gramática

¿Qué hacen?

Escribir According to the illustration, choose the logical verb and write a sentence.

modelo

nosotros (escribir / vivir)

Escribimos una carta.

I. mi amigo y yo
(abrir / compartir)

2. tú (vivir / abrir)

3. mi amiga
(recibir / vivir)

4. mis maestros
(escribir / recibir)

5. yo (abrir / recibir)

6. nosotros
(abrir / vivir)

■ **MÁS PRÁCTICA** *cuaderno p. 54*

■ **PARA HISPANOHABLANTES** *cuaderno p. 52*

Online Workbook
CLASSZONE.COM

ACTIVIDAD 13

♻ ¿Mucho o poco?

Hablar/Escribir Do the people you know do these activities a lot or a little? Use the correct form of the verb and choose **mucho** or **poco** to complete your report.

I. yo (aprender)

2. mis amigos
(vender meriendas)

3. yo (ver la televisión)

4. mi padre (leer)

5. mis primos (comer
y beber)

6. mis amigos y
yo (comer)

7. mi amigo(a) (leer
los periódicos)

8. mi hermano(a)
(recibir cartas)

9. los estudiantes
(abrir los libros)

10. mi madre
(comprender)

ACTIVIDAD 14

¿Lo hacen o no?

Hablar/Escribir Ask three students whether they do these activities. Keep track of their responses. Report your findings to the class.

modelo

comer en la cafetería

Estudiante A: *¿Comes en la cafetería?*

Estudiante B: *No, no como en la cafetería.*

Resumen: *Cristina y Ramón comen en la cafetería. Pedro no come en la cafetería.*

I. vivir en un apartamento

2. aprender a tocar algún instrumento musical

3. ver la televisión todos los días

4. recibir mucho correo electrónico (*e-mail*)

5. comprender las matemáticas

GRAMÁTICA

Regular Present Tense Verbs with Irregular **yo** Forms

These are verbs that have regular present tense forms except for an irregular **yo** form.

conocer *to know, to be familiar with (a person or a place)*

cono**zco**	conocemos
conoces	conocéis
conoce	conocen

These verbs follow the form for regular -er verbs except in the yo form.

hacer
to do, to make

ha**go**	hacemos
haces	hacéis
hace	hacen

Isabel says:

—¡Cono**zco** a **alguien** muy modesto!
I know someone very modest!

Voy a cuidar a **mi hermano.**
*I am going to take care of **my brother.***

Voy a cuidar mi **gato.**
*I am going take care of **my cat.***

Note that whenever a **person** is the object of a verb, the personal **a** must be used after the **verb** except for the verb **tener.**

A may also be used when talking about animals that are pets, but it is not required.

ACTIVIDAD
15 ◀ Gramática

¡A comer!

Hablar/Escribir Say what people in this family are making for lunch. Use the correct form of **hacer** in your sentences.

> **modelo**
>
> *mi hermano / sándwiches*
>
> **Mi hermano** hace **sándwiches.**

I. mi padre / hamburguesas

2. mi mamá y yo / enchiladas

3. mi abuela / pastel

4. mis primas / ensalada de frutas

ACTIVIDAD 16 Gramática

¿A quiénes conocen?

Hablar/Escribir Tell whom these people know.

modelo

la señora / mi maestra
La señora conoce a **mi maestra.**

1. el señor Guzmán / la policía
2. tú / mis maestros
3. ustedes / sus amigos
4. yo / la doctora
5. nosotros / Ricardo
6. yo / alguien simpático

■ **MÁS PRÁCTICA** *cuaderno* p. 55
■ **PARA HISPANOHABLANTES** *cuaderno* p. 53

Online Workbook
CLASSZONE.COM

Conexiones

Las ciencias El Bosque de Chapultepec is called the "lungs" of Mexico City. This vast expanse of plants cleans the air by turning carbon dioxide (which all humans and animals breathe out) into oxygen.

PARA HACER:
Learn about photosynthesis. What is it called in Spanish? Name 5 of its components, including carbon dioxide and oxygen, and give their names in Spanish.

English	Spanish
1. carbon dioxide	_____
2. oxygen	_____
3. _____	
4. _____	
5. _____	

ACTIVIDAD 17

Un día típico

Hablar/Escribir Tell what these people are doing. Use the personal **a**, if necessary.

modelos

yo / beber / ¿?
Yo bebo un refresco.
Ricardo / ayudar / ¿?
Ricardo ayuda a Isabel.

1. un amigo / cuidar / ¿?
2. yo / hacer / ¿?
3. nosotros / esperar / ¿?
4. mis padres / visitar / ¿?
5. tú / escribir / ¿?
6. yo / ver / ¿?

ACTIVIDAD 18

 ### ¿A quién conocen?

Hablar/Escribir You, your friends, and your family know many people. Tell who they are, using the correct form of **conocer.**

modelo

Mi madre conoce a mis maestros.
Mis amigos conocen a mi primo Bob.

1. yo
2. mi amiga
3. mis amigos
4. mi familia y yo
5. mis padres
6. mi hermano

Using the Verb oír

Like **hacer** and **conocer**, the verb **oír** *(to hear)* has an irregular **yo** form in the present tense.

* Some of its forms also require a spelling change where the **i** becomes a **y**.

* Note that the **nosotros(as)** and **vosotros(as)** forms have accents.

You may hear the expression **¡Oye!** used throughout the dialog. It is used to get someone's attention, the way *Hey!* is used in English.

To get Isabel's attention Ricardo might say: —¡**Oye**, Isabel!

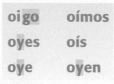

oigo	oímos
oyes	oís
oye	oyen

ACTIVIDAD
19 Gramática

¿A quiénes oyen?

Escribir Write whom each person hears. Complete each sentence with the correct form of the verb **oír.**

modelo

Isabel / su madre

Isabel *oye a **su madre.***

1. Anita / sus amigos
2. los estudiantes / la profesora
3. tú / tu amigo
4. yo / mi hermano
5. Felipe y yo / la señora Ruiz
6. mi primo / mis tíos
7. tus hermanas / tus padres
8. mi amigo y yo / la maestra
9. mi abuela / mi tía
10. Felipe / mi madre

ACTIVIDAD 20 Gramática

¿Qué oyen?

Escribir What does each person hear?

modelo

Mi padre oye **la televisión.**

mi padre

1. mis hermanas   **2.** tú

3. mi amigo y yo   **4.** yo

MÁS PRÁCTICA *cuaderno* p. 56

PARA HISPANOHABLANTES *cuaderno* p. 54

Online Workbook
CLASSZONE.COM

ACTIVIDAD 21

♻ ¿Dónde oyes…?

Hablar Work with another student to say where you hear these things.

modelo

música

Estudiante A: *¿Dónde oyes música?*

Estudiante B: *Oigo música en el auditorio.*

Estudiante A
PREGUNTAS

1. música   5. el doctor
2. la profesora 6. unos pájaros
3. tus amigos   7. el piano
4. la guitarra

Estudiante B
RESPUESTAS

la casa   la clase

la tienda   el auditorio

la escuela

la oficina   el parque

¡A oír bien!

Escuchar Choose the most appropriate response for each statement you hear.

1. **a.** caminar con el perro
   b. tocar la guitarra
   c. hacer ejercicio

2. **a.** ir al parque
   b. comer una hamburguesa
   c. abrir el libro

3. **a.** mandar una carta
   b. ir al teatro
   c. comprar una novela

4. **a.** comer una torta
   b. beber un refresco
   c. visitar a los amigos

Querido...

Escribir Write a letter.

1. Imagine you have a Spanish-speaking pen pal. Write a letter or e-mail to your friend describing what you do every day.

2. Use words such as **primero, después,** and **luego** to tell the order in which you do the activities.

3. Use words such as **siempre, de vez en cuando,** and **rara vez** to indicate how frequently you do each activity.

modelo

Querido Jorge:

¡Hola! ¿Que haces en un día típico? Primero, yo voy a la escuela. Siempre hablo con mis amigos. Después de las clases me gusta ir al parque. De vez en cuando ando en bicicleta. Rara vez camino con el perro. Mi hermana tiene que cuidar el perro. Luego, voy a casa.

Tu amiga,

Elena

■ MÁS COMUNICACIÓN p. R6

Pronunciación

Refrán

La pronunciación y los acentos

1. Words ending in a vowel, or the letters *n* or *s*, are stressed on the next-to-last syllable.

2. Words ending in a consonant other than *n* or *s* are stressed on the last syllable.

3. Words that have written accents are stressed on the syllable with the accent.

A las diez en la cama estés, mejor antes que después.

AUDIO

En voces

LECTURA

PARA LEER

STRATEGY: READING

Following plot Use a chart to help you follow what happens in this legend. Show the beginning, middle, and end of the story. What do the father and the son do at each point of the story?

	Beginning	Middle	End
Father			
Son			

Una leyenda mexicana

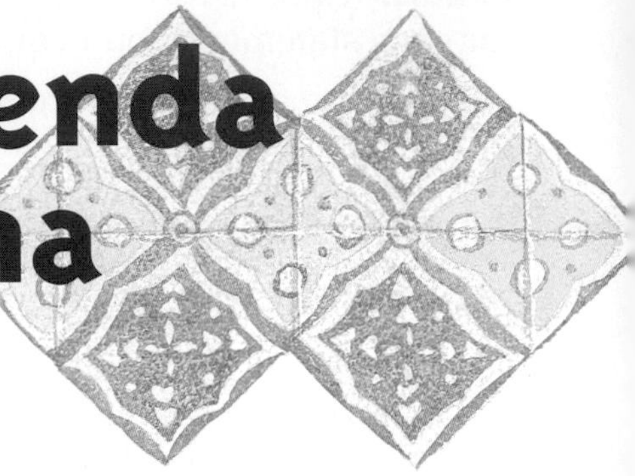

La Casa de los Azulejos[1]

En la Ciudad de México hay una casa muy famosa. Hay muchas leyendas de esta casa. Una de ellas va así...

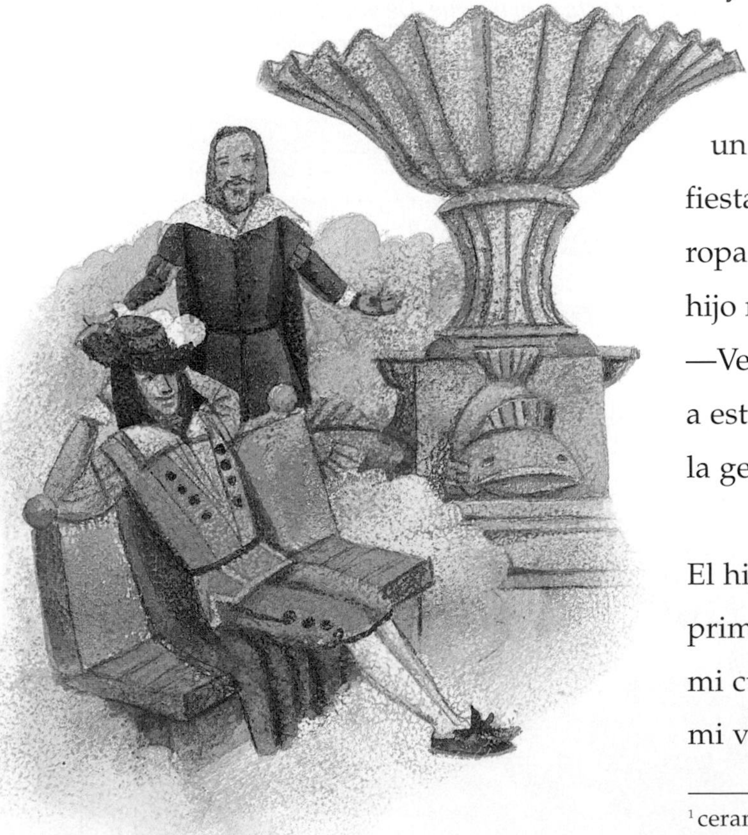

En la época colonial, el señor conde de Valle tiene un hijo que no trabaja y no estudia. Sólo va a muchas fiestas de noche y descansa de día. Sólo quiere llevar ropa elegante. Su padre está muy triste[2]. Piensa[3] que su hijo nunca va a hacer nada[4] bueno. Por fin, un día dice: —Veo, hijo mío, que tú nunca vas a trabajar, nunca vas a estudiar y nunca vas a hacer tu casa de azulejos como la gente buena de esta ciudad.

El hijo escucha con atención las palabras de su papá por primera vez y contesta: —Lo veo a usted muy triste por mi culpa[5]. Quiero cambiar[6] mi vida. Voy a abandonar mi vida de perezoso y voy a trabajar.

[1] ceramic tiles
[2] sad
[3] He thinks
[4] *nunca...nada* is never going to do anything
[5] fault
[6] change

Entonces, el hijo empieza a trabajar mucho. Hace una casa grande y bonita con azulejos por dentro[7] y ¡por fuera[8]! Es para enseñarle a su papá que sí escucha sus palabras.

¡Y todavía existe esta casa! Si vas a la Ciudad de México, puedes visitarla. Es un restaurante muy bonito y famoso.

¿Comprendiste?

1. ¿Cómo es el hijo del conde?
2. ¿Qué hace todos los días?
3. ¿Qué piensa el padre?
4. Por fin, ¿qué hace el hijo?

¿Qué piensas?

1. ¿Es muy importante la influencia de un padre sobre un hijo?
2. En tu opinión, ¿qué es un buen balance para vivir bien?
3. ¿Cómo respondes a los consejos (advice) de otra persona?

---

[7] inside
[8] outside

En colores

VIDEO DVD

CULTURA Y COMPARACIONES

PARA CONOCERNOS

STRATEGY: CONNECTING CULTURES

Compare places Have you lived in or visited a place that has a long history? Is there a special name for that historical area? How old is it? What can you see—buildings, sculptures, murals—that reveals its history? What is its historical importance? What comparisons can you make between it and places in «**El Zócalo: centro de México**»?

Conozco este lugar	Lugar histórico de México
Nombre del lugar: Edad del lugar: Pinturas/Murales: Otras cosas:	Nombre del lugar: Edad del lugar: Pinturas/Murales: Otras cosas:

Un canal del imperio azteca

El Zócalo:

El Zócalo es el centro de la Ciudad de México. Es la plaza principal de la ciudad. Allí estaban[1] la vieja capital colonial española y también la capital azteca de México, Tenochtitlán. En el tiempo de los aztecas, el Zócalo fue[2] un centro ceremonial con pirámides y palacios. Después de conquistar Tenochtitlán en 1521, los españoles construyeron[3] su capital encima de[4] la capital de los aztecas. La Catedral española está aquí, encima del Templo Mayor de los aztecas,

---

[1] there used to be [2] was [3] built [4] on top of

En el Zócalo están **la Catedral** y **el Sagrario**. Son dos símbolos religiosos y ejemplos importantes de la arquitectura y el arte colonial de México.

El Templo Mayor es la pirámide principal de Tenochtitlán. De esta excavación vienen descubrimientos[6] importantes sobre los aztecas.

El calendario azteca o la Piedra del Sol[7] fue descubierto[8] debajo del[9] Zócalo en 1790.

centro de México

una gran pirámide. El Palacio Nacional, el centro del gobierno[5] mexicano, está encima de las ruinas de un palacio azteca. Hoy el Zócalo es el centro de la vida social y religiosa de las personas de esta ciudad.

---

[5] government
[6] discoveries
[7] Sun Stone
[8] was discovered
[9] beneath

More About Mexico
CLASSZONE.COM

¿Comprendiste?

1. ¿Cómo se llama la capital azteca?
2. ¿Qué está encima de las ruinas de un palacio?
3. ¿Qué descubrimientos importantes hay en el Zócalo?
4. ¿Qué lugar del Zócalo representa la vida política de México?
5. ¿Cuáles representan la vida religiosa?

¿Qué piensas?

1. Si vas a la Ciudad de México, ¿por qué es importante ver el Zócalo?
2. ¿Qué importancia tiene el Zócalo en la historia de México?

En uso

REPASO Y MÁS COMUNICACIÓN

OBJECTIVES

- Discuss plans
- Sequence events
- Talk about places and people you know

Now you can...

- discuss plans.

To review

- **ir** + **a** + infinitive, see p. 174.

ACTIVIDAD 1 ¿Qué vas a hacer tú?

Tell what people's afternoon plans are.

modelo

Victoria **Victoria** *va a tocar la guitarra.*

1. Juan y Rubén

2. yo

3. la señora Estrada

4. nosotros

5. tú

6. Benjamín

ACTIVIDAD 2 Nuestra comunidad

Tell who is familiar with the people and places.

modelo

nosotros: la familia Méndez

Nosotros *conocemos a* **la familia Méndez.**

1. ellos: los maestros

3. tú: la tienda de música

5. nosotras: el teatro

2. yo: el museo de arte

4. Marcela: el doctor

6. yo: las policías

Now you can...

- talk about places and people you know.

To review

- the verb **conocer**, see verbs with irregular **yo** forms, p. 179.

Now you can...

• sequence events.

To review

• vocabulary for sequencing events, see p. 176.

ACTIVIDAD 3 Todos los sábados

Use sequencing words (**primero, entonces, después,** etc.) to describe Miguel's schedule.

modelo

__Primero__ , Miguel lee el periódico.

1. _____ correr en el gimnasio, Miguel lee el periódico.
2. _____ correr, él escribe cartas.
3. _____, Miguel come con los amigos.
4. _____ comer, descansa en casa.
5. _____, él pasea en el parque.

10:00	leer el periódico
10:30	correr en el gimnasio
11:30	escribir cartas
1:00	comer con los amigos
3:00	descansar en casa
5:00	pasear en el parque

Now you can...

• discuss plans.

To review

• the present tense of regular **-er** and **-ir** verbs, see p. 177.

• verbs with irregular **yo** forms, see p. 179.

• the verb **oír**, see p. 181.

ACTIVIDAD 4 ¡Muchas actividades!

Where do people do these activities?

modelo

Luz / correr (¿museo o parque?)

Luz corre en el **parque.**

1. Samuel y Sofía / leer unos libros (¿biblioteca o teatro?)
2. yo / ver la televisión (¿gimnasio o casa?)
3. usted / comer fruta (¿museo o cafetería?)
4. nosotros / hacer la tarea (¿supermercado o biblioteca?)
5. yo / oír música (¿auditorio o museo?)
6. la señora Santana / vender ropa (¿cafetería o tienda?)
7. tú / recibir cartas (¿casa o parque?)
8. yo / hacer ejercicio (¿gimnasio o museo?)
9. nosotros / comer chicharrones (¿parque o biblioteca?)
10. Eduardo / oír los pájaros (¿teatro o parque?)
11. Marcelo / comprender la lección (¿clase de matemáticas o cafetería?)
12. Cristina / aprender historia (¿escuela o gimnasio?)

ACTIVIDAD 5 — Y luego...

PARA CONVERSAR

STRATEGY: SPEAKING

Ask for clarification Show your interest by asking for clarification or verification: **Ah, sí, ¿tú vas al museo antes de comer?** Or use other words about the sequence of plans: **entonces, luego, después (de), antes (de),** or a specific time.

Imagine you are a tourist in a Mexican city. Choose four of the following activities. Then talk with a classmate about your plans.

modelo

Primero, voy al Zócalo...

9:00	Excursión al Zócalo
10:30	Museo de Arte Moderno
2:00	Almuerzo
3:30	Tienda de ropa típica
5:00	Paseo en el parque central
8:30	Cena mexicana en el hotel

ACTIVIDAD 6 — En la plaza

You and your classmates are in this Mexican plaza. Talk about what you see and hear and the people you know.

ACTIVIDAD 7 — En tu propia voz

Escritura It's Saturday and you have many things to do. Describe your plans.

Entonces...   **Luego...**   Antes de...

Por la tarde voy a...   Después...

Primero, voy a...

En la comunidad

Tim is a high school student in Wisconsin. He volunteers to help children with their homework, and he often speaks with them in Spanish. He also uses Spanish to understand some of the customers at his part-time job at a store. Do you ever speak Spanish in stores?

En resumen

REPASO DE VOCABULARIO

DISCUSSING PLANS

ir a…	to be going to…

After-school Plans

andar en bicicleta	to ride a bike
caminar con el perro	to walk the dog
cenar	to have dinner, supper
comer chicharrones	to eat pork rinds
cuidar (a)	to take care of
el animal	animal
mi hermano(a)	my brother (sister)
el pájaro	bird
el pez	fish
hacer ejercicio	to exercise
ir al supermercado	to go to the supermarket
leer	to read
la novela	novel
el periódico	newspaper
el poema	poem
la poesía	poetry
la revista	magazine
mandar una carta	to send a letter
pasar un rato con los amigos	to spend time with friends
pasear	to go for a walk
pintar	to paint
preparar	to prepare
la cena	supper, dinner
la comida	food, a meal
tocar el piano	to play the piano
tocar la guitarra	to play the guitar
ver la televisión	to watch television

SEQUENCING EVENTS

antes (de)	before
después (de)	after, afterward
entonces	then, so
luego	later
por fin	finally
primero	first

ACTIVITIES

abrir	to open
aprender	to learn
beber	to drink
compartir	to share
comprender	to understand
hacer	to make, to do
oír	to hear
recibir	to receive
tener hambre	to be hungry
tener sed	to be thirsty
vender	to sell
ver	to see
vivir	to live

PLACES AND PEOPLE YOU KNOW

conocer a alguien	to know, to be familiar with someone

Places

el museo	museum
el parque	park
el teatro	theater
la tienda	store

OTHER WORDS AND PHRASES

cada	each, every
el corazón	heart
la gente	people
el problema	problem
la vida	life

Juego

¿Qué actividades hacen las personas?

Adriana: Le gusta hacer ejercicio y tiene un perro.

José: Le gusta tocar un instrumento. Jakob Dylan, Mary Chapin Carpenter y Melissa Etheridge tocan este instrumento.

Jorge: Es un hermano muy responsable. Tiene una familia grande.

Conexiones

OTRAS DISCIPLINAS Y PROYECTOS

La lengua/Origen de las palabras

When engineers began to build the subway system (**Metro**) in Mexico City in the 1960s, they ran into a problem. They were constantly

digging up artifacts from the Aztec city of Tenochtitlán, dating back to the fourteenth century. The solution? Reroute the **Metro** so that these priceless objects of Mexico's past could stay in their original sites. Today, you can ride through the tunnels of the **Metro** while looking at glass cases containing 500-year-old treasures! The displays are a testimony to the respect Mexicans have for their indigenous past.

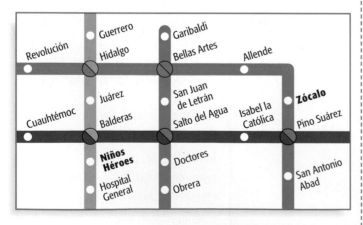

*Look at this map of the **Metro** in Mexico City. Choose 5 station names. Find out their meaning and explain what importance those names have in Mexico City.*

La salud

In Spanish-speaking countries, a popular saying goes, **Gástalo en la cocina y no en la medicina.** Translated this literally means, "Spend your money on the cuisine, not on medicine." It recommends eating healthy foods to maintain health.

In addition to all the usual modern medical remedies, many Mexicans use the same herbs and plant remedies that the Aztecs used. For example, chamomile and mint teas can be used to alleviate tension and stomachaches. Here are more plants that are still used today as home remedies.

Plant	Associated with ...
garlic (**ajo**)	arthritis, heart, stomach
clove (**clavero**)	toothaches
sunflower (**girasol**)	skin
rosemary (**romero**)	stress, headache
thyme (**tomillo**)	lack of appetite, fatigue
aloe (**áloe**)	skin, burns

Which of these plants would you use if you had a sunburn? aching joints? a painful tooth? Explain which you might like to try and why.

Proyecto cultural

If you travel to Mexico, you can still see evidence of cultures dating back thousands of years. Working in a group of three, use the Internet or reference books such as an encyclopedia or a travel guide for Mexico to find out about the indigenous structures that exist in and around Mexico City.

Even today, visitors are permitted to climb the Pyramid of the Moon (above) at the site of Teotihuacán.

1. Choose one of the following places to research.

   • Xochimilco (floating gardens of the Aztecs)

   • El Templo Mayor (part of Tenochtitlán)

   • La Plaza de las Tres Culturas in Mexico City

   • Teotihuacán (ancient city northeast of Mexico City)

2. Each member of your group should be responsible for one aspect of the place chosen—its architecture, its history, its role in the culture.

3. Make an original drawing, map, or model of the structure that you have chosen. You may want to focus only on a detail of a building.

4. Prepare a presentation for the rest of the class using your research and your artwork.

UNIDAD 3

SAN JUAN
PUERTO RICO
EL FIN DE SEMANA

STANDARDS

Communication
- Expressing feelings and emotions
- Discussing what just happened
- Talking on the telephone
- Discussing sports
- Talking about clothes and accessories
- Describing the weather
- Stating preferences and opinions

Cultures
- Regional vocabulary
- Leisure activities in Puerto Rico
- The history, geography, and wildlife of Puerto Rico
- Some important people from Puerto Rico

Connections
- Music: Music and dance in Puerto Rico and the U.S.
- Science: Using the Celsius scale in Spanish-speaking countries and learning the conversion formula

Comparisons
- Music and dance in Puerto Rico and the U.S.
- Sports traditions in Puerto Rico and the U.S.
- Tourist attractions in Puerto Rico and the U.S.

Communities
- Using Spanish for personal interest
- Using Spanish to help others

INTERNET Preview
CLASSZONE.COM
- More About Puerto Rico
- Webquest
- Self-Check Quizzes
- Flashcards
- Writing Center
- Online Workbook
- eEdition Plus Online

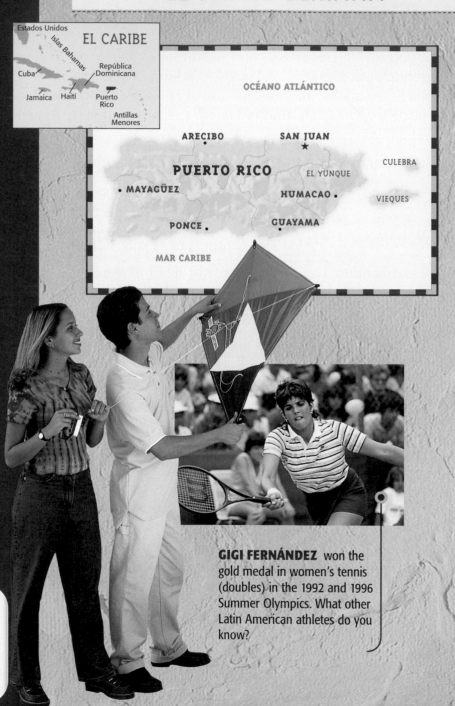

EL CARIBE

Estados Unidos
Islas Bahamas
Cuba
Jamaica
Haití
República Dominicana
Puerto Rico
Antillas Menores

OCÉANO ATLÁNTICO

ARECIBO
SAN JUAN
PUERTO RICO
EL YUNQUE
CULEBRA
MAYAGÜEZ
HUMACAO
VIEQUES
PONCE
GUAYAMA
MAR CARIBE

GIGI FERNÁNDEZ won the gold medal in women's tennis (doubles) in the 1992 and 1996 Summer Olympics. What other Latin American athletes do you know?

POBLACIÓN: 3.808.610

ALTURA: 0 metros (el nivel del mar)

CLIMA: 27° C (80° F)

COMIDA TÍPICA: pasta de guayaba, tostones, pernil

GENTE FAMOSA DE PUERTO RICO: Gigi Fernández (tenista), Luis Muñoz Marín (político), Luis Rafael Sánchez (escritor), Chayanne (cantante)

¿VAS A PUERTO RICO? No necesitas pasaporte. Puerto Rico es una parte de Estados Unidos.

> **More About Puerto Rico**
> CLASSZONE.COM

EL MORRO is a fortress that the Spanish began in 1539 and finished in 1787. How could such a fortress protect the city of San Juan?

EL LORO PUERTORRIQUEÑO became an endangered species in 1971, when only twenty of these parrots were left. Their numbers have now increased. You might see one in El Yunque, the tropical rain forest. What other animals have been saved from extinction?

LUIS MUÑOZ MARÍN (1898–1980) became the island's first elected governor in 1948. In 1952 he signed an agreement making Puerto Rico a commonwealth of the U.S. What other U.S. territories do you know that aren't states?

Luis Muñoz Marín — USA 05 — Governor, Puerto Rico

PASTA DE GUAYABA is a popular dessert. This sweet, thick paste made from the guava fruit is usually eaten with white cheese. What tropical fruits have you eaten?

LOS TAÍNOS were the people living on the island when Columbus arrived in 1493. They left these glyphs. Their language survived in words like **huracán** (hurricane). What other Native American cultures can you name?

195

UNIDAD 3

EL FIN DE SEMANA

- Comunicación

- **Culturas**

- Conexiones

- Comparaciones

- Comunidades

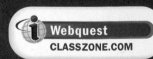

Explore cultures in Puerto Rico through guided Web activities.

Culturas

Have you ever wondered what pastimes young people enjoy most in other countries? What things people there build or create? The things they do and make—from music to monuments—tell you a lot about the people in a culture. In this unit, you will get to know young people and special places in San Juan, Puerto Rico.

Culturas en acción Estás de vacaciones en Puerto Rico. Habla de tus planes para hoy. ¿Vas a escuchar música puertorriqueña? ¿Vas a comer en un restaurante puertorriqueño?

Comunicación

If you were to invite new friends to join you in getting acquainted with Puerto Rico, what would you say to them? Would you use any of the following questions?

¿Comemos algo?   ¿Vamos a caminar?

¿Hay tiendas en el Viejo San Juan?   ¿Qué te gusta hacer?

Comunidades

You can enjoy contributions made by Puerto Ricans in your own community. They may be your neighbors, or famous athletes and entertainers on television.

¿Conoces puertorriqueños famosos? ¿Por qué son famosos?

Comparaciones

Puerto Rico and the United States have some pastimes in common. What do you think are some popular ones, based on the photos you see here?

¿Te gusta el béisbol? ¿Escuchas la música de Puerto Rico?

Conexiones

Knowing what to expect about geography, climate, animal life, and earth sciences would help you enjoy a visit to Puerto Rico. Consider these questions:

¿Qué ropa necesitas en un clima tropical?

¿Hay animales exóticos en el bosque tropical?

¿Leemos la temperatura en *Celsius* o *Fahrenheit* en Puerto Rico?

Fíjate

Each of the following statements relates to one or more of the areas described (**Culturas, Comunicación, Comunidades, Comparaciones, Conexiones**). Determine which one each statement best represents.

1. El loro puertorriqueño es un pájaro bonito.
2. El béisbol es muy popular en Puerto Rico y en Estados Unidos.
3. A los jóvenes les gustan la música y el baile tradicionales de la isla.
4. Vamos a invitar a nuestros amigos a conocer las tradiciones puertorriqueñas.
5. Si visitas Puerto Rico, tienes que visitar la interesante comunidad del Viejo San Juan.

ETAPA

1

¡Me gusta el tiempo libre!

OBJECTIVES

- Extend invitations

- Talk on the phone

- Express feelings

- Say where you are coming from

- Say what just happened

¿Qué ves?

Mira la foto de la calle de San Sebastián en el Viejo San Juan, Puerto Rico.

1. ¿Las casas son viejas?

2. ¿Qué llevan las personas, ropa formal o casual?

3. ¿Cómo se llama la plaza de la calle San Sebastián?

VIEJO SAN JUAN

Muralla histórica

Boulevard del Valle

Plaza de San José

San Sebastián

Boulevard del Valle

Parque de Beneficencia

Sol

Luna

Cristo

Recinto Oeste

San José

Cruz

San Justo

San Francisco

Plaza Colón

Fortaleza

Plaza de Armas

Tanca

Tetuán

Recinto Sur

Estacionamiento

Parque de las Palomas

Marina

Paseo de la Princesa

Terminal de cruceros

En contexto

VOCABULARIO

Look at the illustrations to see what Diana and Ignacio do in their free time. This will help you understand the meaning of the words in blue. It will also help you answer the questions on the next page.

A

Ignacio y Diana tienen **tiempo libre.** Hoy van a unas tiendas para **ir de compras.**

Diana: ¿Quieres acompañarme a comprar unas cosas?
Ignacio: Sí, **me encantaría.**

B

El muchacho de la tienda trabaja mucho. Él está muy **ocupado.**

Diana: ¿Por qué no **alquilamos un video?** ¿**Te gustaría** ver algo?
Ignacio: **¡Claro que sí!**

ocupado

C

¡Para Ignacio y Diana es divertido tomar fotos! Expresan muchas emociones. Primero, Diana está **alegre,** pero Ignacio está **triste.** Luego, Diana está **enojada,** pero Ignacio no. Él está **tranquilo.** Al final, Ignacio está **preocupado,** pero Diana no. Ella está **contenta.**

alegre
triste
enojada
tranquilo
contenta
preocupado

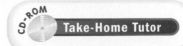

nervioso

enfermo

emocionada

deprimido

D El hombre que trabaja en la tienda está **nervioso**. ¡El cliente de la camisa roja está enojado! La madre cuida a su niño. Él está **enfermo**.

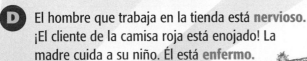

DEPORTES RAMIREZ

CINE BORINQUEN

F En el estadio la comunidad **practica deportes**. En Puerto Rico el deporte favorito es el béisbol. Muchas personas miran. Unas están **emocionadas**, otras están **deprimidas**.

¡TODOS A BAILAR!

Concierto espectacular de
BOMBA y PLENA
¡Músicos sensacionales!

¡Y la actuación especial de los bailarines
Lilián y Alberto!

Sábado 16 de octubre
a las 5 de la tarde
en el Instituto de Cultura

E Ignacio y Diana **van al cine**. Después de ver **la película**, Diana está **cansada**.

el cine

G **Ignacio: Te invito a ir a un concierto.**

Diana: ¡Gracias!

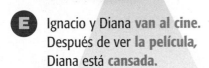
cansada

Preguntas personales

1. ¿Tienes mucho tiempo libre?
2. ¿Te gusta más ir al cine o alquilar un video?
3. ¿Te gusta ir de compras o practicar deportes?
4. ¿Te gusta ir a conciertos? ¿Cómo estás cuando escuchas un concierto?
5. ¿Cuál es tu actividad favorita? ¿Cómo estás cuando haces la actividad?

En vivo

VIDEO DVD AUDIO

DIÁLOGO

Diana

Ignacio

Roberto

La llamada

PARA ESCUCHAR • STRATEGY: LISTENING

Listen for a purpose Listening for specific information is like scanning when reading. Practice listening for one idea. What is the exact day and time of an important event for Ignacio? Why is it important?

El evento	El día	La hora

1▶ Diana: Oye, hermano, voy de compras. ¿Quieres acompañarme?
Ignacio: No, tal vez otro día.
Diana: ¡Qué aburrido!

5▶ Roberto: Tengo muy buenas noticias. ¡Estoy muy emocionado! ¡Mi familia y yo vamos a Puerto Rico a vivir! Llegamos el viernes. ¿Cuándo hablamos?

6▶ Ignacio: Te invito a mi práctica de béisbol. Es el sábado, a las dos. ¿Te gustaría venir?
Roberto: ¡Claro que sí! En el lugar de siempre, ¿no?
Ignacio: Sí, en el mismo lugar de siempre.
Roberto: Bueno, ¡adiós!

7▶ Diana: ¿Tu pana Roberto?
Ignacio: Roberto y su familia vienen a vivir a Puerto Rico de nuevo.
Diana: Estás contento, ¿no?
Ignacio: Sí, pero también estoy nervioso.

2▶ Ignacio: ¡El teléfono!

Diana: Ay, Ignacio. No tienes que contestar; la máquina contesta.

3▶ Mensaje: Es la casa de la familia Ortiz. Deja un mensaje después del tono. ¡Gracias!

Roberto: ¡Oye, Ignacio! Habla tu viejo amigo Roberto. Si estás allí, ¡por favor, contesta!

4▶ Ignacio: ¡Sí, Roberto, estoy aquí! ¡Qué sorpresa! ¿Cómo estás? ¿Dónde estás? En Minnesota, ¿no?

8▶ Diana: Va a ser el Roberto de siempre. Bueno, ¿quieres ir de compras, o no?

Ignacio: Pues, sí, hermanita. Ya no quiero ver más deportes. Vamos.

9▶ Diana: Acabo de comprar unos zapatos.

Ignacio: Yo vengo del cine.

Diana: ¿Hay una película interesante?

Ignacio: A las muchachas sólo les gusta ver las películas de romance, ¿no es verdad?

Diana: ¡No! ¡También nos gusta ver otras!

10▶ Diana: ¿Qué pasa? ¿Estás preocupado?

Ignacio: Es que… dos años en Minnesota… ya no conozco a Roberto.

Diana: ¡No te preocupes! Los buenos amigos son amigos para siempre.

En acción

VOCABULARIO Y GRAMÁTICA

ACTIVIDAD
1

¿Qué pasa?

Escuchar Look at the photos. In what order do the events in the dialog happen? Touch each picture in the correct order.

a.

b.

c.

d.

e.

Ignacio

Escuchar Based on the dialog, tell whether the statements about Ignacio are true or false. Respond to each one with **sí** or **no**. If the statement is false, say what is true.

modelo

Ignacio quiere ver más deportes.

No. Ignacio quiere salir con Diana.

1. Ignacio habla por teléfono.
2. Ignacio vive en Minnesota.
3. Ignacio practica el béisbol el domingo.
4. Ignacio invita a Roberto a su práctica de béisbol.
5. Ignacio pasa por el cine.
6. Ignacio está tranquilo.

♻ El tiempo libre

Hablar/Escribir Tell what Ignacio and Diana do in their free time.

modelo

En su tiempo libre, Diana lee novelas.

escribir una carta   practicar deportes

ir de compras   ver la televisión

1.

2.

3.

4.

ACTIVIDAD 4

♻ ¿Y tú?

Hablar What do you and a classmate like to do in your free time? Find out three activities your partner likes to do. Then switch roles.

modelo

Estudiante A: *¿Te gusta ver la televisión?*

Estudiante B: *Sí, me gusta ver la televisión. o: No, no me gusta ver la televisión.*

ACTIVIDAD 5

♻ El tiempo libre de su amiga

Escuchar Listen to Diana's friend. She is talking about what she does on Saturdays. Then put her activities in order.

a. Alquila un video.

b. Prepara el almuerzo.

c. Hace la tarea.

d. Cuida a su hermano.

e. Va de compras.

También se dice

There are many ways to talk about **un buen amigo.** Diana uses one of them, **pana.**

- **pata:** Peru
- **colega:** Spain
- **vale:** Venezuela
- **cuadro:** Colombia
- **cuate:** Mexico
- **pana:** Puerto Rico, Ecuador, parts of Latin America

In the dialog, Ignacio uses the word **hermanita** when talking to Diana. The ending **-ito(a)** adds meaning to a word. It can mean *very small* or express a special relationship. **Hermanita** means *little sister*, but it also expresses Ignacio's close relationship with his sister. This ending is used in most Spanish-speaking countries.

ACTIVIDAD 6

¿Cómo estás?

Leer/Escribir How do you feel in the following situations? On a separate sheet of paper, write a complete sentence using the best answer choice for you.

1. Cuando tengo un examen difícil...
   a. estoy contento(a).
   b. estoy nervioso(a).
   c. estoy emocionado(a).

2. Cuando escucho mi música favorita...
   a. estoy alegre.
   b. estoy tranquilo(a).
   c. estoy enojado(a).

3. Cuando saco una mala nota...
   a. estoy triste.
   b. estoy enojado(a).
   c. estoy cansado(a).

4. Cuando mi abuelo está enfermo...
   a. estoy contento(a).
   b. estoy preocupado(a).
   c. estoy triste.

5. Cuando no hay clases...
   a. estoy deprimido(a).
   b. estoy enojado(a).
   c. estoy alegre.

6. Cuando tengo mucha tarea...
   a. estoy preocupado(a).
   b. estoy emocionado(a).
   c. estoy tranquilo(a).

Conexiones

La música Puerto Rican teens enjoy going to parties to listen to music and to dance. **La bomba** and **la plena** are traditional dances of Puerto Rico. Both have African roots. The instruments used to play this music are **tambores** (drums), **panderetas** (type of tambourine), **maracas**, and **el cuatro** (small Spanish guitar).

PARA HACER:

Musical instruments can be grouped in these categories: wind (de viento), stringed (de cuerda), and percussion (de percusión). Make a chart using the instruments above.

Instrumento	Categoría
tambores	de percusión

GRAMÁTICA

Expressing Feelings with estar and Adjectives

♻ **¿RECUERDAS?** *p. 153* You learned that the verb **estar** is used to say where someone or something is located.

Estar is also used with **adjectives** to describe how someone feels at a given moment.

agrees

Diana **está preocupada** por Ignacio.
Diana is worried about Ignacio.

agrees

Ignacio **está preocupado** por Roberto.
Ignacio is worried about Roberto.

estoy	estamos
estás	estáis
está	están

Remember that **adjectives** must **agree** in gender and number with the nouns they describe.

ACTIVIDAD 7 — Gramática

¿Cómo están?

Hablar/Escribir Tell how these people are feeling.

> *modelo*
>
> Mario: triste
> **Mario** está **triste**.

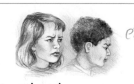

1. ellos: alegre   **2.** mi amigo y yo: enojado(a)

3. tú: nervioso(a)   **4.** yo: preocupado(a)

▓ **MÁS PRÁCTICA** *cuaderno* p. 61

▓ **PARA HISPANOHABLANTES** *cuaderno* p. 59

Online Workbook
CLASSZONE.COM

ACTIVIDAD 8

Reacciones

Hablar Complete each statement with an adjective that shows how these people feel in each situation.

> *modelo*
>
> Cuando mi tía tiene ropa nueva...
> está contenta.

Nota

When **cuando** is not used as a question word, it does not have an accent.

---

1. Cuando vemos una película muy divertida...

2. Cuando tengo un examen de inglés...

3. Cuando mi amigo(a) saca una mala nota...

4. Cuando es tu cumpleaños...

5. Cuando oigo música alegre...

6. Cuando mis amigos(as) no tienen clases...

¿Cuándo estás...?

Hablar Take turns with another student asking and answering questions about when he or she feels certain ways.

modelo

deprimido(a)

Estudiante A: *¿Cuándo estás* **deprimido(a)**?

Estudiante B: *Estoy* **deprimido(a)** *cuando no tengo tiempo para pasar un rato con mis amigos. ¿Y tú?*

Estudiante A: *Estoy* **deprimido(a)** *cuando tengo mucho trabajo.*

1. enojado(a)
2. alegre
3. cansado(a)
4. preocupado(a)
5. nervioso(a)
6. triste

¿Qué hacen? ¿Cómo están?

Hablar Work with a partner. Take turns saying what the people in the pictures are doing and how they feel.

modelo

Ignacio y Diana alquilan un video.

Están contentos.

¿Te gustaría...?

Hablar Ask another student if he or she would like to do these activities with you on Saturday. Switch roles.

modelo

Estudiante A: *¿Te gustaría ir conmigo al museo el sábado?*

Estudiante B: *¡Claro que sí!*

Nota

When you use **mí** and **ti** after **con**, they combine with **con** to form the words **conmigo** and **contigo**.

¿Te gustaría venir **conmigo**?	Sí, me gustaría ir **contigo**.
Would you like to come **with me**?	*Yes, I'd like to go* **with you**.

Vocabulario

Para aceptar o no una invitación

Gracias, pero no puedo.
Thanks, but I can't.

Me gustaría... *I would like...*

¡Qué lástima! *What a shame!*

Tal vez otro día. *Perhaps another day.*

Other useful words:

porque *because*

solo(a) *alone*

temprano *early*

¿Cuándo usas estas frases?

Estudiante A
PREGUNTAS

¿Quieres acompañarme a...?
Te invito a...
¿Te gustaría venir conmigo a...?

Estudiante B
RESPUESTAS

¡Claro que sí!
Sí, me encantaría.
Me gustaría ir contigo a...

Gracias, pero no puedo.
Tal vez otro día.
¡Qué lástima! Gracias, pero no puedo.

Gramática

Saying What Just Happened with **acabar de**

When you want to say that something just happened, use the present tense of

acabar + **de** + *infinitive*

acabo de comer *I just ate*	**acabamos de comer** *we just ate*
acabas de comer *you just ate*	**acabáis de comer** *you just ate*
acaba de comer *he, she, you just ate*	**acaban de comer** *they, you just ate*

Diana says:

—**Acabo de comprar** unos zapatos.

I just bought some shoes.

ACTIVIDAD 12 Gramática

 ### ¿Qué acaban de hacer?

Hablar Say what Ignacio and his friends just did.

modelo

Ignacio y yo: ver una película interesante

Ignacio y yo acabamos de **ver una película interesante.**

1. yo: comprar una novela nueva
2. Ana: bailar con Juan
3. Ignacio y Pedro: escuchar un concierto
4. tú: correr por el parque
5. Lucía y yo: alquilar un video
6. Alma y Dorotea: comer tacos

MÁS PRÁCTICA *cuaderno* p. 62

PARA HISPANOHABLANTES *cuaderno* p. 60

Online Workbook
CLASSZONE.COM

ACTIVIDAD 13

Un poco de lógica

Hablar/Escribir Choose the best option to indicate what these people have just done.

modelo

Estás en casa. (¿ver la televisión o andar en bicicleta?)

Acabas de ver la televisión.

1. Estamos en el cine. (¿sacar una buena nota o ver una película?)
2. Marisa está en la tienda. (¿comprar ropa o caminar con el perro?)
3. Mis primos están en San Juan. (¿patinar sobre hielo o nadar?)
4. Estoy en la biblioteca. (¿ir de compras o buscar un libro?)

ACTIVIDAD 14 — ¿Cómo están?

PARA CONVERSAR

STRATEGY: SPEAKING

Personalize After completing this activity, make the expressions your own by describing how you feel after doing these things.

Hablar Work in pairs to tell how these people are when they finish the activity.

modelo

¿Cómo está tu padre…? (trabajar mucho)

Estudiante A: *¿Cómo está tu padre cuando acaba de trabajar mucho?*

Estudiante B: *Está cansado.*

1. ¿Cómo está tu amigo(a)…? (estudiar mucho)
2. ¿Cómo está tu amigo(a)…? (pasear por el parque)
3. ¿Cómo estás tú…? (terminar un examen)
4. ¿Cómo están tus padres…? (escuchar un concierto)
5. ¿Cómo estás tú…? (leer una revista)
6. ¿Cómo está tu maestro(a)…? (hablar mucho)
7. ¿Cómo está tu mamá…? (ir de compras)
8. ¿Cómo está tu familia…? (ir al cine)

MÁS COMUNICACIÓN p. R7

GRAMÁTICA

Saying Where You Are Coming From with venir

 ¿RECUERDAS? *p. 88* Do you remember the forms of the verb **tener?**

tengo	tenemos
tienes	tenéis
tiene	tienen

▶ **Venir** (*to come*) is similar to **tener,** except that the **nosotros(as)** and **vosotros(as)** forms have **-ir** endings, while **tener** uses **-er** endings.

vengo	venimos
vienes	venís
viene	vienen

Ignacio says:
—Roberto y su familia **vienen** a Puerto Rico…
*Roberto and his family **are coming** to Puerto Rico…*

Later he says:
—Yo **vengo** del cine.
*I'm **coming** from the movie theater.*

¡Bienvenidos a San Juan!

Escribir Roberto is in the San Juan airport. He is coming from Minneapolis. Write where these people are coming from.

modelo

Carlos __viene__ de Miami.

1. Tú _____ de San Antonio.
2. Los señores puertorriqueños _____ de Nueva York.
3. Yo _____ de la Ciudad de México.
4. Nosotros _____ de Los Ángeles.
5. Ana _____ de Santa Fe.
6. Tú _____ de Miami.
7. Mis padres _____ de Minnesota.
8. Ustedes _____ de mi ciudad.
9. Felipe _____ de San Antonio.
10. La profesora Morales _____ de Chicago.

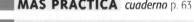
MÁS PRÁCTICA *cuaderno* p. 63

PARA HISPANOHABLANTES *cuaderno* p. 61

Online Workbook
CLASSZONE.COM

NOTA CULTURAL

The name **Puerto Rico** was given to the island by the Spanish. Its port is one of the world's busiest. Guess what **Puerto Rico** means in English.

♻ ¿De dónde vienen?

Leer/Hablar Take turns with another student describing where these people are coming from.

biblioteca	concierto	museo
café	escuela	parque
cafetería	gimnasio	tienda
ciudad		

modelo

Tú acabas de ver una película.

Vienes **del cine.**

Nota

Remember how **a** contracts with **el** to form **al**? The preposition **de** also contracts with **el** to form **del**.

1. Acabo de buscar un libro.
2. Ustedes acaban de ver una exhibición de arte, ¿no?
3. Ignacio y Diana acaban de comer.
4. Acabo de caminar con el perro.
5. Acabas de tomar un examen de historia, ¿no?
6. Roberto acaba de comprar ropa.
7. Ellas acaban de escuchar una canción de Ricky Martin.
8. Magdalena acaba de hacer ejercicio.
9. ¿Usted acaba de visitar a su abuela?
10. La profesora acaba de beber un refresco.

¿Qué pasa?

Leer/Hablar Work with a classmate to tell the story pictured here. Take turns describing each scene.

modelo

Estudiante A: *Carlos y Andrés hablan en el parque.*

Estudiante B: *Están aburridos.*

GRAMÁTICA

Saying What Someone Likes to Do Using gustar + infinitive

 ¿RECUERDAS? *p. 43* You learned to use **me gusta, te gusta,** and **le gusta** + *infinitive* to talk about the activities a person likes to do.

me gusta **correr**
te gusta **correr**
le gusta **correr**

Here are more phrases to use to talk about what people like to do.

nos gusta correr   *we like to run*
os gusta correr   *you (familiar plural) like to run*
les gusta correr   *they/you (plural) like to run*

When you want to emphasize or identify the person that you are talking about, use: **a** +

| name |
| noun |
| pronoun |

→ **A Diana** le gusta **ir** de compras.
Diana likes to shop.

A su hermana le gusta **ir** de compras.
His sister likes to shop.

A ella le gusta **ir** de compras.
She likes to shop.

These are the **pronouns** that follow **a**.

a mí → me gusta
a ti → te gusta
a usted, él, ella → le gusta

a nosotros(as) → nos gusta
a vosotros(as) → os gusta
a ustedes, ellos(as) → les gusta

 **ACTIVIDAD 18** Gramática

¿A quién le gusta?

Leer/Escribir Diana is writing a letter to her friend, Elena, describing things that she and her friends do. Complete her letter with **a mí, a ti, a él, a ella, a nosotros,** or **a ustedes.**

MÁS PRÁCTICA *cuaderno p. 64*

PARA HISPANOHABLANTES
cuaderno p. 62

Online Workbook
CLASSZONE.COM

Querida Elena:
      ¿Qué hago aquí en San Juan? Bueno, primero estudio mucho porque __1__ me gusta sacar buenas notas. Después de las clases, normalmente voy a la cafetería con mis amigos Pablo y Linda. Pablo siempre compra dos hamburguesas. ¡ __2__ le gusta mucho comer!
      Cuando tenemos tiempo libre, vamos al cine. __3__ nos gusta ver películas de acción. A veces, Pablo y yo vamos al museo. Linda no va porque __4__ no le gusta el arte.
      Y tú, ¿qué haces? ¿ __5__ te gusta estudiar? ¿Qué haces con tus amigos? ¿ __6__ les gusta ir al cine o a un museo?
      Bueno, espero tu carta.
      Tu amiga,
      Diana

¿A quién le gusta ir a...?

Hablar/Escribir Tell what these people like to do.

a mis padres

a mis amigos(as)

a mi profesor(a) de...

a mí

a mi hermano(a)

a mi primo(a)

modelo

A mis padres les gusta ir a los museos.

1. a los museos
2. al gimnasio
3. de compras
4. a la biblioteca
5. al cine
6. a la ciudad

♻ ¿Qué hacen?

Hablar Ask others what they and their friends like to do.

escribir poesía

practicar deportes

¿?

alquilar videos

andar en bicicleta

ir de compras

leer novelas

patinar

modelo

nadar

Estudiante A: *¿A ustedes les gusta nadar?*

Estudiantes B y C: *No nos gusta nadar, pero sí nos gusta bailar.*

Una conversación telefónica

Escuchar Listen to the conversation between Ignacio and Roberto. Then say if the sentences below are true or false. Correct the false ones.

1. El señor Campos contesta el teléfono.
2. Roberto no está en casa.
3. Ignacio invita a Roberto a ir a un concierto.
4. Roberto no tiene tiempo libre el sábado.
5. El sábado es el cumpleaños de su hermano.
6. Ignacio y Roberto van al cine el domingo.
7. La película es a las cuatro.

Vocabulario

El teléfono

contestar *to answer*

dejar un mensaje *to leave a message*

la guía telefónica *phone book*

la llamada *call*

llamar *to call*

la máquina contestadora *answering machine*

marcar *to dial*

Speaking on the phone:

¿Puedo hablar con...?	*May I speak with...?*
Un momento.	*One moment.*
Regresa más tarde.	*He/She will return later.*
Dile/Dígale que me llame.	*Tell (familiar/formal) him or her to call me.*
Quiero dejar un mensaje para...	*I want to leave a message for...*
Deje/a un mensaje después del tono.	*Leave (formal/familiar) a message after the tone.*

¿Qué dices cuando hablas por teléfono?

ACTIVIDAD 22

♻ ¿Puedo hablar con...?

Hablar/Leer Practice Diana's telephone conversation with another student. Then answer the questions.

Señor Ruiz: Hola.

Diana: Buenas tardes, señor Ruiz. Soy Diana.

Señor Ruiz: ¡Ah! Diana, ¿cómo estás?

Diana: Muy bien, gracias, señor. ¿Puedo hablar con Gloria, por favor?

Señor Ruiz: Pues, Gloria no está en este momento. Está en la biblioteca. Regresa más tarde.

Diana: Dígale que me llame, por favor.

Señor Ruiz: Sí, cómo no.

Diana: Gracias, adiós.

Señor Ruiz: Hasta luego.

1. ¿Quién hace la llamada?
2. ¿Quién contesta?
3. ¿Cómo está Diana?
4. ¿Dónde está Gloria?
5. ¿Cuándo regresa Gloria?
6. ¿Con quién quiere hablar Diana?

ACTIVIDAD 23

¡Te invito!

Hablar/Escribir You call a friend's house to invite him or her to join you in an activity. Change roles.

modelo

Señor Gómez: *Hola.*

Luisa: *Buenas tardes. Soy Luisa. ¿Puedo hablar con Ana?*

Señor Gómez: *Un momento, por favor. ¡Ana! Es Luisa.*

Ana: *Hola, Luisa.*

Luisa: *Hola, Ana. Te invito a…*

■ **MÁS COMUNICACIÓN** p. R7

Online Workbook
CLASSZONE.COM

También se dice

There are many ways to answer the phone.

- **Hola:** Puerto Rico
- **Aló:** Chile, Colombia, Venezuela
- **Bueno:** Mexico
- **Diga:** Spain
- **Hable:** Argentina
- **Oigo:** Uruguay

Pronunciación 🎧

Refrán **Pronunciación de la *b* y la *v*** The b and v are pronounced alike. At the beginning of a phrase and after the letters **m** or **n**, they are pronounced like the English *b* in the word *boy*. In the middle of a word, a softer sound is made by vibrating the lips. Practice the following words.

bueno   vamos   acaba   novela   hombre

Now try this **refrán**. Can you guess what it means?

No hay mal que por bien no venga.

La **b** es de **burro**.   La **v** es de **vaca**.

doscientos diecisiete
San Juan   Etapa 1

217

En voces

AUDIO

LECTURA

PARA LEER

STRATEGY: READING

Using context You can use context to understand a word's meaning. Context includes what is written before and after the word. Write the words that help you understand what these words mean.

Word	Context
voz	
areito	

El bohique[1] y los niños

Hace sol[2] en las islas del Caribe. Unos niños taínos[3] pasan un buen rato en la playa[4]. Enseñan a hablar a los loros[5]. El bohique está en su casa. El bohique es una persona muy importante. Es la persona que sabe toda la historia de su pueblo[6]. Es la persona que comunica la historia a su pueblo. El bohique empieza[7] a contar[8] un **areito**. Un areito es una canción[9], leyenda o historia.

Cuando los niños escuchan la voz del bohique, uno dice[10]:—Vamos a ir a la casa del bohique. ¡Va a contar un areito! ¡Va a contar la historia de nuestra gente!

---

[1] storyteller
[2] It's sunny
[3] original inhabitants of Puerto Rico
[4] beach
[5] parrots
[6] people, civilization
[7] begins
[8] to tell
[9] song
[10] says

218 doscientos dieciocho
Unidad 3

—¡Sí! —dicen todos los niños—. ¡Vamos a escucharlo!

—¡Escuchen! Acaba de empezar el bohique. Escucho los tambores[11].

—Y tocan las maracas también.

—¡Vamos a cantar con el bohique!

—A mí me gustan los areitos. Me gusta bailar cuando canta el bohique.

—¡Escuchen! El bohique empieza a contar el areito.

El bohique empieza: «Dicen que de las primeras personas, los taínos, el sol crea todo el mundo...»

Gracias al bohique que cuenta las historias, los niños aprenden de la vida de su pueblo.

_____
[11] drums

Online Workbook
CLASSZONE.COM

¿Comprendiste?

1. ¿Dónde están los niños taínos?
2. ¿Qué hacen?
3. ¿Qué hace el bohique?
4. ¿Qué aprenden los niños gracias al bohique?

¿Qué piensas?

1. ¿Qué maneras hay para comunicar una historia?
2. ¿En qué maneras les comunican los padres su cultura a sus hijos?

ETAPA 1

En uso
REPASO Y MÁS COMUNICACIÓN

OBJECTIVES

- Extend invitations
- Talk on the phone
- Express feelings
- Say where you are coming from
- Say what just happened

Now you can...

- extend invitations.
- talk on the phone.

To review

- vocabulary for invitations, see p. 200 and p. 210.
- vocabulary for talking on the phone, see p. 216.

ACTIVIDAD 1 Una invitación por teléfono

Complete Mateo's conversations.

conmigo   contigo   lástima   mensaje   tal vez

puedo   gracias   dígale   regresa

Sra. Ruiz: Hola.

Mateo: Buenas tardes, señora. Soy Mateo. ¿ __1__ hablar con Laura?

Sra. Ruiz: No está en este momento. __2__ más tarde. ¿Quieres dejar un __3__ ?

Mateo: Sí, gracias. __4__ que me llame, por favor.

Más tarde...

Mateo: Hola.

Laura: Hola, Mateo. Soy Laura.

Mateo: Oye, ¿te gustaría ir al cine __5__ mañana?

Laura: __6__ , pero no puedo. Tengo que trabajar. __7__ otro día.

Mateo: ¡Qué __8__ ! ¿Y el sábado?

Laura: Sí, me encantaría ir __9__ .

Now you can...

- express feelings.

To review

- **gustar** with infinitives, see p. 215.

ACTIVIDAD 2 Están contentos

Say what these people like to do.

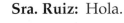

modelo

Carlos: pasear

*A **Carlos** le gusta **pasear**.*

1. mis padres: alquilar un video
2. tú: escuchar un concierto
3. mis hermanos y yo: practicar deportes
4. la vecina: ir al cine
5. yo: ver la televisión
6. Berta y José: ir de compras
7. Ignacio: pasear
8. nosotros: hablar por teléfono

Now you can...
• express feelings.

To review
• **estar** with adjectives, see p. 208.

ACTIVIDAD
3 Un festival internacional

Tell how these people are feeling.

alegre   emocionado(a)   triste   nervioso(a)   enojado(a)

modelo

Julia: le gusta bailar

Julia está alegre porque **le gusta bailar.**

1. Ignacio y Diana: tienen que estudiar

2. Rogelio: sus amigos no van

3. tú: vas a cantar

4. yo: tengo que trabajar

5. ustedes: su grupo favorito va a tocar

6. nosotros: vamos a ver a nuestros amigos

Now you can...
• say what just happened.

• say where you are coming from.

To review
• **acabar de,** see p. 211.

• the verb **venir,** see p. 212.

ACTIVIDAD
4 Muchas actividades

Tell what these people have just done and where they are coming from.

modelo

mis amigos: hacer ejercicio

Mis amigos acaban de **hacer ejercicio.** *Vienen del gimnasio.*

1. yo: ver una exhibición de arte

2. tú: practicar deportes

3. Ernesto: leer revistas y periódicos

4. Hugo y Raquel: escuchar música

5. mi madre y yo: comprar comida

6. los Fernández: ver una película

7. usted: ir de compras

8. nosotros: comer papas fritas

ACTIVIDAD 5

Por teléfono

You wish to invite a friend to do something with you. Call two people. One refuses your invitation, but the other accepts. Agree on the time and day.

ACTIVIDAD 6

 **¡De visita!**

Imagine that you are in Puerto Rico at the home of a friend. Your friend's friends come over to meet you. Talk with your friend to find out (1) who they are, (2) how they're feeling (and why), and (3) where they are coming from.

modelo

Tú: *¿Quién es la muchacha?*

Tu amigo(a): *Es mi amiga Rosa. Está cansada porque acaba de practicar deportes. Viene del gimnasio.*

¿Quién es?	¿Cómo está?	¿Por qué?	¿De dónde viene?
un(a) amigo(a)	alegre	acaba de ¿ ?	la escuela
¿ ?	¿ ?	acaba de ¿ ?	¿ ?

ACTIVIDAD 7

 *En tu propia voz*

Escritura Write a letter to your pen pal about your leisure activities.

• ¿Cuáles son tres de tus actividades favoritas?

• Pregúntale a tu amigo(a) sobre tres actividades específicas.

Conexiones

La música Would you like to hear **bomba y plena** music? Check your local library or the international section of a music store for recordings. You can probably find many kinds of music with Spanish influences. What other kinds of music do you like? You can check the Internet to find out what is popular in Spain. Listen to five songs from any source and complete the following chart. Then say why you do or don't like the songs.

Título	Sí, me gusta/No, no me gusta	¿Por qué?

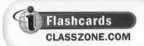

En resumen
REPASO DE VOCABULARIO

EXTENDING INVITATIONS

¿Quieres acompañarme a…?	Would you like to come with me to…?
Te invito.	I'll treat you. I invite you.
¿Te gustaría…?	Would you like…?

Accepting

¡Claro que sí!	Of course.
Me gustaría…	I would like…
Sí, me encantaría.	Yes, I would love to.

Declining

Gracias, pero no puedo.	Thanks, but I can't.
¡Qué lástima!	What a shame!
Tal vez otro día.	Maybe another day.

Activities

alquilar un video	to rent a video
el concierto	concert
ir al cine	to go to a movie theater
ir de compras	to go shopping
la película	movie
practicar deportes	to play sports
el tiempo libre	free time

EXPRESSING FEELINGS

alegre	happy
cansado(a)	tired
contento(a)	content, happy, pleased
deprimido(a)	depressed
emocionado(a)	excited
enfermo(a)	sick
enojado(a)	angry
nervioso(a)	nervous
ocupado(a)	busy
preocupado(a)	worried
tranquilo(a)	calm
triste	sad

TALKING ON THE PHONE

contestar	to answer
dejar un mensaje	to leave a message
la guía telefónica	phone book
la llamada	call
llamar	to call
la máquina contestadora	answering machine
marcar	to dial
el teléfono	telephone

Phrases for talking on the phone

Deje/a un mensaje después del tono.	Leave (formal/familiar) a message after the tone.
Dile/Dígale que me llame.	Tell (familiar/formal) him/her to call me.
¿Puedo hablar con…?	May I speak with…?
Quiero dejar un mensaje para…	I want to leave a message for…
Regresa más tarde.	He/She will return later.
Un momento.	One moment.

WHERE YOU ARE COMING FROM

del/de la	from the
venir	to come

SAYING WHAT JUST HAPPENED

acabar de…	to have just…

OTHER WORDS AND PHRASES

conmigo	with me
contigo	with you
cuando	when, whenever
¡No te preocupes!	Don't worry!
porque	because
solo(a)	alone
temprano	early
ya no	no longer

Juego

¿Adónde van en su tiempo libre?

1. A Miguel le gusta escuchar música.
2. A Mariela le gusta ver las películas de Antonio Banderas.
3. A Martina y a Martín les gusta comprar ropa.

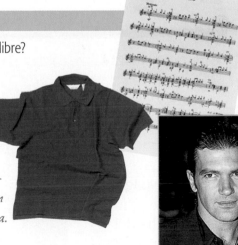

ETAPA

2

¡Deportes para todos!

OBJECTIVES

- Talk about sports

- Express preferences

- Say what you know

- Make comparisons

¿Qué ves?

Mira la foto de un campo de béisbol en San Juan.

1. Para ti, ¿el béisbol es interesante?

2. ¿Quién practica, Ignacio o Roberto?

3. ¿Cuál es la fecha del campeonato de béisbol?

4. ¿En qué día de la semana es el campeonato?

224

Campeonato de béisbol

Los Toros Valientes

vs.

Los Huracanes

domingo
17 de abril
a las 6 de la tarde
en el campo de deportes

Entrada: $3

En contexto

VOCABULARIO

Diana and Ignacio are looking at equipment in a sporting goods store. Look at the illustrations to understand the meaning of the words in blue. This will help you answer the questions on the next page.

¡Hola! Ignacio y yo estamos en **la tienda de deportes**. ¡Vamos a ver qué hay!

A

A mí me gusta andar en **patineta**. Uso **un casco** cuando ando en patineta y cuando uso **patines**.

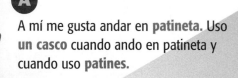

los patines

las bolas

el casco

la patineta

B

Aquí hay de todo para practicar deportes como **el baloncesto, el voleibol, el fútbol** y el **fútbol americano**. ¡Y hay **una bola** especial para cada deporte! El baloncesto y el voleibol se practican en **una cancha**. El fútbol y el fútbol americano se practican en **un campo**. A veces se practican en **un estadio**.

¡los deportes!

las canchas

El baloncesto   El voleibol

el estadio

El fútbol americano   los campos   El fútbol

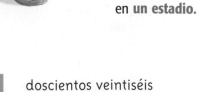

D ¿Te gusta **levantar pesas**?

la pesa

Tienda de Deportes Peña

la raqueta

E Para practicar **el tenis** usas **una raqueta** y una bola.

F En Puerto Rico, es divertido **esquiar** en el agua o practicar **el surfing**.

esquiar

C

Practicas el **béisbol** con **un guante, un bate** y **una pelota**. Ésta es una foto del **equipo** de béisbol de Ignacio.

el guante

la pelota

el bate

el surfing

el equipo

Online Workbook
CLASSZONE.COM

Preguntas personales

1. ¿Practicas deportes?
2. ¿Practicas el baloncesto o el voleibol?
3. ¿Te gusta más mirar el fútbol o el fútbol americano?
4. ¿Cuál es tu deporte favorito?
5. ¿Qué usas cuando practicas tu deporte favorito?

En vivo

VIDEO DVD AUDIO

DIÁLOGO

Ignacio Claudio Roberto Sr. Castillo

El campo de béisbol

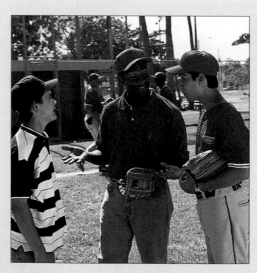
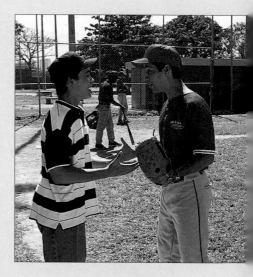

PARA ESCUCHAR • STRATEGY: LISTENING

Listen for "turn-taking" tactics In English conversation we often say *uh, yeah, well, say,* or *listen* to signal that we are getting ready to speak. Listen carefully to the Spanish. What words or expressions do you hear that signal, "It's my turn to talk"?

1▶ Claudio: Oye, ¿qué haces?
Ignacio: Espero a mi amigo.
Claudio: ¡Ah! ¿Sabe él a qué hora empieza la práctica?
Ignacio: Sí.

5▶ Ignacio: Sr. Castillo, le presento a Roberto. Viene de Minneapolis.
Sr. Castillo: Mucho gusto. ¿Qué deportes juegan en Minneapolis?
Roberto: ¡Son locos con el fútbol americano!

6▶ Ignacio: ¿Les gusta jugar al fútbol?
Roberto: Sí, pero no es tan popular como el fútbol americano. Mucha gente en los Estados Unidos piensa que el fútbol americano es más interesante que el fútbol.

7▶ Roberto: Me gusta jugar al baloncesto y al tenis. Pienso que el tenis es menos divertido que el baloncesto. También me gusta nadar.
Ignacio: Me gusta correr más que nadar.

2 ▶ Claudio: ¿Quieres practicar un poco conmigo?

Ignacio: No, gracias. Prefiero esperar a Roberto aquí.

3 ▶ Roberto: ¡Ignacio! ¡Qué gusto!

Ignacio: ¡Roberto! ¡Cuánto tiempo!

Roberto: ¡Ahora tengo un amigo para hablar de deportes!

4 ▶ Roberto: ¿Prefieres este bate o éste?

Ignacio: Yo prefiero este bate. ¿Juegas al béisbol en Minneapolis?

Roberto: Sí.

8 ▶ Sr. Castillo: ¿Piensas jugar en el equipo de baloncesto?

Roberto: Sí. También quiero jugar en el equipo de béisbol. ¿Puedo practicar con ustedes?

Sr. Castillo: ¡Claro! ¡Vamos!

9 ▶ Ignacio: Necesito tu ayuda. Quiero participar en un concurso.

Roberto: ¿Y qué piensas hacer?

Ignacio: Tengo una idea. Me gustaría hablar contigo sobre el proyecto.

10 ▶ Roberto: Claro, está bien. ¿Por qué no vienes a casa mañana por la mañana?

Ignacio: Así también saludo a tu familia.

Roberto: ¿Por qué no invitas a Diana?

Ignacio: Está bien. Nos vemos como a las diez.

En acción
VOCABULARIO Y GRAMÁTICA

ACTIVIDAD
1

¿Qué pasa?

Escuchar Complete the following statements about the dialog.

1. Ignacio espera _____.
   a. a Diana
   b. a su amigo Roberto
   c. al señor Castillo

2. Roberto viene de _____.
   a. Minneapolis
   b. Miami
   c. Puerto Rico

3. Roberto piensa que el _____ es muy popular en Minneapolis.
   a. béisbol
   b. fútbol americano
   c. baloncesto

4. A Ignacio le gusta _____ más que nadar.
   a. jugar al béisbol
   b. correr
   c. patinar

5. Ignacio necesita la ayuda de Roberto para el _____.
   a. béisbol
   b. tenis
   c. concurso

También se dice

There are different ways to say *ball*.

- **la bola:** Puerto Rico
- **el balón:** Spain
- **la pelota:** Latin America, Spain

In Puerto Rico, **una pelota** is a baseball. **Balón** and **cesto** (basket) are combined to mean *basketball*. **Básquetbol** is sometimes used as a name for this sport.

ACTIVIDAD 2

Conversaciones

Escuchar Based on what you heard in the dialog, choose the sentence that tells what is being said in the photo.

1.
a. ¡Ignacio! ¡Qué gusto!
b. Espero a mi amigo.

2.
a. Necesito tu ayuda.
b. Sr. Castillo, le presento a Roberto.

3.
a. ¡Vamos a jugar!
b. ¡Cuánto tiempo!

4.
a. ¿Prefieres este bate o éste?
b. ¿Qué deportes juegan en Minneapolis?

ACTIVIDAD 3

De vacaciones

Leer/Escribir Imagine you're going to sports camp. Read the list of sports offered. On a piece of paper, write them in order of your preference. (Number 1 is the sport you're most interested in. Number 5 is the sport you're least interested in.)

¡A jugar!
una semana de...

- baloncesto
- béisbol
- esquiar
- fútbol
- fútbol americano
- hockey
- nadar
- surfing
- tenis
- voleibol

♻ ¿Qué te gusta?

Hablar Work with a classmate. Look at the pictures below. Choose five sports and ask your partner if she or he likes to play each of those sports. Switch roles.

jugar al tenis

modelo

Estudiante A: *¿Te gusta jugar al tenis?*

Estudiante B: *Sí, me gusta jugar al tenis.*
   o: *No, no me gusta jugar al tenis.*

nadar

jugar al fútbol americano

andar en patineta

patinar

jugar al béisbol

esquiar en agua

levantar pesas

jugar al fútbol

jugar al baloncesto

Una fanática para los deportes

Hablar/Escribir Have you ever seen anybody as crazy about sports as this person? Give the name of each piece of equipment.

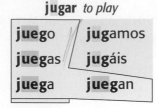

GRAMÁTICA

Talking About Playing a Sport: The Verb jugar

When you talk about playing a sport, you use the verb **jugar**. The forms of **jugar** are unique. In some of them, the **u** changes to **ue**.

jugar *to play*

juego	**jugamos**
juegas	**jugáis**
juega	**juegan**

When you use **jugar** with the name of a sport, use

jugar a + *sport*

Ignacio asks Roberto:

—¿**Juegas al** béisbol en Minneapolis?
*Do **you play** baseball in Minneapolis?*

Coach Castillo asks:

—¿Qué deportes **juegan** en Minneapolis?
*What sports do **they play** in Minneapolis?*

Vocabulario

Más sobre los deportes

al aire libre *outdoors*

andar en patineta *to skateboard*

ganar *to win*

el gol *goal*

la gorra *baseball cap*

el hockey *hockey*

el partido *game*

la piscina *pool*

sobre hielo *on ice*

Use these adjectives and others you know to describe sports.

favorito(a) *favorite*

peligroso(a) *dangerous*

¿Qué frase usas para hablar de tu deporte favorito?

ACTIVIDAD **6** Gramática

¿A qué juegan?

Hablar/Escribir Diana's new friend asks her what sports she and her friends play. Complete her sentences with the correct form of **jugar**.

Mis amigos y yo __1__ a muchos deportes. Yo __2__ al voleibol. No ganamos siempre, pero me gusta mucho __3__ . Yo también __4__ al baloncesto, y ¡sí! ganamos mucho. Antonio y Marco __5__ al fútbol americano y al béisbol. Andrea __6__ al tenis y al voleibol conmigo. Bueno, ¿a qué __7__ tú?

MÁS PRÁCTICA *cuaderno* p. 69

PARA HISPANOHABLANTES *cuaderno* p. 67

Online Workbook
CLASSZONE.COM

234 doscientos treinta y cuatro
Unidad 3

ACTIVIDAD
7

¿Juegan a...?

Hablar/Escribir Use the clues to decide what sport these people play.

modelo

Susana (patines y hielo)
Susana juega al hockey.

1. yo (gorra, guante, bate)
2. Antonio y Raúl (casco, bola, aire libre)
3. Anita (bola, cancha o gimnasio)
4. tú (raqueta y bola)

ACTIVIDAD
8

¿Quién juega a qué?

Hablar Tell what sports you, your friends, and family members play.

modelo

mi hermana

Mi hermana juega al **tenis.**

1. yo
2. mi hermano(a)
3. mis amigos(as)
4. mi amigo(a)
5. mis amigos(as) y yo
6. mi padre
7. mis abuelos
8. mi hermana y yo
9. mi madre
10. ¿?

Conexiones

Los estudios sociales Although Puerto Rico is a part of the U.S., it is not a state. It is an **estado libre asociado.** Puerto Ricans are U.S. citizens. They use U.S. dollars as currency. They elect a governor and a legislature. However, Puerto Ricans cannot vote for members of Congress or the president, unless they are living in one of the 50 states.

PARA HACER:

Use the library or the Internet to find out:

• When did Puerto Rico become part of the U.S.?

• Under what circumstances did this occur?

GRAMÁTICA

Stem-Changing Verbs: e → ie

You learned that the **u** in **jugar** sometimes changes to **ue**. When you use the verb **pensar** (*to think, to plan*), the **e** in its **stem** sometimes changes to **ie**. **Pensar** means *to plan* only when followed by an infinitive.

stem changes to

p**e**nsar → p**ie**nso

In stem-changing verbs, it is always the next-to-last syllable that changes.

pensar *to think, to plan*

p**ie**nso	p**e**nsamos
p**ie**nsas	p**e**nsáis
p**ie**nsa	p**ie**nsan

Roberto says:

—Yo **pref**i**ero** este bate.
I prefer this bat.

The coach asks:

—¿**P**i**e**nsas **jugar** en el equipo de baloncesto?
Do you plan to play on the basketball team?

Vocabulario

Stem-Changing Verbs: e → ie

cerrar *to close*
empezar *to begin*
entender *to understand*
merendar *to have a snack*
perder *to lose*
preferir *to prefer*
querer *to want*

¿Cuándo usas una de estas palabras?

Note that when one verb follows another, the first verb is **conjugated** and the second is in its **infinitive** form.

ACTIVIDAD 9 — Gramática

¡Todos piensan jugar!

Hablar These people all plan to play a sport. Say what they are planning to play.

modelo

ustedes
Ustedes piensan jugar al **fútbol**.

1. nosotros

2. Diana

3. los chicos

4. tú

5. yo

6. usted

¿Qué hacen?

PARA CONVERSAR

STRATEGY: SPEAKING

Monitor yourself Listen. How do you sound? Do you hear errors? If so, stop and correct yourself. It is OK to do so.

Hablar/Escribir Explain what happens one day at school.

modelo

la clase / empezar / por la mañana
La clase empieza por la mañana.

1. los estudiantes / cerrar / libro
2. yo / perder / partido
3. el equipo / querer hacer / gol
4. tú / querer jugar / tenis
5. nosotros / entender / matemáticas
6. el partido / empezar / a las cuatro
7. ellos / merendar / cafetería
8. yo / preferir nadar / piscina

MÁS PRÁCTICA *cuaderno* p. 70

PARA HISPANOHABLANTES
cuaderno p. 68

¿Qué pasa aquí?

Escribir Choose two verbs from the list. Then write two sentences to describe each picture.

| cerrar | entender | pensar | preferir |
| empezar | merendar | perder | querer |

modelo

Nosotros **queremos** ganar el partido.
Perdemos y estamos tristes.

1.

2.

3.

4.

ACTIVIDAD 12

Un día de clases

Hablar Work with a partner. Take turns making statements about school using the words as a guide.

modelo

yo / preferir

Estudiante A: *Yo prefiero la clase de música.*

Estudiante B: *Pues, yo prefiero la clase de español.*

1. los estudiantes / entender bien
2. yo / querer
3. mis amigos y yo / merendar
4. mi amigo(a) / pensar
5. el equipo de... / perder
6. la clase de... / empezar

Conexiones
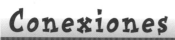

La educación física Although baseball is the favorite sport in Puerto Rico, soccer is the most popular sport in most Spanish-speaking countries. Every four years, teams from around the world compete in the World Cup (**la Copa Mundial**). Latin American teams are frequently finalists, if not winners. Brazil, for example, has won five times. In 1998, though, Brazil lost the championship game to host country France.

PARA HACER:

1. Describe the colors of these team shirts. What colors do you think they represent?

2. Find out the name of another popular sport in a Spanish-speaking country. Learn how it is played and demonstrate it with your classmates.

Chile

Colombia

Argentina

Estados Unidos

Saying What You Know: The Verb saber

¿RECUERDAS? *pp. 179, 181* You learned that some verbs have irregular **yo** forms.

conocer ➝ cono**zco**
hacer ➝ ha**go**
oír ➝ o**igo**

Saber is another verb that has an irregular **yo** form. You use **saber** when you talk about factual information you know.

saber *to know*

s**é**	sabemos
sabes	sabéis
sabe	saben

Claudio asks Ignacio:

—¿**Sabe** él a qué hora empieza la práctica?
*Does **he know** what time practice starts?*

To say that someone knows how to do something, use: **saber** + ***infinitive***.

Sé patinar muy bien.
I know how to skate very well.

13 Gramática

¡Saben hacer mucho!

Escribir/Hablar Complete each item using **saber**. Then say if you know how to do each activity.

1. Él _____ bailar.
2. Yo _____ nadar.
3. Nosotros _____ hablar español.
4. María _____ jugar al tenis.
5. Los chicos _____ jugar al voleibol.
6. Tú _____ patinar.
7. Ella _____ tocar el piano.
8. Ustedes _____ cantar.

MÁS PRÁCTICA *cuaderno* p. 71
PARA HISPANOHABLANTES *cuaderno* p. 69

14

Los deportistas

Escuchar Many of Diana's friends know how to play various sports. Listen to Diana's descriptions and explain what they know how to play.

1. Gisela y César
2. Pablo
3. ella y su hermano
4. Roberto y su hermano
5. Diana

Online Workbook
CLASSZONE.COM

ACTIVIDAD 15

¿Qué saben hacer?

Hablar Work with a partner. Take turns asking and answering questions about what these people know how to do.

modelo

tu hermano(a)

Estudiante A: *¿Qué sabe hacer tu hermana?*

Estudiante B: *Mi hermana sabe cantar y bailar.*

1. tus amigos(as)
2. tú
3. el (la) maestro(a) de español
4. tú y tus amigos(as)
5. tu mamá (papá)
6. tu hermano(a)
7. tus abuelos
8. tú y tus hermanos(as)

■ MÁS COMUNICACIÓN p. R8

NOTA CULTURAL

When Spanish speakers started playing baseball in large numbers, they "adopted" many English baseball terms into Spanish. Can you recognize these words?

la base   el bate

el jonrón   el diamante

GRAMÁTICA

Phrases for Making Comparisons

▶ Several phrases are used to compare things. Roberto and Ignacio use these when they discuss sports.

* **más… que**
  more… than

  …el fútbol americano es **más** interesante **que** el fútbol.
  *…football is **more** interesting **than** soccer.*

* **menos… que**
  less… than   *agrees*

  …**el tenis** es **menos** divertid**o que** el baloncesto.
  *…tennis is **less** entertaining **than** basketball.*

  > Adjectives must agree in gender and number with the **nouns** that precede them.

* **tan… como**
  as… as

  …el fútbol no es **tan** popular **como** el fútbol americano.
  *…soccer is not **as** popular **as** football.*

▶ These phrases are also used to compare actions.

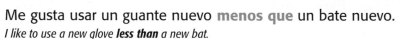

* **más que…**
  more than…

  Me gusta correr **más que** nadar.
  *I like to run **more than** (I like to) swim.*

* **menos que…**
  less than…

  Me gusta usar un guante nuevo **menos que** un bate nuevo.
  *I like to use a new glove **less than** a new bat.*

* **tanto como…**
  as much as…

  A él le gusta jugar al fútbol **tanto como** al béisbol.
  *He likes to play soccer **as much as** baseball.*

▶ When you talk about numbers, you must use **más de** or **menos de**.

más de dos o tres minutos   en **menos de** cinco minutos
more than *two or three minutes*   *in **less than** five minutes*

▶ There are a few irregular comparative words.

mayor	**menor**	**mejor**	**peor**
older	*younger*	*better*	*worse*

240   doscientos cuarenta
Unidad 3

¿Más o menos?

Hablar/Escribir Complete the sentences by using **más… que** or **menos… que**, according to the pictures.

modelo

La pelota de béisbol es <u>menos</u> grande <u>que</u> la bola de baloncesto.

1. El bate es _____ delgado _____ el casco.

2. La patineta es _____ larga _____ la bicicleta.

3. Elisa es _____ alta _____ Marta.

4. Mario es _____ fuerte _____ Ricardo.

¿Tan o tanto?

Hablar/Escribir Say that the following are equal by completing each sentence with **tan… como** or **tanto como.**

modelo

Julio es guapo. / Víctor es guapo.

Julio es tan guapo como Víctor.

Me gusta leer. / Me gusta escribir.

Me gusta leer tanto como escribir.

1. Él es simpático. / Ella es simpática.
2. Me gusta nadar. / Me gusta correr.
3. La chica es bonita. / La mujer es bonita.
4. Nos gusta correr. / Nos gusta bailar.
5. Yo trabajo. / Tú trabajas.

¿De o que?

Escribir Use the correct word (**de** or **que**) to complete these sentences about athletes.

1. Ignacio tiene más _____ cinco bates.
2. Todas las semanas Ignacio practica más _____ cinco veces.
3. Roberto juega peor _____ Diana.
4. La chica rubia quiere jugar menos _____ la morena.
5. Hay menos _____ ocho personas en el equipo de baloncesto.

MÁS PRÁCTICA *cuaderno* p. 72

PARA HISPANOHABLANTES *cuaderno* p. 70

Online Workbook
CLASSZONE.COM

ACTIVIDAD 19

¿Qué piensas tú?

Hablar Work with another student to compare the sports. Switch roles.

interesante

modelo

Estudiante A: *Para ti, ¿qué deporte es más **interesante, el tenis** o **el béisbol**?*

Estudiante B: *Para mí, **el tenis** es más **interesante** que **el béisbol**.*

Estudiante A: *Para mí, **el tenis** es tan **interesante** como **el béisbol**.*

Estudiante A
PREGUNTAS

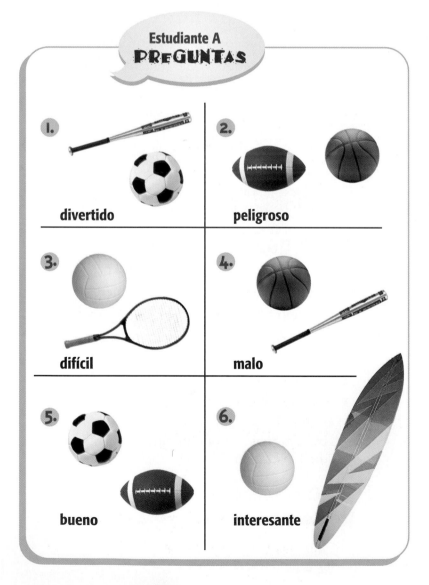

1. **divertido**

2. **peligroso**

3. **difícil**

4. **malo**

5. **bueno**

6. **interesante**

Estudiante B
RESPUESTAS

Para mí, ... es más... que...

Para mí, ... es menos... que...

Para mí, ... es tan... como...

APOYO PARA ESTUDIAR

Comparatives

When comparing, picture these visual cues:

(+) más…que   (−) menos…que

(=) tan…como

Think about extremes that would illustrate **más** and **menos**, such as **UN ELEFANTE [(+) más grande]** and **un ratón [(−) menos grande]**. Now think of two athletes or performers that are very different about whom you have an opinion. How would you compare them?

¡Lógicamente!

Escuchar Everyone is talking about sports. Listen to what they have to say. Then choose the most logical response.

1. a. ¡Qué bien! Tenemos más de cinco minutos.
   b. ¡Ay! Tenemos menos de cinco minutos.

2. a. ¿Tienes tu raqueta?
   b. ¿Tienes tu tarea?

3. a. Sí, me gusta nadar.
   b. ¡Claro que sí! Me gusta patinar.

4. a. No necesita un guante.
   b. ¿Va a la tienda de deportes?

5. a. Prefiere nadar.
   b. Prefiere levantar pesas.

¿Cuál es tu deporte favorito?

Hablar/Escribir Which is your favorite sport?

1 Interview two students about sports. Ask the following questions.

2 Write their responses on a chart like the one below.

3 Write a summary of what they said.

modelo

Estudiante A: *¿A qué deportes sabes jugar?*

Estudiante B: *Yo sé jugar al voleibol.*

Estudiante C: *Y yo sé jugar al fútbol.*

Estudiante A (Resumen): *Ana sabe jugar al voleibol. Víctor sabe jugar al fútbol.*

La encuesta	Estudiante B	Estudiante C
1. ¿A qué deportes sabes jugar?		
2. ¿A qué deportes juegas mucho?		
3. ¿A qué deporte prefieres jugar?		
4. ¿Qué deporte prefieres ver?		
5. Compara el deporte que prefieres ver con el deporte que prefieres jugar.		
6. ¿Cuál es tu equipo favorito?		

MÁS COMUNICACIÓN p. R8

Online Workbook
CLASSZONE.COM

Pronunciación

Trabalenguas

Pronunciación de la ñ The letter **ñ** does not exist in English, but the sound does. It is the sound made by the combination of the letters *ny* in the English word *canyon*. To practice the sound, pronounce the following tongue twister.

ñ

La **ñ** *es la* **n** *con bigote.*

¡Mañana la araña se baña!

En colores
CULTURA Y COMPARACIONES

PARA CONOCERNOS

STRATEGY:
CONNECTING CULTURES

Reflect on sports traditions Can you think of any sports in the U.S. that have players from other countries? What sports are they? Are some countries associated with certain sports more than others? Why do you think that might be true? Use this chart to organize your answers.

Deporte	País 1	País 2	País 3
el béisbol	Cuba	Japón	
el hockey	Canadá	Rusia	

Do you associate other countries with areas such as science, music, or art? If so, which ones? Why?

Béisbol
El pasatiempo nacional

En Puerto Rico el béisbol es muy popular. La temporada[1] de béisbol es de octubre a marzo. Los equipos que juegan forman la liga de invierno[2] y hay un partido casi todos los días.

Cada ciudad principal tiene un equipo. Unos jugadores[3] de las ligas mayores y menores[4] de Estados Unidos participan junto con los jugadores puertorriqueños.

---

[1] season   [2] winter league   [3] players   [4] major and minor leagues

Roberto Clemente (1934–1972), jugador de los Piratas de Pittsburgh, es el puertorriqueño más famoso del béisbol. El primer latino elegido[5] para el Salón de la Fama[6] en 1973, Clemente empezó[7] su carrera con el equipo de Santurce, Puerto Rico. Hoy, en la ciudad de San Juan, el estadio principal de béisbol se llama Coliseo Roberto Clemente.

---

[5] elected   [6] Hall of Fame   [7] began

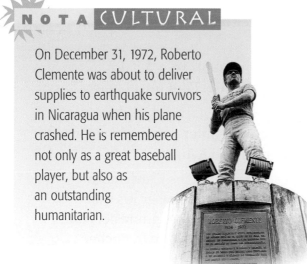

En el resto del Caribe el béisbol es tan importante como en Puerto Rico. Muchos jugadores importantes vienen de esta región. Juan Marichal de la República Dominicana está en el Salón de la Fama. Andrés Galarraga de Venezuela, Edgar Rentería de Colombia, Liván Hernández de Cuba y Fernando Valenzuela de México son otras figuras latinoamericanas importantes de las ligas mayores de béisbol de Estados Unidos.

José Cruz, Jr. e Iván Rodríguez son dos jugadores de Puerto Rico.

More About Puerto Rico
CLASSZONE.COM

¿Comprendiste?

1. ¿En qué meses juegan los equipos de la liga de invierno?
2. ¿De dónde vienen los jugadores de la liga de invierno?
3. ¿Quién es el primer latino elegido para el Salón de la Fama?
4. ¿Qué países latinos tienen jugadores en las ligas mayores?

¿Qué piensas?

1. ¿Por qué juegan en Puerto Rico los jugadores de las ligas mayores y menores de Estados Unidos?
2. ¿Por qué vienen a Estados Unidos los jugadores de otros países?

En uso

REPASO Y MÁS COMUNICACIÓN

OBJECTIVES
- Talk about sports
- Express preferences
- Say what you know
- Make comparisons

ACTIVIDAD 1 ¿Dónde juegas?

Tell where people play their favorite sports.

modelo

mi padre: tenis (¿en la piscina o en la cancha?)
Mi padre *juega al* **tenis en la cancha**.

1. tú: baloncesto
   (¿en el campo o en la cancha?)

2. usted: voleibol
   (¿en la cancha o sobre hielo?)

3. yo: fútbol
   (¿en la cancha o en el campo?)

4. los vecinos: béisbol
   (¿al aire libre o en el gimnasio?)

5. Tomás y yo: fútbol americano
   (¿en el estadio o en la piscina?)

6. mi hermano: hockey
   (¿en la cancha o sobre hielo?)

ACTIVIDAD 2 ¡Vamos a jugar!

Complete the conversation with the appropriate verbs in the correct form.

cerrar   pensar   querer   entender   preferir   empezar

Eva: Rita, ¿ __1__ ir a un partido de béisbol conmigo mañana? El partido __2__ a las siete.

Rita: Gracias, pero no me gusta ver el béisbol. Yo __3__ los deportes individuales, como el surfing. Para mí, el béisbol es aburrido. No __4__ por qué te gusta.

Eva: Pues, yo __5__ que el béisbol es muy interesante. Y mañana mi equipo favorito, los Cardenales, va a jugar.

Rita: Mis hermanos también __6__ ver jugar a los Cardenales mañana, pero yo no. Mi mamá y yo __7__ pasar los sábados en las tiendas. Pero, a veces vamos al nuevo gimnasio. Abre a las siete de la mañana y __8__ a las nueve de la noche.

Now you can...

- talk about sports.

To review

- the verb **jugar**, see p. 234.

Now you can...

- express preferences.

To review

- stem-changing verbs: **e→ie**, see p. 236.

Now you can...
• say what you know.

To review
• the verb **saber**, see p. 239.

ACTIVIDAD 3 Somos deportistas

Tell what sports these people know how to play and what equipment they use.

modelo

Bárbara
Bárbara sabe patinar.
Usa **patines**.

ustedes
Ustedes saben
jugar al voleibol. Usan **una bola**.

1. Guillermo   **2.** nosotros   **3.** yo

4. mis amigos   **5.** tú   **6.** yo

Now you can...
• make comparisons.

To review
• phrases for making comparisons, see p. 240.

ACTIVIDAD 4 Comparaciones

Express your opinions about sports.

modelo

correr / nadar (menos / divertido)

Correr es **menos divertido** que **nadar**.
o: **Nadar** es **menos divertido** que **correr**.
o: **Correr** es **tan divertido** como **nadar**.

1. el baloncesto / el tenis (menos / interesante)

2. el surfing / el béisbol (más / aburrido)

3. nadar / levantar pesas (más / bueno)

4. esquiar / patinar (más / peligroso)

5. el fútbol americano / el baloncesto (más / popular)

6. el voleibol / el fútbol (menos / difícil)

7. el tenis / el béisbol (más / malo)

8. patinar / levantar pesas (menos / fácil)

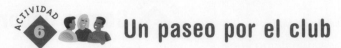

¿Qué opinas tú?

PARA CONVERSAR
STRATEGY: SPEAKING
Give reasons for your preferences Support your choices in different ways. Compare (1) how you feel about the sports, (2) what you know or don't know about them, or (3) basic similarities and differences among them. Think of different ways of explaining your choices.

Talk with another student about sports. Tell which sports you prefer and why.

modelo

Tú: *¿Prefieres levantar pesas o jugar al voleibol?*

Otro(a) estudiante: *Prefiero jugar al voleibol. El voleibol es más interesante que levantar pesas.*

Tú: *Para mí, levantar pesas es más divertido.*

Un paseo por el club

Imagine you work in a sports club. Complete the following sentences to describe the club to your friends.

Hay equipos de...

Muchas personas juegan al...

Tenemos cancha de...

El club abre...

Para jugar al voleibol, hay...

Los sábados jugamos al...

Al aire libre jugamos...

Los viernes hay clases de...

Para las personas que les gusta nadar, hay...

En tu propia voz

Escritura Create a brochure about the sports club where you work (**Actividad 6**). Include information about the activities available and the schedule.

En la comunidad

Sarah is a Florida student who uses Spanish at her job as a restaurant hostess and sends e-mails in Spanish. She also used her Spanish when she went to Venezuela as a volunteer with a medical mission group. Sarah spoke Spanish to the patients and translated doctors' questions and instructions. Do you use Spanish to help others?

En resumen
REPASO DE VOCABULARIO

TALKING ABOUT SPORTS

el equipo	team
ganar	to win
el gol	goal
jugar (ue)	to play
el partido	game
la tienda de deportes	sporting goods store

Sports

andar en patineta	to skateboard
el baloncesto	basketball
el béisbol	baseball
esquiar	to ski
el fútbol	soccer
el fútbol americano	football
el hockey	hockey
levantar pesas	to lift weights
el surfing	surfing
el tenis	tennis
el voleibol	volleyball

Equipment

el bate	bat
la bola	ball
el casco	helmet
la gorra	baseball cap
el guante	glove
los patines	skates
la patineta	skateboard
la pelota	baseball
la raqueta	racket

Locations

al aire libre	outdoors
el campo	field
la cancha	court
el estadio	stadium
la piscina	swimming pool
sobre hielo	on ice

EXPRESSING PREFERENCES

preferir (ie)	to prefer
querer (ie)	to want

SAYING WHAT YOU KNOW

saber	to know

MAKING COMPARISONS

más de	more than
más… que	more…than
mayor	older
mejor	better
menor	younger
menos de	less than
menos… que	less…than
peor	worse
tan… como	as…as
tanto como	as much as

OTHER WORDS AND PHRASES

cerrar (ie)	to close
empezar (ie)	to begin
entender (ie)	to understand
favorito(a)	favorite
loco(a)	crazy
merendar (ie)	to have a snack
peligroso(a)	dangerous
pensar (ie)	to think, to plan
perder (ie)	to lose

Juego

A Ángela, a Marco y a Juanito les gusta practicar diferentes deportes. ¿Cuáles son? Busca sus nombres. Con las otras letras, identifica su deporte preferido.

1. ALSAEGSPENARALEVANT
2. GINAMURFSOCR
3. NIAUJOTTBLOFU

ETAPA 3

El tiempo en El Yunque

OBJECTIVES

- Describe the weather

- Discuss clothing and accessories

- State an opinion

- Describe how you feel

- Say what is happening

¿Qué ves?

Mira la foto de El Yunque, el bosque tropical.

1. ¿Hay muchas plantas verdes?

2. ¿Ignacio está ocupado o no?

3. ¿Diana y Roberto están alegres o preocupados?

4. ¿Cómo se llama el lugar?

VEREDA
↑ EL YUNQUE
EL YUNQUE TRAIL
BOSQUE NACIONAL
DEL CARIBE

BAÑO GRANDE
CUERPOS CIVILES DE CONSERVACIÓN
CIVILIAN CONSERVATION CORPS

En contexto

VOCABULARIO

Roberto has experienced all kinds of weather in Minnesota and Puerto Rico. Take a look at the pictures in his scrapbook to understand the meaning of the words in blue. This will also help you answer the questions on the next page.

A ¿Qué tiempo **hace** en Minnesota? En **el invierno** hace mal **tiempo**. ¡Hace **frío** y hay mucha **nieve**! Cuando va a **nevar**, necesitas **un gorro, una bufanda** y **un abrigo**.

yo

yo en el invierno

el gorro

la bufanda

el abrigo   la nieve

B Cuando va a **llover**, necesitas **un paraguas**. A la madre de Roberto le gusta caminar bajo **la lluvia** con su paraguas **de cuadros**.

mamá con paraguas

el paraguas

de cuadros

C En Puerto Rico, en **el verano hace calor**. Cuando **hay sol**, es divertido ir a **la playa** y nadar en **el mar**.

mi primo en el verano

el mar

el traje de baño

la playa

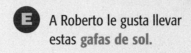

las gafas de sol

E A Roberto le gusta llevar estas **gafas de sol.**

mi amiga María

con rayas

F En **el bosque** tropical El Yunque, hay **árboles, plantas** y **flores** muy interesantes.

D La chica lleva una camisa **con rayas.** Es verano.

el bosque

la planta

la flor

EL YUNQUE

el árbol

EL TIEMPO

el sol

Temperaturas

9 de marzo

	ALTA	BAJA
San Juan	87°	73°
Minneapolis	30°	15°

Online Workbook
CLASSZONE.COM

Preguntas personales

1. Cuando va a llover, ¿llevas un paraguas?
2. En el lugar donde vives, ¿hace calor o hace frío en el invierno?
3. ¿Prefieres ropa de cuadros o ropa con rayas?
4. ¿Qué ropa llevas en el invierno?
5. ¿Qué hay en un bosque tropical?

En vivo

DIÁLOGO

¡Qué tiempo!

Diana   Roberto   Ignacio

ROPA
DE
INVIERNO

PARA ESCUCHAR • STRATEGY: LISTENING

Sort and categorize details Minneapolis and San Juan are a world apart, yet in at least one way they are similar. How? What does Roberto say? What differences are mentioned? Use a Venn diagram to sort these details.

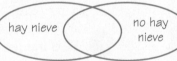

MINNEAPOLIS   SAN JUAN

hay nieve   no hay nieve

1 ▶ **Diana:** ¡Qué mona tu bufanda! Me gusta tu gorro. ¿Hace mucho frío en Minneapolis?

ROPA

5 ▶ **Diana:** ¡Ay! Pues, ya tienes ropa de verano.
Roberto: Claro que la tengo. ¡En Minneapolis no es invierno todo el año!

6 ▶ **Roberto:** ¡Qué día bonito! Hace muy buen tiempo. Tengo ganas de ir a El Yunque.
Diana: Perfecto, porque el proyecto de Ignacio para el concurso es sobre el bosque tropical. Y está preparando el proyecto este mes.

7 ▶ **Ignacio:** Sí, y necesito sacar fotos del bosque. Y las quiero sacar hoy mismo.
Roberto: Tengo suerte, ¿no lo creen?
Diana: Creo que tienes mucha suerte.
Ignacio: Tengo prisa. Es buena hora para sacar fotos porque hay sol.

2 ▶ Roberto: En el invierno, sí, ¡hace mucho frío! ¡Brrr! Tengo frío cuando pienso en los inviernos de Minneapolis.

3 ▶ Diana: ¿Nieva mucho?

Roberto: Bueno, en el invierno, nieva casi todas las semanas. Pero en verano, es como aquí. Hace mucho calor.

4 ▶ Ignacio: ¿Qué vas a hacer con toda esta ropa de invierno? Aquí nadie la necesita.

Roberto: Tienes razón. Voy a necesitar shorts, trajes de baño y gafas de sol.

8 ▶ Ignacio: ¡Qué bonito! Los árboles, las flores…

Roberto: Sí, muy bonita.

Ignacio: No es como Minneapolis, ¿verdad, Roberto?

Roberto: Tienes razón, Ignacio.

9 ▶ Ignacio: Mi proyecto va a estar bien chévere, ¿no creen?… ¿No creen?…

…Sí, Ignacio, creo que tu proyecto va a ser muy impresionante.

10 ▶ Ignacio: ¡Está lloviendo! ¡Y no tengo paraguas!

Roberto: Te estamos esperando, hombre.

En acción

VOCABULARIO Y GRAMÁTICA

ACTIVIDAD
1

¿Frío o calor?

Escuchar/Leer Based on the dialog, does each statement refer to Puerto Rico or to Minnesota? Some statements may refer to both places.

modelo

Es importante tener paraguas.

Puerto Rico y Minnesota

1. Los árboles y las flores son tan bonitos.
2. Tengo ganas de ir a El Yunque.
3. La gente no necesita ropa de invierno.
4. En el invierno, hace mucho frío.
5. Hay un bosque tropical.
6. Nieva mucho en el invierno.
7. En el verano, hace calor.
8. En el invierno, necesitas shorts, traje de baño y gafas de sol.

ACTIVIDAD 2

En el bosque tropical

Escuchar/Leer Based on the dialog, tell whether each statement is true or false. If the statement is true, say **cierto**. If it is false, say **falso.**

modelo

En El Yunque hay muchas plantas.
Cierto.

1. El proyecto de Ignacio para el concurso es sobre el béisbol.
2. Las plantas y flores son feas.
3. Ignacio quiere sacar fotos del bosque.
4. Los chicos tienen un paraguas.
5. Ignacio no tiene cámara.
6. En El Yunque siempre hace buen tiempo.

También se dice

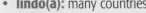

There are different ways to say _cute._

- **bonito(a):** Mexico and other countries
- **mono(a):** Puerto Rico, Spain
- **lindo(a):** many countries

¡Qué linda!

ACTIVIDAD 3

♻ ¿Qué hay en la mochila?

Hablar Work with a classmate. Take turns describing the contents of Willie's backpack.

modelo

Hay una gorra
anaranjada.

¿En qué estación?

Hablar/Leer Identify the season in which the following comments were probably made. Some items may have more than one right answer.

modelo

¡Vamos a la playa!

El verano.

1. Mira los árboles. ¡Qué colores tan bonitos!
2. Pero, ¿dónde está mi bronceador?
3. ¡Por fin no nieva!
4. ¿Quieres ir conmigo al lago a patinar sobre hielo?
5. ¡Ay, llueve otra vez! ¿Dónde está mi impermeable?
6. Vamos al río a nadar, ¿quieres?
7. Como no tengo clases, tengo mucho tiempo libre.

Vocabulario

Las estaciones

el verano

tomar el sol

el desierto

el bronceador

los shorts

el otoño

el viento

la montaña

el río

el invierno

el lago

cero grados

la primavera

la tormenta

el impermeable

¿Qué actividad te gusta hacer en cada estación?

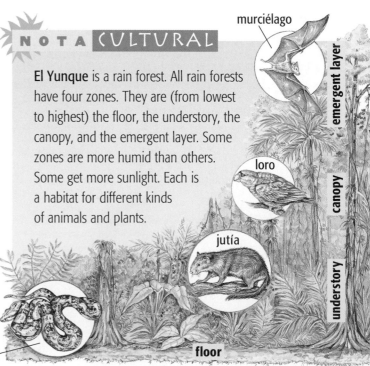

N O T A CULTURAL

El Yunque is a rain forest. All rain forests have four zones. They are (from lowest to highest) the floor, the understory, the canopy, and the emergent layer. Some zones are more humid than others. Some get more sunlight. Each is a habitat for different kinds of animals and plants.

murciélago

emergent layer

loro

canopy

jutía

understory

serpiente

floor

Un año de actividades

Hablar Work with a partner. Find out what activities your classmate and his/her friends and family like to do throughout the year. Choose from the following.

modelo

Estudiante A: *¿Qué hacen tus amigos en el invierno?*

Estudiante B: *Mis amigos juegan al baloncesto en el invierno.*

tú

tu amigo(a)

tus amigos(as)

tu hermano(a) menor

tu hermano(a) mayor

tú y tu familia

en la primavera

en el verano

en el otoño

en el invierno

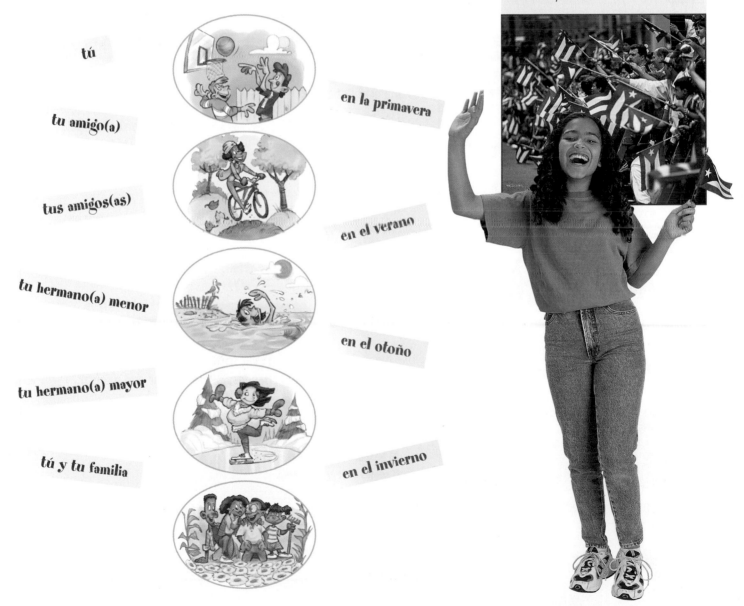

NOTA CULTURAL

The National Puerto Rican Day Parade on Fifth Avenue in New York City is the largest parade in the country. Millions of people watch it, and tens of thousands of people march in it every June.

¡Organízalos!

Escribir You are working in a store. Arrange the articles according to the season.

modelo

Las gorras van en la sección de verano.

LA PRIMAVERA   EL OTOÑO

EL VERANO   EL INVIERNO

 1.

 2.

 3.

 4.

 5.

 6.

 7.

 8.

 9.

GRAMÁTICA

Describing the Weather

To talk about weather, you will often use the verb **hacer**.

¿Qué tiempo hace?
What's it like out?

Hace...
It's...

(mucho) calor.	*(very) hot.*
(mucho) fresco.	*(very) cool.*
(mucho) frío.	*(very) cold.*
(mucho) sol.	*(very) sunny.*
(mucho) viento.	*(very) windy.*
(muy) buen tiempo.	*(very) nice outside.*
(muy) mal tiempo.	*(very) bad outside.*

Diana asks Roberto:

—¿**Hace mucho frío** en Minneapolis?
Is it very cold in Minneapolis?

Roberto replies:

—En el invierno, sí, ¡**hace mucho frío**!
*In the winter, yes, **it's very cold**!*

When you talk about wind or sun, you can also use **hay**.

Hay...
It's...

(mucho) sol.	*(very) sunny.*
(mucho) viento.	*(very) windy.*

Use the verbs **llover** and **nevar** to say it is raining or snowing. They are verbs with stem changes, just like **jugar** and **pensar.**

Llueve mucho en el bosque tropical.
*It **rains** a lot in the tropical rain forest.*

Nieva mucho en Minnesota.
*It **snows** a lot in Minnesota.*

To say that it's cloudy, use the expression **está nublado.**

No vamos a la playa porque **está nublado.**
*We're not going to the beach because **it's cloudy**.*

El tiempo

Escuchar Listen to the descriptions. What season is it in each case?

a. primavera
c. otoño
b. verano
d. invierno

♻ ¿Qué te gusta hacer?

Hablar Work with a partner. Take turns asking and answering questions about what you like to do in different kinds of weather. Use the pictures to respond logically.

modelo

hace frío

Estudiante A: ¿Qué te gusta hacer cuando **hace frío?**

Estudiante B: Me gusta patinar sobre hielo.

I. hay sol

2. hace calor

3. hace mal tiempo

4. nieva

Conexiones

Las ciencias In the middle of summer in Puerto Rico, it's possible to travel to South America to go skiing. Why? Countries south of the equator have seasons that are opposite of those north of the equator. In the months of June, July, and August, the sun shines directly on the northern hemisphere; during December, January, and February, the southern hemisphere gets the sun's direct rays.

PARA HACER:

Tell in which seasons and months you could do the following activities at Bariloche, the famous Argentine resort.

• nadar
• esquiar
• patinar sobre hielo
• jugar al hockey

ACTIVIDAD 9 **Gramática**

¿Qué tiempo hace?

Hablar/Escribir Use at least two weather expressions and say what season it is to describe each scene.

modelo

Hace frío. Hay sol. Es invierno.

I.

2.

3.

4.

5.

6.

■ **MÁS PRÁCTICA** *cuaderno* p. 77

■ **PARA HISPANOHABLANTES** *cuaderno* p. 75

Online Workbook
CLASSZONE.COM

ACTIVIDAD 10

♻ **¿Qué llevas?**

Hablar The clothing you wear usually depends on the weather. Work with another student to explain what you are going to wear in each case.

modelo

hace calor

Estudiante A: *Hace calor. ¿Qué vas a llevar hoy?*

Estudiante B: *Voy a llevar una camiseta y shorts. Llevo shorts mucho cuando hace calor.*

I. hace mucho frío

2. hace fresco

3. hace mucho calor

4. hay sol

5. llueve

6. hay viento

7. hay nieve

8. ¿?

El tiempo hoy

Hablar/Leer Work in a group of three. Take turns asking and answering questions about the weather in the cities that are listed on the newspaper page below. Use the following questions.

¿Qué tiempo hace en…?   ¿Hace buen/mal tiempo en…?

¿Cuál es la temperatura en…?   ¿Dónde hace/hay…?

EL TIEMPO
4 de enero

	Tiempo	Temperatura mínima	máxima
San Juan	☀	70°	82°
Buenos Aires	☀	75°	90°
Los Ángeles	☔	50°	64°
Madrid	☁	37°	46°
México	☁	48°	61°
Miami	☀	59°	70°
Nueva York	❄	28°	32°
Quito	☀	50°	59°
San Antonio	🌬	39°	51°

Clave: sol ☀   lluvia ☔   nieve ❄   nublado ☁   viento 🌬

Conexiones

La geografía Altitude (height above sea level) and latitude (distance from the equator) affect temperatures at all locations.

PARA HACER:
Locate the following cities on a map and learn about their climates. Describe how the altitude and latitude affect temperatures. Refer to the chart on the left. (For example: Quito está en el ecuador, pero está muy alto. No hace mucho calor.)

	Altitud	Latitud
Buenos Aires	0m	34°S
Madrid	655m	40°N
Ciudad de México	2239m	19°N
Quito	2850m	0°

También se dice

There are different ways to say the following:

sunglasses
- **gafas de sol:** Puerto Rico, Spain, Ecuador
- **lentes de sol:** many countries

T-shirt
- **camiseta:** Puerto Rico and many countries
- **playera:** Mexico
- **polera:** Chile
- **remera:** Argentina

shorts
- **shorts:** Puerto Rico
- **pantalones cortos:** many countries
- **pantalonetas:** Colombia, Ecuador

Special Expressions Using **tener**

♻ **¿RECUERDAS?** *p. 173* You learned to say that someone is hungry or thirsty using the verb **tener**. You also learned how to tell age using **tener**.

tener **hambre**
tener **sed**
tener… **años**

You can use the verb **tener** in many expressions.

tener… *to be…*

calor *hot*	
cuidado *careful*	
frío *cold*	
miedo *afraid*	
prisa *in a hurry*	
razón *right*	
sueño *sleepy*	
suerte *lucky*	

tener ganas de… + *infinitive* *to feel like…*

bailar *dancing*
cantar *singing*

Roberto says:
—**Tengo suerte.** *I'm lucky.*

Ignacio says:
—**Tengo prisa.** *I'm in a hurry.*

 ACTIVIDAD 12 **Gramática**

♻ **Tiene ganas de…**

Hablar/Escribir What do these people feel like doing?

modelo

Diana: ir a la playa

Diana tiene ganas de **ir a la playa.**

1. nosotras: caminar
2. usted: ver la televisión
3. ellos: practicar deportes
4. él: patinar
5. tú: ¿?
6. yo: ¿?

■ **MÁS PRÁCTICA**
cuaderno p. 78

■ **PARA HISPANOHABLANTES**
cuaderno p. 76

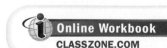
Online Workbook
CLASSZONE.COM

ACTIVIDAD **13**

¿Qué pasa aquí?

Hablar How do these people feel? Describe each picture with an expression using **tener**.

1. la prima de Roberto

2. su vecino

3. su amiga

4. su amigo

5. su hermana

ACTIVIDAD 14

¿Cómo estás?

Hablar Work with a partner. Take turns asking how you feel in each situation. Use the following words.

modelo

No comes por muchas horas.

Estudiante A: *¿Cómo estás cuando no comes por muchas horas?*

Estudiante B: *¡Tengo hambre!*

calor
suerte
razón
prisa
frío
miedo

1. Hace mucho sol.
2. Saben que el examen va a ser muy, muy difícil.
3. Contestas bien una pregunta.
4. Ustedes van a llegar tarde a clase.
5. Hace mucho frío y no tienes bufanda.
6. ¡Ganas la lotería!

MÁS COMUNICACIÓN p. R9

GRAMÁTICA ◆ Direct Object Pronouns

The **direct object** in a sentence receives the action of the verb. Direct objects answer the question *whom?* or *what?* about the verb. Nouns used as **direct objects** can be replaced by **pronouns**.

Singular		Plural	
me		**nos**	
me		us	
te		**os**	
you (familiar)		you (familiar)	
lo	masculine	**los**	masculine
you (formal), him, it		you, them	
la	feminine	**las**	feminine
you (formal), her, it		you, them	

The **direct object** noun is placed after the **conjugated verb**.

Diana says: Roberto answers:

replaced by

—Pues, ya **tienes ropa de verano.**
*You already have **summer clothing**.*

—Claro que **la tengo**.
*Of course I have **it**.*

The direct object **pronoun** is placed directly **before** the **conjugated verb**.

When an infinitive follows the conjugated verb, the direct object **pronoun** can be placed:

before the **conjugated verb** or **attached** to the **infinitive**

Ignacio says: *replaced by*

—Necesito sacar **fotos** del bosque. Y **las quiero sacar** hoy mismo.
*I need to take pictures of the rain forest. I want to take **them** today.*

He could also have said: *replaced by*

—Necesito sacar **fotos** del bosque. Y **quiero sacar**las hoy mismo.

ACTIVIDAD 15 Gramática

La fiesta

Leer/Escribir Diana and Sara are writing to each other on the Internet. Complete their conversation about their friend Juan's upcoming party. Use the appropriate pronouns.

Diana: Sara, ¿Juan ___1___ invita a ti a su fiesta?

Sara: Sí, ___2___ invita. ¿A ustedes ___3___ invita?

Diana: Sí, ___4___ invita.

Sara: ¿Invita a Tina y a Graciela?

Diana: No, no ___5___ conoce.

Sara: ¿Y a Roberto?

Diana: Sí, ___6___ invita.

Sara: ¿Invita a Julio y a Fernando?

Diana: Sí, ___7___ invita. Son sus mejores amigos.

Sara: ¿Y a Mónica?

Diana: No, no ___8___ invita. Ella es su hermana.

■ **MÁS PRÁCTICA** *cuaderno* p. 79

■ **PARA HISPANOHABLANTES** *cuaderno* p. 77

Online Workbook
CLASSZONE.COM

Juego

¿Qué describe la oración?

Hace buen tiempo.

a.

b.

ACTIVIDAD 16

♻ ¿Qué compran?

Hablar Work with a partner. Take turns asking what the following people are buying.

modelo

Roberto

Estudiante A: *¿Roberto compra el guante de béisbol?*

Estudiante B: *Sí, lo compra.*

1. Diana

2. Ignacio

3. Roberto

4. Ignacio

5. Diana

6. Diana

¿Qué pasa?

Escuchar Listen to the conversation, and then decide if the sentences are true or false.

1. Cuando llueve, Raúl ve la televisión.
2. Raúl lee revistas. Las lee cuando llueve.
3. María lleva paraguas. Lo lleva cuando llueve.
4. Raúl necesita gafas de sol para ir a la playa.
5. María tiene bronceador. Va a llevarlo a la playa.

¿Cuándo necesitamos...?

Hablar Work with a partner. Take turns asking and answering questions about when things are needed.

modelo

un bate

Estudiante A: *¿Cuándo necesitamos **un bate**?*

Estudiante B: *Lo necesitamos cuando jugamos al béisbol.*

1. un abrigo	6. los shorts
2. un paraguas	7. una bufanda
3. los trajes de baño	8. el bronceador
4. las gafas de sol	9. un impermeable
5. una pelota	10. un gorro

Una visita

Hablar Work with a partner. You are going to visit a friend in San Juan. Your partner wants to know what you are going to take with you. Be sure to ask about at least six items. Switch roles.

modelo

Estudiante A: *¿Vas a llevar tu traje de baño?*

Estudiante B: *Sí, voy a llevarlo. (No, no voy a llevarlo.) **o:** Sí, lo voy a llevar. (No, no lo voy a llevar.)*

Nota

You learned that **llevar** means *to wear.* In this example, **llevar** means *to take along.*

1.
2.
3.
4.
5.
6.
7.
8.

GRAMÁTICA — Present Progressive

When you want to say that an action is happening now, use the **present progressive**.

estoy **esperando**	estamos **esperando**
estás **esperando**	estáis **esperando**
está **esperando**	están **esperando**

Ignacio says:

—¡**Está lloviendo**!
It's raining!

Roberto replies:

—Te **estamos esperando**…
We're waiting for you…

▶ To form this tense, use:

the present tense of **estar** + *present participle*

▶ To form the present participle of a verb, drop the **ending** of the infinitive and add **-ando** or **-iendo**.

-ar verbs	esper**ar** ←	**ando**	esper**ando**
-er verbs	com**er** ←	**iendo**	com**iendo**
-ir verbs	escrib**ir** ←	**iendo**	escrib**iendo**

....

▶ When the **stem** of an **-er** or **-ir** verb ends in a vowel, change the **-iendo** to **-yendo**.

le**er**	→	le**yendo**
o**ír**	→	o**yendo**
cre**er**	→	cre**yendo**

Están haciendo...

Hablar Choose the most logical option to tell what the people below are doing, given the various situations.

modelo

Hace frío.
Pablo: ¿nadando / esquiando?
Creo que **Pablo** *está* **esquiando**.

Nota

Creer (*to think, to believe*) can be used to state an opinion.

Creo que sí. **Creo que no.**

1. Hace mucho calor. Elena: ¿descansando en casa / patinando sobre hielo?

2. Nieva. Yo: ¿haciendo ejercicio en el parque / esquiando?

3. Llueve. Tú: ¿leyendo en casa / corriendo por la playa?

4. Estás en Puerto Rico. ¿visitando El Yunque / aprendiendo francés?

5. Ustedes están tranquilos. ¿descansando / escribiendo una composición larga?

■ **MÁS PRÁCTICA** *cuaderno* p. 80

■ **PARA HISPANOHABLANTES** *cuaderno* p. 78

ACTIVIDAD 21

♻ ¡Están ocupados!

Hablar Everyone is doing his or her favorite activity. What is each person doing?

modelo

Diana

Diana está comprando libros.

bailar

comer fruta

escribir la tarea

leer cuentos   ¿?

jugar al béisbol

1. Pablo y Marta
2. la familia
3. yo
4. nosotros
5. tus padres
6. tú

ACTIVIDAD 22

¡Qué buenas vacaciones!

Escribir Elena and her family are on vacation at the beach. Describe what is happening. Use the questions as a guide.

la señora Álvarez

el señor Álvarez

Pablo   Ana   Marta

Elena

- ¿Qué tiempo hace?
- ¿Qué están haciendo las personas?
- ¿Cómo están? ¿Tienen frío? ¿Tienen hambre?

MÁS COMUNICACIÓN p. R9

Online Workbook
CLASSZONE.COM

Pronunciación 🎧

Trabalenguas

Pronunciación de la _j_ y la _g_ The letter **j** is pronounced somewhat like the _h_ in the English word _hope_, but a bit stronger. Before the letters **e** and **i**, the Spanish **g** is pronounced just like the **j**. Listen to this tongue twister, then try it yourself to practice.

«Ji, ji, ji» ríen Javier y Jorge cuando miran a Jazmín la jirafa ingerir jarabe.

PARA LEER
STRATEGY: READING

Skim Skimming a reading before you begin can give you valuable information about what you are going to read. Skim this selection and write down what you learn by looking at these things.

Look at	Learn
title	
pictures	
text	

Una leyenda taína

En las islas del Caribe los bohiques cuentan[1] una leyenda de la creación del mundo. Dicen[2] que de las primeras personas, los taínos, el sol crea todo el mundo.

Los taínos viven en cuevas[3] en las montañas. En una de las cuevas vive un hombre que se llama Marocael. Marocael cuida la cueva de su gente.

Un día el sol le habla a Marocael: —Marocael, Marocael, ¡te invito a mi casa!

Marocael está aterrorizado y contesta: —Muchas gracias, pero tengo que cuidar la cueva de mi gente.

El sol habla otra vez y dice: —Por favor, vamos a pasar buen rato.

—No, muchas gracias —contesta Marocael. —Estoy muy contento en mi cueva.

---

[1] tell   [2] they say   [3] caves

Y Marocael empieza a regresar a su cueva cuando
el sol, furioso, habla fuerte y dice: —¡Ahora vienes
conmigo, Marocael!— Y el sol lleva a Marocael de la
cueva a su casa.

Cuando la gente de la cueva se despierta[4], busca a
Marocael pero no lo encuentra[5]. El sol convierte a
Marocael en una de las primeras piedras[6] de la tierra.
Y cuando la gente sale[7] de la cueva, el sol convierte a
cada uno de ellos en algo diferente. Así de la primera
gente, el sol crea no sólo las piedras pero también las
plantas, los pájaros, los peces y los árboles.

---

[4] wake up   [6] stones
[5] find   [7] go out

¿Comprendiste?

1. ¿Dónde tiene lugar (*take place*)
   la leyenda?
2. Según la leyenda, ¿dónde viven
   los taínos?
3. ¿Quién cuida la cueva?
4. ¿Qué le dice el sol al señor?
5. ¿Qué hace el sol con el señor?

¿Qué piensas?

1. What is the main idea of the story?
2. Why do you think the first people
   lived in caves?
3. Can you compare this story with
   others that you know?

En colores

VIDEO DVD

CULTURA Y COMPARACIONES

PARA CONOCERNOS
STRATEGY: CONNECTING CULTURES

Define travel and tourism Look at a travel brochure. (Get one from a travel agency or hotel.) What does it contain? What does it *not* contain? Do you think there is a difference between being a *traveler* and being a *tourist*? List the interests of each. Explain your ideas.

Viajero	Turista

Una excursión por la isla

Roberto tiene ganas de pasear por Puerto Rico otra vez. Diana e Ignacio lo llevan de excursión por la isla. En la Oficina de Turismo ven este folleto[1].

---
[1] brochure

Descubra la isla de Puerto Rico
¡La hija del mar y del sol!

El mar y Puerto Rico tienen una unión fuerte. Las primeras personas de la isla, los taínos, llegan en canoas. Cristóbal Colón también llega a la isla por el mar. Y por el mar Puerto Rico sufre[2] ataques por muchos años. Los españoles construyen[3] El Morro en el siglo XVI[4] como protección contra los ingleses, los holandeses y los piratas. Hoy una excursión por San Juan siempre incluye[5] una visita a esta gran fortaleza.

---
[2] suffers
[3] build
[4] 16th century
[5] includes
[6] waves
[7] national anthem
[8] indigenous, native
[9] land

Puerto Rico: Diversión para todos

El himno nacional[7] de Puerto Rico, «La Borinqueña», habla de Borinquen, una palabra que viene del nombre indígena[8] de la isla. Sus palabras explican la relación entre la tierra[9], el mar y el sol.

«**Ésta es la linda tierra,
que busco yo.
Es Borinquen la hija,
la hija del mar y del sol.**»

Tanto para el turista como para el puertorriqueño, el mar ofrece muchas actividades. En las playas es posible practicar muchos deportes: nadar, practicar el surfing o esquiar. El surfing es muy popular. En Puerto Rico hay playas que tienen olas[6] grandes, donde hay competiciones internacionales.

More About Puerto Rico
CLASSZONE.COM

¿Comprendiste?

1. ¿Cuál es el grupo que llega primero a Puerto Rico?
2. ¿De quiénes vienen los ataques contra los españoles de Puerto Rico?
3. ¿Cuáles son unos deportes populares en las playas de Puerto Rico?
4. ¿De qué deporte hacen competiciones internacionales?
5. En el himno nacional de Puerto Rico, ¿qué es Borinquen?

¿Qué piensas?

1. Si algún día vas a Puerto Rico, ¿qué vas a hacer? ¿Te gustaría visitar lugares históricos o pasar toda tu visita en la playa? ¿Por qué?
2. ¿Cómo imaginas tu vacación perfecta? ¿Adónde vas? ¿Qué tiempo hace?

Hazlo tú

¿Cuáles son los deportes más populares en tu comunidad? Trabaja con otro(a) estudiante para preparar un folleto sobre las atracciones de tu estado.

3

En uso

REPASO Y MÁS COMUNICACIÓN

OBJECTIVES

- Describe the weather
- Discuss clothing and accessories
- State an opinion
- Describe how you feel
- Say what is happening

ACTIVIDAD 1 ¿Qué tiempo hace?

Explain what the weather is like.

1. Miami 92°
2. Boston 31°
3. Portland 34°
4. San Juan 85°
5. Washington 67°
6. Los Ángeles 75°

ACTIVIDAD 2 ¿Cuándo lo usas?

Tell when and why you use the following.

modelo

¿el traje de baño?: verano

Estudiante A: *¿Cuándo usas **el traje de baño**?*

Estudiante B: *Lo uso en el **verano** porque hace calor.*

1. ¿los shorts?: verano
2. ¿el gorro?: invierno
3. ¿los suéteres?: otoño
4. ¿la bufanda?: invierno
5. ¿el paraguas?: primavera
6. ¿las gafas de sol?: verano

ACTIVIDAD 3 Opiniones

How much do you know about Puerto Rico? Respond to the following statements.

modelo

Hace mal tiempo todo el año.   *Hay playas bonitas.*

Creo que no.   *Creo que sí.*

1. En el invierno hay mucha nieve.
2. En El Yunque hay plantas y animales muy interesantes.
3. Cuando está nublado, los puertorriqueños toman el sol.
4. El surfing es popular en Puerto Rico.

Now you can...

- describe the weather.

To review

- weather expressions, see p. 260.

Now you can...

- describe the weather.
- discuss clothing and accessories.

To review

- direct object pronouns, see p. 265.

Now you can...

- state an opinion.

To review

- weather expressions, see p. 260.

doscientos setenta y cuatro
Unidad 3

ACTIVIDAD 4 Los problemas de Roberto

Describe Roberto's problems.

calor   frío   ganas   prisa   sed

hambre   miedo   sueño   razón   suerte

1. Cuando Roberto tiene _____, nunca hay comida.
2. Roberto siempre tiene _____, pero siempre llega tarde.
3. Cuando hay una tormenta, Roberto tiene mucho _____.
4. En el invierno en Minnesota, Roberto no lleva un abrigo y siempre tiene _____.
5. Cuando Roberto tiene _____ de nadar, siempre llueve.
6. Roberto tiene mucha _____, pero no hay agua.
7. Cuando camina en el desierto, Roberto tiene mucho _____.
8. Cuando Roberto participa en un concurso, nunca tiene _____.
9. Roberto piensa que 2 + 2 = 5. No tiene _____.
10. A las once de la noche Roberto siempre tiene _____.

ACTIVIDAD 5 ¡Está lloviendo!

Describe what these people are doing, according to Josefina.

1. Emilio y yo
2. Dani y Pati
3. mi padre
4. yo
5. mi madre
6. Emilio

Now you can...
• describe how you feel.

To review
• **tener** expressions, see p. 264.

Now you can...
• say what is happening.

To review
• the present progressive, see p. 270.

ACTIVIDAD 6 ¿Adónde voy?

PARA CONVERSAR

STRATEGY: SPEAKING

Get specific information To find out someone's vacation plans, ask questions about all the specifics. Ask about weather (**el tiempo**), clothing (**la ropa**), or activities (**actividades y deportes**) at their destination. The model shows you how.

Imagine that you are going to one of the places listed below on the left. Your classmates will ask you questions to guess where you are going.

el desierto

el bosque tropical

la playa en verano

las montañas en invierno

el lago en otoño

modelo

Otro(a): *¿Va a nevar?*

Tú: *No, no va a nevar.*

Otro(a): *¿Vas a llevar el traje de baño?*

Tú: *Sí, voy a llevarlo.*

Otro(a): *¿Vas a practicar el surfing?*

Tú: *Sí, voy a practicarlo.*

Otro(a): *¿Vas a la playa?*

Tú: *Sí, voy a la playa.*

ACTIVIDAD 7 Por teléfono

You are on vacation. You are talking with a friend on the phone. Describe the weather, how you feel, and what your family is doing on your vacation.

ACTIVIDAD 8 En tu propia voz

Escritura Your Puerto Rican friend is coming to live with your family for a year. Write a letter describing the weather during each season of the year, the clothes he or she will need to bring, and the things you can do in each season.

En la primavera hace...

Para el frío, necesitas llevar...

En el verano hace...

Llueve mucho en...

Conexiones

Las ciencias The Fahrenheit temperature scale is used in Puerto Rico. However, most Spanish-speaking countries use the Celsius scale. On this scale, water freezes at 0° and boils at 100°. To convert, use these formulas.

$100°C \times 9/5 + 32 = 212°F$ $212°F - 32 \times 5/9 = 100°C$

Convert the temperatures in the chart and write what seasons they might represent. Explain the other weather conditions. Choose a location in the Spanish-speaking world. Find out its average temperature and weather conditions in each season.

C	F	Estación	Tiempo
0°			
10°			
	68°		
25°			
30°			
	95°		

En resumen

REPASO DE VOCABULARIO

DESCRIBING THE WEATHER

¿Qué tiempo hace?	What is the weather like?
Está nublado.	It is cloudy.
Hace…	It is…
buen tiempo	nice outside
calor	hot
fresco	cool
frío	cold
mal tiempo	bad outside
sol	sunny
viento	windy
Hay…	It's…
sol	sunny
viento	windy
el grado	degree
llover (ue)	to rain
la lluvia	rain
nevar (ie)	to snow
la nieve	snow
el sol	sun
la temperatura	temperature
el tiempo	weather
la tormenta	storm
el viento	wind

Seasons

las estaciones	seasons
el invierno	winter
el otoño	fall
la primavera	spring
el verano	summer

DESCRIBING HOW YOU FEEL

tener…	to be…
calor	hot
cuidado	careful
frío	cold
miedo	afraid
prisa	in a hurry
razón	right
sueño	sleepy
suerte	lucky
tener ganas de…	to feel like…

STATING AN OPINION

creer	to think, to believe
Creo que sí/no.	I think so. / I don't think so.

CLOTHING AND ACCESSORIES

Clothing

el abrigo	coat
la bufanda	scarf
el gorro	cap
el impermeable	raincoat
los shorts	shorts
el traje de baño	bathing suit

Styles

con rayas	striped
de cuadros	plaid, checked

Accessories

el bronceador	suntan lotion
las gafas de sol	sunglasses
el paraguas	umbrella

OTHER WORDS AND PHRASES

sacar fotos	to take pictures
tomar el sol	to sunbathe

Places

el bosque	forest
el desierto	desert
el lago	lake
el mar	sea
la montaña	mountain
la playa	beach
el río	river

Vegetation

el árbol	tree
la flor	flower
la planta	plant

Juego

Es julio. Hace frío y nieva mucho. Mucha gente esquía en las montañas. ¿En qué país están?

a. **México**

b. **Estados Unidos**

c. **Chile**

Conexiones

OTRAS DISCIPLINAS Y PROYECTOS

La historia

Taíno chiefs lived in round conically roofed dwellings called **caney**.

Did you know that the Taino and Arawak peoples lived in the Caribbean before the Spaniards arrived in the fifteenth century? Along with the Caribi people from the Orinoco River region of Venezuela, they were all called **caribi** by the Spaniards. Thus we have the name for the entire region: the Caribbean (**el Caribe**, in Spanish).

El Caribe

EE.UU.
ISLAS BAHAMAS
REPÚBLICA DOMINICANA
CUBA
HAITÍ
PUERTO RICO
MÉXICO
ANTILLAS MAYORES
JAMAICA
MAR CARIBE
ANTILLAS MENORES
CENTROAMÉRICA
SUDAMÉRICA   RÍO ORINOCO

What do you know about the civilizations that lived in your area before Europeans arrived? Look at a map. Can you find any place names that derive from Native American languages? Make a list.

Las ciencias

As you have seen in this unit, **El Yunque** is a rich and beautiful rain forest. The plants and trees in rain forests convert carbon dioxide into oxygen, which all animals need in order to breathe. Rain forests provide a large amount of the world's oxygen, which is one reason why they are so important.

Rain forests also provide homes for many unique varieties of birds, insects, lizards, toads, frogs, and snakes. When large portions of rain forests are destroyed, plants, animals, and the Earth's atmosphere are all endangered.

*There are 16 species of tree frogs in Puerto Rico. Read about **los coquíes** in an encyclopedia or on the Internet. Find out and list in Spanish what colors they are. Also find out why they have the name they do.*

El coquí, the tree frog, is the most recognized animal in Puerto Rico.

Proyecto cultural

It's the World Cup finals, and it'll be 4 more years until the next final is played. Soccer fans all over the Spanish-speaking world are anticipating the game with great excitement! Work with a classmate to plan a party to watch the final soccer match of the **Copa Mundial.**

1. Discuss what music and what foods you would like to have at your party. Make a list of your favorites, beginning with **Me gusta escuchar (comer)...**

2. Then make a colorful invitation to the party in Spanish. Tell when, where, and at what time the party will take place. Draw or find pictures related to soccer to use on the invitation. Share the invitation with the class by putting it on the bulletin board.

3. Finally, work together to write a phone dialog between you and a guest who is responding to the invitation. Explain what guests should wear to the party. Ask the guest how she or he feels about being invited. If the guest cannot come, be sure she or he says why not (for example: **Tengo que hacer la tarea...**).

Arístides Rojas (**Paraguay**) jumps for the ball during the **España** vs. **Paraguay** game in the **Copa Mundial.**

RECURSOS

1 Unidad 1 Etapa 1 p. 40 — ¿Quién es?

(Estudiante A — texto invertido)

Estudiante A The people in the neighborhood are being introduced at a town meeting, but it is hard to hear. Find out from your partner who they are.

modelo

Estudiante A: *¿Quién es el policía?*

Estudiante B: *Es…*

1. el policía…
2. el maestro… Hernán Campos
3. las estudiantes…
4. el doctor… Raúl Guzmán
5. las maestras… Beatriz Simón y Laura Valdez
6. el estudiante…
7. la doctora…
8. los maestros… Patricio Díaz y Esteban Castillo

Estudiante B The people in the neighborhood are being introduced at a town meeting, but it is hard to hear. Find out from your partner who they are.

modelo

Estudiante A: *¿Quién es el policía?*

Estudiante B: *Es el señor Ruiz.*

1. el policía… el señor Ruiz
2. el maestro…
3. las estudiantes… Carolina y Olivia
4. el doctor…
5. las maestras…
6. el estudiante… Felipe
7. la doctora… Ana Colón
8. los maestros…

2 Unidad 1 Etapa 1 p. 45 — ¿Le gusta…?

(Estudiante A — texto invertido)

Estudiante A Daniela only likes to do the activities pictured. Find out from your partner if Gustavo likes to do the same.

modelo

Estudiante A: *¿le gusta nadar?*

Estudiante B: *…*

Estudiante B Gustavo only likes to do the activities pictured. Find out from your partner if Daniela likes to do the same.

modelo

Estudiante B: *¿Le gusta correr?*

Estudiante A: *…*

3 Unidad 1 Etapa 2 p. 67
¿Cómo es?

Estudiante A Describe the person to your partner. Include what you think his personality might be like. Then draw the person your partner describes to you.

Estudiante B Draw the person your partner describes to you. Then describe your picture to your partner. Include what you think her personality might be like.

4 Unidad 1 Etapa 2 p. 71
¿De qué color son?

Estudiante B: *Lleva zapatos…*

Estudiante A: *¿De qué color son los zapatos?*

modelo

Estudiante A Ask about the colors of Esteban's clothes. Then describe the colors of Chela's clothing for your partner. Are they wearing anything the same color?

Estudiante B Describe the colors of Esteban's clothing for your partner. Then ask about the colors of Chela's clothes. Are they wearing anything the same color?

modelo

Estudiante A: *¿De qué color son los zapatos?*

Estudiante B: *Lleva zapatos negros.*

5 — Unidad 1, Etapa 3 p. 91
¿Cuántos años tiene?

Estudiante A Complete the chart with the ages of members of the Zavala family.

modelo

Estudiante A: ¿Cuántos años tiene Josefa?
Estudiante B: *Tiene...*

Nombre	Edad
1. Josefa	
2. Víctor	65
3. Victoria	38
4. José	
5. Lupita	
6. Eva	4

Estudiante B Complete the chart with the ages of members of the Zavala family.

modelo

Estudiante A: ¿Cuántos años tiene Josefa?
Estudiante B: Tiene cincuenta y nueve años.

Nombre	Edad
1. Josefa	59
2. Víctor	
3. Victoria	
4. José	33
5. Lupita	15
6. Eva	

6 — Unidad 1, Etapa 3 p. 97
La familia Zavala

Estudiante A Your partner is looking at the Zavala family tree. Find out the names of various family members.

modelo

Estudiante A: ¿Quién es la hermana de José?
Estudiante B: ...

1. hermana / José
2. tío / Eva
3. abuelo / Pepe
4. hermano / Lupita
5. madre / Victoria
6. hijo / Víctor
7. prima / Eva
8. padre / Lupita
9. tía / Pepe
10. hija / Paquita

Estudiante B Your partner wants to know the names of members of the Zavala family. Answer his or her questions according to the family tree.

modelo

Estudiante A: ¿Quién es la hermana de José?
Estudiante B: Victoria es la hermana de José.

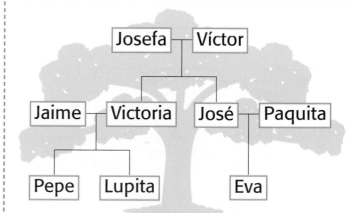

7 · Unidad 2 Etapa 1 p. 125 — ¿Qué clase tiene?

Estudiante A Find out about the following students' classes by completing the chart with your partner.

modelo

Estudiante A: ¿Qué clase tiene Rosa?

Estudiante B: Tiene...

Estudiante A: ¿Qué usa en la clase de...?

Estudiante B: Usa...

Nombre	Clase	Usa...
Rosa		
César	inglés	pluma
Jesús		
Gilberto	matemáticas	calculadora
yo	¿?	¿?
Estudiante B	¿?	¿?

Estudiante B Find out about the following students' classes by completing the chart with your partner.

modelo

Estudiante A: ¿Qué clase tiene Rosa?

Estudiante B: Tiene historia.

Estudiante A: ¿Qué usa en la clase de historia?

Estudiante B: Usa un cuaderno.

Nombre	Clase	Usa...
Rosa	historia	cuaderno
César		
Jesús	computación	ratón
Gilberto		
Estudiante A	¿?	¿?
yo	¿?	¿?

8 · Unidad 2 Etapa 1 p. 131 — ¿Siempre o nunca?

Estudiante A Ask your partner if Gabriela has to do the following activities in her class. Can you guess what class it is?

modelo

Estudiante A: ¿Gabriela tiene que estudiar?

Estudiante B: Gabriela tiene que estudiar...

1. ¿Gabriela tiene que estudiar?
2. ¿leer?
3. ¿llevar uniforme?
4. ¿cantar?
5. ¿correr?
6. ¿mirar videos?
7. ¿escuchar al profesor?

Estudiante B Answer your partner's questions about Gabriela's class.

modelo

Estudiante A: ¿Gabriela tiene que estudiar?

Estudiante B: Gabriela tiene que estudiar de vez en cuando.

Gabriela: la clase de educación física	
siempre	llevar uniforme
todos los días	correr
mucho	escuchar al profesor
a veces	mirar videos
de vez en cuando	estudiar
rara vez	leer
nunca	cantar

MÁS COMUNICACIÓN

9 Unidad 2 Etapa 2 p. 152
¿A qué hora?

Estudiante A Ask what time your partner will do the following activities. Draw clocks to indicate the times. Then tell your partner what time you will do them.

modelo

Estudiante A: ¿A qué hora vas al doctor?

Estudiante B: Voy al doctor a las… ¿Y tú?

Estudiante A: Voy al doctor a las nueve y cuarto de la mañana.

Por la mañana
1. 9:15 - ir al doctor
2. 10:50 - tomar una prueba
3. 12:00 - comprar papel

Por la tarde
4. 1:20 - tomar almuerzo
5. 2:45 - ir a casa
6. 4:30 - visitar a amigos
7. 5:10 - terminar la tarea
8. 7:45 - descansar

Estudiante B Tell your partner what time you will do the following activities. Then draw clocks to indicate what time your partner will do them.

modelo

Estudiante A: ¿A qué hora vas al doctor?

Estudiante B: Voy al doctor a las nueve menos cuarto de la mañana. ¿Y tú?

Estudiante A: Voy al doctor a las…

Por la mañana
8:45 - ir al doctor
12:00 - tomar almuerzo

Por la tarde
1:05 - tomar una prueba
2:15 - comprar papel
3:50 - ir a casa
4:20 - terminar la tarea
6:30 - visitar a amigos
9:00 - descansar

10 Unidad 2 Etapa 2 p. 157
¿Doble visión?

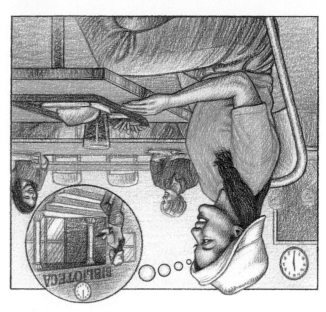

Estudiante A You and your partner have similar drawings. Ask each other questions to find at least five differences between the two drawings.

Estudiante B You and your partner have similar drawings. Ask each other questions to find at least five differences between the two drawings.

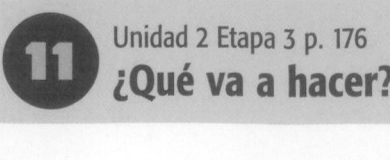

11 Unidad 2 Etapa 3 p. 176
¿Qué va a hacer?

12 Unidad 2 Etapa 3 p. 183
¿En qué orden?

Left column (Activity 11)

(upside-down portion)

6. cuidar el pájaro
5. ver la televisión
4. pintar
3. ir al supermercado
2. leer una novela
1. pasear

Estudiante B: …

Estudiante A: ¿Marcos va a pasear?

modelo

Estudiante A Find out about Marcos. Ask if he is going to do the following activities.

Estudiante B Answer your partner's questions about Marcos according to your drawing.

modelo

Estudiante A: ¿Marcos va a pasear?

Estudiante B: Sí, Marcos va a pasear.

Right column (Activity 12)

(upside-down portion)

9:00	
8:30	escribir un poema
8:00	
7:30	ir a la biblioteca
7:00	
6:30	hacer ejercicio
6:00	

Estudiante A: Entonces, ella hace ejercicio.
Estudiante B: Primero, ella… ¿Qué hace después de…?
Estudiante A: ¿Qué hace primero?

modelo

the order of her evening activities.
school. Work with your partner to determine
activities, but she left her other calendar at
Estudiante A Susana likes to organize her

Estudiante B Susana likes to organize her activities, but she left her other calendar at home. Work with your partner to determine the order of her evening activities.

modelo

Estudiante A: ¿Qué hace primero?

Estudiante B: Primero, ella lee el periódico. ¿Qué hace después de leer el periódico?

Estudiante A: Entonces, ella…

6:00	leer el periódico
6:30	
7:00	escuchar música
7:30	
8:00	comer una merienda
8:30	
9:00	ver la televisión

13 Unidad 3 Etapa 1 p. 212
Muchas emociones

14 Unidad 3 Etapa 1 p. 217
Por teléfono

Estudiante A You and your partner are talking about friends. You know what each person has done and your partner knows how each is feeling. Exchange information.

modelo

Josefina: ayudar a su padre

Estudiante A: *¿Cómo está Josefina?*
Estudiante B: *Está... ¿Qué acaba de hacer?*
Estudiante A: *Acaba de ayudar a su padre.*

1. Milagros: sacar una mala nota
2. Carlos: visitar a su abuelo enfermo
3. Ricardo: tomar un examen
4. Martina: mirar un video

Estudiante A Practice making phone calls. Begin a conversation and then choose logical responses from the list. Your partner will begin the second conversation.

Conversación 1

Soy... ¿Cómo estás?
¿Te gustaría ir al cine por la noche?
Está bien. Hasta luego.
¡Qué lástima!
Buenos días. ¿Puedo hablar con...?

Conversación 2

Muy bien. Adiós.
¿Cuál es tu teléfono?
No está aquí. Regresa más tarde.
¡Claro que sí!

Estudiante B You and your partner are talking about friends. You know how each person is feeling and your partner knows what each has just done. Exchange information.

modelo

Josefina

Estudiante A: *¿Cómo está Josefina?*
Estudiante B: *Está tranquila. ¿Qué acaba de hacer?*
Estudiante A: *Acaba de...*

2. Carlos
4. Martina
1. Milagros
3. Ricardo

Estudiante B Your partner has just called you on the phone. Choose from the responses to carry on a logical conversation. Then begin a second conversation.

Conversación 1

Gracias, pero no puedo.

¡Muy bien! Voy a patinar por la tarde.

Nos vemos.

Tal vez otro día.

Soy... ¿Quién habla?

Conversación 2

Quiero dejar un mensaje para ella.

253-5652

Buenas tardes. ¿Puedo hablar con Carolina?

Dile que me llame, por favor.

Gracias. Adiós.

15 — Unidad 3 Etapa 2 p. 240 — Los deportes

Óscar

modelo

Estudiante A: *Óscar juega al baloncesto. ¿Y Aída?*

Estudiante B: …

Estudiante A By looking at Óscar's equipment, you can see which sports he plays. With your partner, determine how many sports he and Aída have in common.

Estudiante B By looking at Aída's equipment, you can see which sports she plays. With your partner, determine how many sports she and Óscar have in common.

modelo

Estudiante A: *Óscar juega al baloncesto. ¿Y Aída?*

Estudiante B: *No, no juega al baloncesto, pero patina.*

Aída

---

16 — Unidad 3 Etapa 2 p. 243 — En la escuela

6. la clase de historia / la clase de arte
5. la cafetería / el gimnasio
4. la oficina / la biblioteca
3. las tareas / las pruebas
2. tu maestro(a) de educación física / tu maestro(a) de matemáticas
1. la clase de español / la clase de inglés

modelo

el (la) maestro(a) de historia / el (la) maestro(a) de español

Estudiante A: *¿Cómo son la maestra de historia y el maestro de español?*

Estudiante B: *La maestra de historia es más simpática que el maestro de español.*

o: *El maestro de español es más simpático que la maestra de historia.*

Estudiante A Ask your partner to compare school experiences.

Estudiante B Answer your partner's questions about school, using the following expressions.

modelo

más simpático(a)

Estudiante A: *¿Cómo son la maestra de historia y el maestro de español?*

Estudiante B: *La maestra de historia es más simpática que el maestro de español.*

o: *El maestro de español es más simpático que la maestra de historia.*

1. tan fácil como
2. mayor
3. peor
4. menos interesante
5. menos grande
6. más divertida

17 Unidad 3 Etapa 3 p. 265
Los dibujos

Estudiante A Fernando feels differently at 7:30, 1:00, 6:00, and 9:00. Ask about Fernando.

modelo

Estudiante A: ¿Cómo está Fernando a las siete y media?

Estudiante B: …

1. 7:30
2. 9:00
3. 6:00
4. 1:00

Estudiante B Fernando feels differently at 7:30, 1:00, 6:00, and 9:00. Answer your partner's questions about Fernando, using **tener** expressions.

9:00

7:30

1:00

6:00

18 Unidad 3 Etapa 3 p. 269
¿Lo tiene?

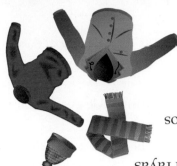

Estudiante A Catalina is going to the beach. Find out if she has the following items with her. Then tell which items Antonio has for his trip to the mountains.

modelo

Estudiante A: ¿Tiene Catalina los patines?

Estudiante B: …

los patines

1. las gafas de sol
2. el traje de baño con rayas
3. la merienda
4. los shorts de cuadros
5. el bronceador
6. una revista

Estudiante B Catalina is going to the beach. Answer your partner's questions about Catalina. Then find out if Antonio has the following items for his trip to the mountains.

modelo

los patines

Estudiante A: ¿Tiene Catalina los patines?

Estudiante B: No, no los tiene.

7. el gorro
8. la chaqueta
9. el impermeable
10. la bufanda con rayas
11. las gafas de sol
12. el suéter

Juegos—respuestas

UNIDAD 1

Etapa 1   **En uso,** p. 51: A Marisol no le gusta hacer las actividades con la letra **c.**

Etapa 2   **En uso,** p. 77: b

Etapa 3   **En acción,** p. 93: El hermano de Marco tiene un año.; **En uso,** p. 105:
1. El abuelo tiene 61 años. 2. Carlos tiene 37 años. 3. Antonio tiene 2 años.

UNIDAD 2

Etapa 1   **En uso,** p. 137: 1. las matemáticas, 2. la computación, 3. el inglés,
4. la música

Etapa 2   **En uso,** p. 163: Marco va al auditorio. Maricarmen va a la biblioteca.
Josefina va a la oficina.

Etapa 3   **En acción,** p. 173: El perro tiene sed.; **En uso,** p. 191: Adriana camina
con el perro. José toca la guitarra. Jorge cuida a sus hermanos.

UNIDAD 3

Etapa 1   **En uso,** p. 223: 1. Miguel va a un concierto. 2. Mariela va al cine.
3. Martina y Martín van de compras (a la tienda).

Etapa 2   **En uso,** p. 249: 1. Ángela: levantar pesas, 2. Marco: surfing,
3. Juanito: fútbol

Etapa 3   **En acción,** p. 266: b; **En uso,** p. 277: c. Chile

Vocabulario adicional

Here are lists of additional vocabulary to supplement the words you know. They include musical instruments, animals, and classes.

Los instrumentos

el acordeón	accordion
la armónica	harmonica
el arpa (fem.)	harp
el bajo	bass
el bajón	bassoon
el banjo	banjo
la batería	drum set
el clarinete	clarinet
el corno francés	French horn
el corno inglés	English horn
la flauta	flute
la flauta dulce	recorder
el flautín	piccolo
la mandolina	mandolin
el oboe	oboe
el órgano	organ
la pandereta	tambourine
el saxofón	saxophone
el sintetizador	synthesizer
el tambor	drum
el trombón	trombone
la trompeta	trumpet
la tuba	tuba
la viola	viola
el violín	violin
el violonchelo	cello
el xilófono	xylophone

Más animales

la araña	spider
el burro	donkey
la cabra	goat
el chapulín	grasshopper
el cisne	swan
el conejillo de Indias	guinea pig
el conejo	rabbit
el ganso	goose
el gerbo	gerbil
el hámster	hamster
la hormiga	ant
el hurón	ferret
la lagartija	small lizard
el loro	parrot
el mono	monkey
el mapache	raccoon
la mariposa	butterfly
la oveja	sheep
la paloma	pigeon, dove
el pato	duck
el pavo	turkey
la rana	frog
la rata	rat
el ratón	mouse
el sapo	toad
la serpiente	snake
la tortuga	turtle

Las clases

el alemán	German
el álgebra (fem.)	algebra
la biología	biology
el cálculo	calculus
la composición	writing
la contabilidad	accounting
la física	physics
el francés	French
la geografía	geography
la geología	geology
la geometría	geometry
el italiano	Italian
el japonés	Japanese
el latín	Latin
la química	chemistry
el ruso	Russian
la salud	health
la trigonometría	trigonometry

Gramática—resumen

Grammar Terms

Adjective (pp. 65, 67): a word that describes a noun

Adverb (p. 125): a word that describes a verb, an adjective, or another adverb

Article (pp. 62, 64): a word that identifies the class of a noun (masculine or feminine, singular or plural); English articles are *a, an,* or *the*

Comparative (p. 240): a phrase that compares two things

Conjugation (p. 122): a verb form that uses the stem of an infinitive and adds endings that reflect subject and tense

Direct Object (p. 265): the noun, pronoun, or phrase that receives the action of the main verb in a sentence

Gender (p. 65): a property that divides adjectives, nouns, pronouns, and articles into masculine and feminine groups

Infinitive (p. 43): the basic form of a verb; it names the action without giving tense, person, or number

Interrogative (p. 154): a word that asks a question

Noun (p. 62): a word that names a thing, person, animal, place, feeling, or situation

Number (p. 67): a property that divides adjectives, nouns, pronouns, articles, and verbs into singular and plural groups

Preposition (p. 90): a word that shows the relationship between its object and another word in the sentence

Pronoun (p. 38): a word that can be used in place of a noun

Subject (p. 38): the noun, pronoun, or phrase in a sentence that performs the action and is the focus of attention

Tense (p. 122): when the action of a verb takes place

Nouns, Articles, and Pronouns

Nouns

Nouns identify things, people, animals, places, feelings, or situations. Spanish nouns are either masculine or feminine. They are also either **singular** or **plural**. **Masculine nouns** usually end in **-o** and **feminine nouns** usually end in **-a.**

To make a noun **plural**, add **-s** to a word ending in a vowel and **-es** to a word ending in a consonant.

Singular Nouns		Plural Nouns	
Masculine	**Feminine**	**Masculine**	**Feminine**
amigo	amiga	amigos	amigas
chico	chica	chicos	chicas
hombre	mujer	hombres	mujeres
suéter	blusa	suéteres	blusas
zapato	falda	zapatos	faldas

Articles

Articles identify the class of a noun: masculine or feminine, singular or plural. **Definite articles** are the equivalent of the English word *the*. **Indefinite articles** are the equivalent of *a, an,* or *some*.

Definite Articles		
	Masculine	**Feminine**
Singular	**el** amigo	**la** amiga
Plural	**los** amigos	**las** amigas

Indefinite Articles		
	Masculine	**Feminine**
Singular	**un** amigo	**una** amiga
Plural	**unos** amigos	**unas** amigas

Pronouns

A **pronoun** takes the place of a noun. The pronoun used is determined by its function or purpose in the sentence.

Subject Pronouns	
yo	nosotros(as)
tú	vosotros(as)
usted	ustedes
él, ella	ellos(as)

Pronouns Used After Prepositions	
de **mí**	de **nosotros(as)**
de **ti**	de **vosotros(as)**
de **usted**	de **ustedes**
de **él, ella**	de **ellos(as)**

Direct Object Pronouns	
me	nos
te	os
lo, la	los, las

Adjectives

Adjectives describe nouns. In Spanish, adjectives must match the **number** and **gender** of the nouns they describe. When an adjective describes a group with both genders, the masculine form is used. To make an adjective plural, apply the same rules that are used for making a noun plural. Most adjectives are placed after the noun.

Adjectives		
	Masculine	**Feminine**
Singular	el chico **guapo**	la chica **guapa**
	el chico **paciente**	la chica **paciente**
	el chico **fenomenal**	la chica **fenomenal**
	el chico **trabajador**	la chica **trabajadora**
Plural	los chicos guapo**s**	las chicas guapa**s**
	los chicos paciente**s**	las chicas paciente**s**
	los chicos fenomenal**es**	las chicas fenomenal**es**
	los chicos trabajador**es**	las chicas trabajadoras

Adjectives cont.

Sometimes adjectives are placed before the noun and **shortened**. **Grande** is shortened before any singular noun. Several others are shortened before a masculine singular noun.

Shortened Forms	
bueno	**buen** chico
malo	**mal** chico
grande	**gran** chico(a)

Possessive adjectives identify to whom something belongs. They agree in gender and number with the noun possessed, not with the person who possesses it.

Possessive Adjectives				
	Masculine		**Feminine**	
Singular	**mi** amigo	**nuestro** amigo	**mi** amiga	**nuestra** amiga
	tu amigo	**vuestro** amigo	**tu** amiga	**vuestra** amiga
	su amigo	**su** amigo	**su** amiga	**su** amiga
Plural	**mis** amigos	**nuestros** amigos	**mis** amigas	**nuestras** amigas
	tus amigos	**vuestros** amigos	**tus** amigas	**vuestras** amigas
	sus amigos	**sus** amigos	**sus** amigas	**sus** amigas

Interrogatives

Interrogative words are used to ask questions.

Interrogatives		
¿Adónde?	¿Cuándo?	¿Por qué?
¿Cómo?		¿Qué?
¿Cuál(es)?	¿Dónde?	¿Quién(es)?

Comparatives and Superlatives

Comparatives

Comparatives are used when comparing two different things.

Comparatives		
más (+) **más** interesante **que...** Me gusta correr **más que** nadar.	menos (−) **menos** interesante **que...** Me gusta nadar **menos que** correr.	tan(to) (=) **tan** interesante **como...** Me gusta leer **tanto como** escribir.

There are a few irregular comparatives. When talking about the age of people, use **mayor** and **menor**.

Age	Quality
mayor menor	mejor peor

When talking about numbers, **de** is used instead of **que**.

    más (menos) de cien...

Superlatives

Superlatives are used to distinguish one item from a group. They describe which item has the most or least of a quality.

Superlatives	Masculine	Feminine
Singular	**el** chico **más** alto **el** chico **menos** alto	**la** chica **más** alta **la** chica **menos** alta
Plural	**los** chicos **más** altos **los** chicos **menos** altos	**las** chicas **más** altas **las** chicas **menos** altas

GRAMÁTICA—RESUMEN

RECURSOS
Gramática—resumen   **R15**

Verbs: Present Tense

Regular Verbs

Regular verbs ending in **-ar, -er,** or **-ir** always have regular endings in the present.

-ar Verbs		-er Verbs		-ir Verbs	
hablo	hablamos	como	comemos	vivo	vivimos
hablas	habláis	comes	coméis	vives	vivís
habla	hablan	come	comen	vive	viven

Verbs with Irregular yo Forms

Some verbs have regular forms in the present except for their **yo** forms.

Infinitive → Yo form		
conocer	→	conozco
hacer	→	hago
saber	→	sé

Stem-Changing Verbs

u → ue	
juego	jugamos
juegas	jugáis
juega	juegan

Jugar is the only verb with a **u → ue** stem change.

e → ie	
cierro	cerramos
cierras	cerráis
cierra	cierran

Other **e → ie** verbs: **empezar, entender, merendar, nevar, pensar, perder, preferir, querer.**

GRAMÁTICA—RESUMEN

Irregular Verbs

estar	
estoy	estamos
estás	estáis
está	están

ir	
voy	vamos
vas	vais
va	van

oír	
oigo	oímos
oyes	oís
oye	oyen

ser	
soy	somos
eres	sois
es	son

tener	
tengo	tenemos
tienes	tenéis
tiene	tienen

venir	
vengo	venimos
vienes	venís
viene	vienen

Verbs: Present Participles

Present participles are used with a conjugated form of **estar** to talk about something that is in the process of happening.

Regular Participles		
-ar Verbs	**-er Verbs**	**-ir Verbs**
esper**ando**	com**iendo**	escrib**iendo**

y Spelling Change
creer → creyendo
leer → leyendo
oír → oyendo

GLOSARIO
español-inglés

This Spanish-English glossary contains all of the active vocabulary words that appear in the text as well as passive vocabulary from readings, culture sections, and extra vocabulary lists. Most inactive cognates have been omitted. The active words are accompanied by the number of the unit and **etapa** in which they are presented. For example, **a veces** can be found in 2.1 (*Unidad* 2, *Etapa* 1). **EP** refers to the *Etapa preliminar*. Stem-changing verbs are indicated by the change inside the parentheses—**jugar (ue)**, as are verbs that are irregular only in the **yo** form.

a to, at
  A la(s)... At.... o'clock. **2.2**
  ¿A qué hora es...? (At)
    What time is...? **2.2**
  a veces sometimes **2.1**
el abrigo coat **3.3**
abril April **1.3**
abrir to open **2.3**
la abuela grandmother **1.3**
el abuelo grandfather **1.3**
los abuelos grandparents **1.3**
aburrido(a) boring **1.2**
acabar de... to have just... **3.1**
el acordeón accordion
Adiós. Good-bye. **EP**
adónde (to) where **2.2**
la aduana customs **1.1**
agosto August **1.3**
el agua (fem.) water **2.2**
el águila eagle
ahora now **1.3**
  ¡Ahora mismo! Right now! **2.1**
al to the **2.2**
  al aire libre outdoors **3.2**
alegre happy **3.1**
el alemán German
el álgebra (fem.) algebra
el almuerzo lunch **2.2**
alquilar un video
  to rent a video **3.1**
alto(a) tall **1.2**
amarillo(a) yellow **1.2**

el (la) amigo(a) friend **1.1**
anaranjado(a) orange **1.2**
andar
  andar en bicicleta
    to ride a bike **2.3**
  andar en patineta
    to skateboard **3.2**
el animal animal **2.3**
antes (de) before **2.3**
el año year **1.3**
  ¿Cuántos años tiene...?
    How old is...? **1.3**
  Tiene... años.
    He/She is... years old. **1.3**
el apartamento apartment **1.1**
el apellido last name, surname **EP**
el apoyo support
aprender to learn **2.3**
la araña spider
el árbol tree **3.3**
la armónica harmonica
el arpa (fem.) harp
el arte art **2.1**
asado(a) roasted
el auditorio auditorium **2.2**
el avión airplane
ayudar (a) to help **2.1**
azul blue **1.2**

bailar to dance **1.1**
bajo(a) short (height) **1.2**
el bajo bass

el bajón bassoon
el baloncesto basketball **3.2**
el banjo banjo
el bate bat **3.2**
la batería drum set
beber to drink **2.3**
  ¿Quieres beber...?
    Do you want to drink...? **2.2**
  Quiero beber...
    I want to drink... **2.2**
el béisbol baseball **3.2**
la biblioteca library **2.2**
la biología biology
bien well **1.1**
  (No muy) Bien, ¿y tú/usted?
    (Not very) Well, and you? **1.1**
bienvenido(a) welcome **1.1**
blanco(a) white **1.2**
la blusa blouse **1.2**
el bohique storyteller
la bola ball **3.2**
la bolsa bag **1.2**
bonito(a) pretty **1.2**
el borrador eraser **2.1**
el bosque forest **3.3**
el bronceador suntan lotion **3.3**
bueno(a) good **1.2**
  Buenas noches.
    Good evening. **EP**
  Buenas tardes.
    Good afternoon. **EP**
  Buenos días. Good morning. **EP**
la bufanda scarf **3.3**
el burro donkey
buscar to look for, to search **2.1**

C

la cabra goat
cada each, every **2.3**
la cafetería
  cafeteria, coffee shop **2.2**
el calcetín sock **1.2**
la calculadora calculator **2.1**
el cálculo calculus
calor
  Hace calor. It is hot. **3.3**
  tener calor to be hot **3.3**
los camarones shrimp
caminar con el perro
  to walk the dog **2.3**
la camisa shirt **1.2**
la camiseta T-shirt **1.2**
el campo field **3.2**
la cancha court **3.2**
cansado(a) tired **3.1**
cantar to sing **1.1**
la carretera highway
la casa house **1.1**
el casco helmet **3.2**
castaño(a) brown (hair) **1.2**
catorce fourteen **1.3**
la cena supper, dinner **2.3**
cenar to have dinner, supper **2.3**
cero zero **EP**
cerrar (ie) to close **3.2**
el chapulín grasshopper
la chaqueta jacket **1.2**
chévere awesome
  ¡Qué chévere!
    How awesome! **1.3**
la chica girl **1.1**
los chicharrones pork rinds **2.3**
el chico boy **1.1**
cien one hundred **1.3**
las ciencias science **2.1**
cinco five **EP**
cincuenta fifty **1.3**
el cisne swan
la cita appointment **2.2**
la ciudad city **1.3**
el clarinete clarinet
¡Claro que sí! Of course! **3.1**
la clase class, classroom **2.1**
el color color **1.2**
  ¿De qué color…?
    What color…? **1.2**

comer to eat **1.1**
  ¿Quieres comer…?
    Do you want to eat…? **2.2**
  Quiero comer…
    I want to eat… **2.2**
cómico(a) funny, comical **1.2**
la comida food, a meal **2.3**
como like, as
cómo how **2.2**
  ¿Cómo es?
    What is he/she like? **1.2**
  ¿Cómo está usted?
    How are you? *(formal)* **1.1**
  ¿Cómo estás?
    How are you? *(familiar)* **1.1**
  ¿Cómo se llama?
    What is his/her name? **EP**
  ¿Cómo te llamas?
    What is your name? **EP**
compartir to share **2.3**
la composición writing
comprar to buy **2.2**
comprender to understand **2.3**
la computación
  computer science **2.1**
la computadora computer **2.1**
la comunidad community **1.1**
con with **1.3**
  con rayas striped **3.3**
  Con razón. That's why. **2.1**
el concierto concert **3.1**
el concurso contest **1.1**
el conejillo de Indias guinea pig
el conejo rabbit
conmigo with me **3.1**
conocer (conozco) to know,
  to be familiar with **2.3**
  conocer a alguien to know, to
    be familiar with someone **2.3**
la contabilidad accounting
el contenido contents
contento(a) content, happy,
  pleased **3.1**
contestar to answer **2.1**
contigo with you **3.1**
el corazón heart **2.3**
el corno francés French horn
el corno inglés English horn
corto(a) short (length) **1.2**
correr to run **1.1**
creer to think, to believe **3.3**
  Creo que sí/no. I think so./
    I don't think so. **3.3**
el cuaderno notebook **2.1**

cuál(es) which (ones), what **2.2**
  ¿Cuál es la fecha?
    What is the date? **1.3**
  ¿Cuál es tu teléfono? What is
    your phone number? **EP**
cuando when, whenever **3.1**
cuándo when **2.2**
cuántos(as) how many
  ¿Cuántos años tiene…?
    How old is…? **1.3**
cuarenta forty **1.3**
cuatro four **EP**
la cuerda string
el cuero leather
cuidar (a) to take care of **2.3**
el cumpleaños birthday **1.3**

D

de of, from, about **1.1**
  de cuadros plaid, checked **3.3**
  de la mañana in the morning **2.2**
  de la noche at night **2.2**
  de la tarde in the afternoon **2.2**
  De nada. You're welcome. **1.1**
  de vez en cuando once in
    a while **2.1**
dejar to leave (behind)
  dejar un mensaje
    to leave a message **3.1**
  **Deje un mensaje después
    del tono.** Leave a message
    after the tone. **3.1**
  Quiero dejar un mensaje para…
    I want to leave a message
    for… **3.1**
del from the **3.1**
delgado(a) thin **1.2**
el deporte sport
  practicar deportes
    to play sports **3.1**
deprimido(a) depressed **3.1**
la derecha right
descansar to rest **2.2**
el desierto desert **3.3**
después (de) after, afterward **2.3**
el día day **EP**
  Buenos días. Good morning. **EP**
  ¿Qué día es hoy?
    What day is today? **EP**
  todos los días every day **2.1**
el diccionario dictionary **2.1**

diciembre December **1.3**
diecinueve nineteen **1.3**
dieciocho eighteen **1.3**
dieciséis sixteen **1.3**
diecisiete seventeen **1.3**
diez ten **EP**
difícil difficult, hard **2.1**
el diós god
divertido(a) enjoyable, fun **1.2**
doce twelve **1.3**
el (la) doctor(a) doctor **1.1**
domingo Sunday **EP**
dónde where **2.2**
   ¿De dónde eres?
      Where are you from? **EP**
   ¿De dónde es?
      Where is he/she from? **EP**
dos two **EP**
durante during **2.2**

la edad age **1.3**
la educación física physical
   education **2.1**
él he **1.1**
ella she **1.1**
ellos(as) they **1.1**
emocionado(a) excited **3.1**
empezar (ie) to begin **3.2**
Encantado(a). Delighted/Pleased
   to meet you. **EP**
en in **1.1**
   en vez de instead of
enero January **1.3**
enfermo(a) sick **3.1**
enojado(a) angry **3.1**
enseñar to teach **2.1**
entender (ie) to understand **3.2**
entonces then, so **2.3**
entrar (a, en) to enter **2.1**
el equipo team **3.2**
escribir to write **1.1**
el escritorio desk **2.1**
la escritura writing
escuchar to listen (to) **2.1**
la escuela school **2.1**
el español Spanish **2.1**
esperar to wait for, to expect **2.1**
la esposa wife
el esposo husband

esquiar to ski **3.2**
las estaciones seasons **3.3**
el estadio stadium **3.2**
estar to be **2.2**
el (la) estudiante student **1.1**
estudiar to study **2.1**
los estudios sociales
   social studies **2.1**
la etapa step
el examen test **2.1**

fácil easy **2.1**
la falda skirt **1.2**
la familia family **1.1**
favorito(a) favorite **3.2**
febrero February **1.3**
la fecha date **1.3**
   ¿Cuál es la fecha?
      What is the date? **1.3**
felicidades congratulations **1.3**
feliz happy **1.3**
feo(a) ugly **1.2**
fíjate take a look
el fin de semana weekend
la física physics
la flauta flute
la flauta dulce recorder
el flautín piccolo
la flor flower **3.3**
el folleto brochure
la foto picture
   sacar fotos to take pictures **3.3**
el francés French
frío
   Hace frío. It is cold. **3.3**
   tener frío to be cold **3.3**
la frontera border
la fruta fruit **2.2**
fuerte strong **1.2**
el fútbol soccer **3.2**
el fútbol americano football **3.2**

las gafas de sol sunglasses **3.3**
ganar to win **3.2**
el ganso goose

el (la) gato(a) cat **1.2**
la gente people **2.3**
la geografía geography
la geología geology
la geometría geometry
el gerbo gerbil
el gimnasio gymnasium **2.2**
el gobierno government
el gol goal **3.2**
gordo(a) fat **1.2**
la gorra baseball cap **3.2**
el gorro cap **3.3**
Gracias. Thank you. **1.1**
   Gracias, pero no puedo.
      Thanks, but I can't. **3.1**
el grado degree **3.3**
grande big, large; great **1.2**
el guante glove **3.2**
guapo(a) good-looking **1.2**
la guía telefónica phone book **3.1**
el guerrero warrior
gustar to like
   Le gusta… He/She likes… **1.1**
   Me gusta… I like… **1.1**
   Me gustaría… I'd like… **3.1**
   Te gusta… You like… **1.1**
   ¿Te gustaría…?
      Would you like…? **3.1**
el gusto pleasure
   El gusto es mío.
      The pleasure is mine. **EP**
   Mucho gusto.
      Nice to meet you. **EP**

hablar to talk, to speak **2.1**
   ¿Puedo hablar con…?
      May I speak with…? **3.1**
hacer (hago) to make, to do **2.3**
   hacer ejercicio to exercise **2.3**
   Hace buen tiempo.
      It is nice outside. **3.3**
   Hace calor. It is hot. **3.3**
   Hace fresco. It is cool. **3.3**
   Hace frío. It is cold. **3.3**
   Hace mal tiempo.
      It is bad outside. **3.3**
   Hace sol. It is sunny. **3.3**
   Hace viento. It is windy. **3.3**
   ¿Qué tiempo hace?
      What is the weather like? **3.3**

ESPAÑOL–INGLÉS

la **hamburguesa** hamburger **2.2**
el **hámster** hamster
hasta until
    Hasta luego. See you later. **EP**
    Hasta mañana.
        See you tomorrow. **EP**
hay there is, there are **1.3**
    hay que one has to, must **2.1**
    Hay sol. It's sunny. **3.3**
    Hay viento. It's windy. **3.3**
hazlo do it
la **hermana** sister **1.3**
la **hermanastra** stepsister
el **hermanastro** stepbrother
el **hermano** brother **1.3**
los **hermanos** brother(s) and
    sister(s) **1.3**
la **hija** daughter **1.3**
el **hijo** son **1.3**
los **hijos** son(s) and daughter(s),
    children **1.3**
la **historia** history **2.1**
el **hockey** hockey **3.2**
Hola. Hello. **EP**
el **hombre** man **1.1**
el **horario** schedule **2.2**
la **hormiga** ant
hoy today **EP**
    Hoy es… Today is… **EP**
    ¿Qué día es hoy?
        What day is today? **EP**
el **hurón** ferret

Igualmente. Same here. **EP**
el **impermeable** raincoat **3.3**
la **impresora** printer **2.1**
el **inglés** English **2.1**
inteligente intelligent **1.2**
interesante interesting **1.2**
el **invierno** winter **3.3**
invitar to invite
    Te invito. I'll treat you.
        I invite you. **3.1**
ir to go **2.2**
    ir a… to be going to… **2.3**
    ir al cine to go to a movie
        theater **3.1**
    ir al supermercado to go to
        the supermarket **2.3**
    ir de compras to go shopping **3.1**

la **isla** island
el **italiano** Italian

el **japonés** Japanese
los **jeans** jeans **1.2**
joven young **1.3**
el **juego** game
jueves Thursday **EP**
el (la) **jugador(a)** player
jugar (ue) to play **3.2**
julio July **1.3**
junio June **1.3**

la **lagartija** small lizard
el **lago** lake **3.3**
el **lápiz** pencil **2.1**
largo(a) long **1.2**
el **latín** Latin
la **lección** lesson **2.1**
la **lectura** reading
leer to read **1.1**
el **letrero** sign
levantar pesas to lift weights **3.2**
el **libro** book **2.1**
la **literatura** literature **2.1**
la **llamada** call **3.1**
llamar to call **3.1**
    Dile/Dígale que me llame.
        Tell him or her to call me. **3.1**
llegar to arrive **2.1**
    llegar a ser to become
llevar to wear, to carry **2.1**;
    to take along **3.3**
llover (ue) to rain **3.3**
la **lluvia** rain **3.3**
loco(a) crazy **3.2**
el **loro** parrot
luego later **2.3**
    Hasta luego. See you later. **EP**
el **lugar** place **1.1**
lunes Monday **EP**

la **madrastra** stepmother
la **madre** mother **1.3**
el (la) **maestro(a)** teacher **1.1**
el **maíz** corn
malo(a) bad **1.2**
mandar una carta
    to send a letter **2.3**
la **mandolina** mandolin
mañana tomorrow **EP**
    Hasta mañana.
        See you tomorrow. **EP**
    Mañana es… Tomorrow is… **EP**
la **mañana** morning **2.2**
    de la mañana
        in the morning **2.2**
    por la mañana
        during the morning **2.2**
el **mapache** raccoon
la **máquina contestadora**
    answering machine **3.1**
el **mar** sea **3.3**
marcar to dial **3.1**
la **mariposa** butterfly
marrón brown **1.2**
martes Tuesday **EP**
marzo March **1.3**
más more **1.3**
    más de more than **3.2**
    más… que more… than **3.2**
las **matemáticas** mathematics **2.1**
la **materia** subject **2.1**
mayo May **1.3**
mayor older **1.3**
Me llamo… My name is… **EP**
la **media hermana** half-sister
la **medianoche** midnight **2.2**
el **medio hermano** half-brother
el **mediodía** noon **2.2**
mejor better **3.2**
menor younger **1.3**
menos to, before **2.2**; less **3.2**
    menos de less than **3.2**
    menos… que less… than **3.2**
merendar (ie) to have a snack **3.2**
la **merienda** snack **2.2**
el **mes** month **1.3**
mi my **1.3**
miércoles Wednesday **EP**
mirar to watch, to look at **2.1**

mismo(a) same **2.1**
la mochila backpack **2.1**
el momento moment
    Un momento. One moment. **3.1**
el mono monkey
la montaña mountain **3.3**
morado(a) purple **1.2**
moreno(a) dark hair and skin **1.2**
la muchacha girl **1.1**
el muchacho boy **1.1**
mucho often **2.1**
mucho(a) much, many **1.1**
la mujer woman **1.1**
el mundo world **1.1**
el museo museum **2.3**
la música music **2.1**
muy very **1.3**

nadar to swim **1.1**
necesitar to need **2.1**
negro(a) black **1.2**
nervioso(a) nervous **3.1**
nevar (ie) to snow **3.3**
ni nor
la nieta granddaughter
el nieto grandson
los nietos grandchildren
la nieve snow **3.3**
el niño boy
la niña girl
no no **EP**; not **1.1**
    ¡No digas eso! Don't say that! **1.2**
    ¡No te preocupes!
      Don't worry! **3.1**
la noche night, evening
    Buenas noches.
      Good evening. **EP**
    de la noche at night **2.2**
    por la noche
      during the evening **2.2**
el nombre name, first name **EP**
nosotros(as) we **1.1**
la novela novel **2.3**
noventa ninety **1.3**
noviembre November **1.3**
nublado cloudy
    Está nublado. It is cloudy. **3.3**
nuestro(a) our **1.3**
nueve nine **EP**

nuevo(a) new **1.2**
nunca never **2.1**

o or **1.1**
el oboe oboe
ochenta eighty **1.3**
ocho eight **EP**
octubre October **1.3**
ocupado(a) busy **3.1**
la oficina office **2.2**
oír to hear **2.3**
el ojo eye **1.2**
once eleven **1.3**
el órgano organ
el otoño fall **3.3**
otro(a) other, another **1.2**
la oveja sheep

paciente patient **1.2**
el padrastro stepfather
el padre father **1.3**
los padres parents **1.3**
el país country **1.1**
el pájaro bird **2.3**
la paloma pigeon, dove
la pandereta tambourine
la pantalla screen **2.1**
los pantalones pants **1.2**
    los pantalones cortos shorts
la papa potato
las papas fritas french fries **2.2**
el papel paper **2.1**
el paraguas umbrella **3.3**
el parque park **2.3**
el partido game **3.2**
pasar to happen, to pass (by) **2.1**
    pasar un rato con los amigos to
      spend time with friends **2.3**
pasear to go for a walk **2.3**
patinar to skate **1.1**
los patines skates **3.2**
la patineta skateboard **3.2**
    andar en patineta
      to skateboard **3.2**
el pato duck

el pavo turkey
la película movie **3.1**
peligroso(a) dangerous **3.2**
pelirrojo(a) redhead **1.2**
el pelo hair **1.2**
la pelota baseball **3.2**
pensar (ie) to think, to plan **3.2**
peor worse **3.2**
pequeño(a) small **1.2**
perder (ie) to lose **3.2**
perezoso(a) lazy **1.2**
el periódico newspaper **2.3**
pero but **1.1**
el (la) perro(a) dog **1.2**
    caminar con el perro
      to walk the dog **2.3**
el pez fish **2.3**
pintar to paint **2.3**
la piña pineapple
la piscina swimming pool **3.2**
el pizarrón chalkboard **2.1**
el placer pleasure
    Es un placer. It's a pleasure. **EP**
la planta plant **3.3**
la playa beach **3.3**
la pluma pen **2.1**
poco a little **2.1**
poder (ue) to be able
    ¿Puedo hablar con…?
      May I speak with…? **3.1**
el poema poem **2.3**
la poesía poetry **2.3**
el (la) policía police officer **1.1**
por
    por favor please **2.2**
    por fin finally **2.3**
    por la mañana
      during the morning **2.2**
    por la noche
      during the evening **2.2**
    por la tarde
      during the afternoon **2.2**
    por qué why **2.2**
porque because **3.1**
practicar deportes to play sports **3.1**
preferir (ie) to prefer **3.2**
preocupado(a) worried **3.1**
preparar to prepare **2.1**
presentar to introduce
    Te/Le presento a…
      Let me introduce you to… **1.1**
la primavera spring **3.3**
el primero first of the month **1.3**

primero(a) first **6.2**
el (la) primo(a) cousin **1.3**
el problema problem **2.3**
el programa program
pronto soon **2.1**
propio(a) own
la prueba quiz **2.1**
el pueblo people, civilization
pues well **1.2**

que that
qué what **2.2**
   ¿A qué hora es…?
     (At) What time is…? **2.2**
   ¡Qué (divertido)! How (fun)! **1.2**
   ¿Qué día es hoy?
     What day is today? **EP**
   ¿Qué hora es? What time is it? **2.2**
   ¡Qué lástima! What a shame! **3.1**
   ¿Qué lleva?
     What is he/she wearing? **1.2**
   ¿Qué tal? How is it going? **1.1**
   ¿Qué tiempo hace?
     What is the weather like? **3.3**
querer (ie) to want **3.2**
   ¿Quieres beber…?
     Do you want to drink…? **2.2**
   ¿Quieres comer…?
     Do you want to eat…? **2.2**
   Quiero beber…
     I want to drink… **2.2**
   Quiero comer…
     I want to eat… **2.2**
   Quiero dejar un mensaje para…
     I want to leave a message
     for… **3.1**
quién(es) who **2.2**
   ¿De quién es…? Whose is…? **1.3**
   ¿Quién es? Who is it? **1.3**
   ¿Quiénes son? Who are they? **1.3**
la química chemistry
quince fifteen **1.3**

la rana frog
la raqueta racket **3.2**

rara vez rarely **2.1**
la rata rat
el ratón mouse **2.1**
la razón reason **2.1**
   Con razón. That's why. **2.1**
   tener razón to be right **3.3**
el receso break **2.2**
recibir to receive **2.3**
el recurso resource
el refrán saying
el refresco soft drink **2.2**
regresar to return
   Regresa más tarde.
     He/She will return later. **3.1**
Regular. So-so. **1.1**
el reloj clock, watch **2.2**
el repaso review
el resumen summary
la revista magazine **2.3**
rico(a) rich
el río river **3.3**
rojo(a) red **1.2**
la ropa clothing **1.2**
rosado(a) pink **1.2**
rubio(a) blond **1.2**
el ruso Russian

sábado Saturday **EP**
saber (sé) to know **3.2**
sacar
   sacar fotos to take pictures **3.3**
   sacar una buena nota to get
     a good grade **2.1**
la sala living room
   la sala de espera waiting room
la salud health
el sapo toad
la sartén frying pan
el saxofón saxophone
Se llama… His/Her name is… **EP**
seis six **EP**
la semana week **EP**
   el semestre semester **2.2**
la señal sign
el señor Mr. **1.1**
la señora Mrs. **1.1**
la señorita Miss **1.1**
septiembre September **1.3**

ser to be **1.1**
   Es la…/Son las…
     It is… o'clock. **2.2**
   ser de… to be from… **1.1**
serio(a) serious **1.2**
la serpiente snake
sesenta sixty **1.3**
setenta seventy **1.3**
los shorts shorts **3.3**
sí yes **EP**
   Sí, me encantaría.
     Yes, I would love to. **3.1**
siempre always **2.1**
siete seven **EP**
el siglo century
simpático(a) nice **1.2**
el sintetizador synthesizer
sobre on, about
   sobre hielo on ice **3.2**
el sol sun **3.3**
   las gafas de sol sunglasses **3.3**
   Hace sol. It is sunny. **3.3**
   Hay sol. It's sunny. **3.3**
   tomar el sol to sunbathe **3.3**
sólo only **1.3**
solo(a) alone **3.1**
el sombrero hat **1.2**
el sonido sound
la sorpresa surprise
su your, his, her, its,
   their **1.3**
el suéter sweater **1.2**
el surfing surfing **3.2**

Tal vez otro día.
   Maybe another day. **3.1**
también also, too **1.1**
   también se dice
     you can also say
el tambor drum
tan… como as… as **3.2**
tanto como as much as **3.2**
tarde late **2.1**
la tarde afternoon **2.2**
   Buenas tardes.
     Good afternoon. **EP**
   de la tarde in the afternoon **2.2**
   por la tarde
     during the afternoon **2.2**

la **tarea** homework **2.1**

el **teatro** theater **2.3**

la **tecla** key (of an instrument)

el **teclado** keyboard **2.1**

el **teléfono** telephone **3.1**

   ¿Cuál es tu teléfono? What is your phone number? **EP**

la **temperatura** temperature **3.3**

temprano early **3.1**

tener to have **1.3**

   ¿Cuántos años tiene…? How old is…? **1.3**

   tener calor to be hot **3.3**

   tener cuidado to be careful **3.3**

   tener frío to be cold **3.3**

   tener ganas de… to feel like… **3.3**

   tener hambre to be hungry **2.3**

   tener miedo to be afraid **3.3**

   tener prisa to be in a hurry **3.3**

   tener que to have to **2.1**

   tener razón to be right **3.3**

   tener sed to be thirsty **2.3**

   tener sueño to be sleepy **3.3**

   tener suerte to be lucky **3.3**

   Tiene… años. He/She is… years old. **1.3**

el **tenis** tennis **3.2**

terminar to finish **2.2**

Terrible. Terrible./Awful. **1.1**

la **tía** aunt **1.3**

el **tiempo** time **3.1**; weather **3.3**

   Hace buen tiempo. It is nice outside. **3.3**

   Hace mal tiempo. It is bad outside. **3.3**

   ¿Qué tiempo hace? What is the weather like? **3.3**

   el tiempo libre free time **3.1**

la **tienda** store **2.3**

   la tienda de deportes sporting goods store **3.2**

la **tierra** land

el **tío** uncle **1.3**

los **tíos** uncle(s) and aunt(s) **1.3**

la **tiza** chalk **2.1**

tocar to play (an instrument)

   tocar el piano to play the piano **2.3**

   tocar la guitarra to play the guitar **2.3**

todo(a) all **1.3**

   todos los días every day **2.1**

tomar to take, to eat or drink **2.2**

   tomar el sol to sunbathe **3.3**

la **tormenta** storm **3.3**

la **torta** sandwich (sub) **2.2**

la **tortuga** turtle

trabajador(a) hard-working **1.2**

trabajar to work **1.1**

el **trabalenguas** tongue twister

el **traje de baño** bathing suit **3.3**

tranquilo(a) calm **3.1**

trece thirteen **1.3**

treinta thirty **1.3**

tres three **EP**

la **trigonometría** trigonometry

triste sad **3.1**

el **trombón** trombone

la **trompeta** trumpet

tu your (familiar) **1.3**

tú you (familiar singular) **1.1**

la **tuba** tuba

la **unidad** unit

uno one **EP**

usar to use **2.1**

el **uso** use

usted you (formal singular) **1.1**

ustedes you (plural) **1.1**

el **vaso** glass

   el vaso de glass of **2.2**

veinte twenty **1.3**

veintiuno twenty-one **1.3**

vender to sell **2.3**

venir to come **3.1**

ver (veo) to see **2.3**

   Nos vemos. See you later. **EP**

   ver la televisión to watch television **2.3**

el **verano** summer **3.3**

la **verdad** truth **2.2**

   Es verdad. It's true. **1.2**

verde green **1.2**

el **vestido** dress **1.2**

la **vida** life **2.3**

viejo(a) old **1.3**

el **viento** wind **3.3**

   Hace viento. It is windy. **3.3**

   Hay viento. It's windy. **3.3**

viernes Friday **EP**

la **viola** viola

el **violín** violin

el **violonchelo** cello

visitar to visit **2.2**

vivir to live **2.3**

   Vive en… He/She lives in… **1.1**

   Vivo en… I live in… **1.1**

vivo(a) alive

el **voleibol** volleyball **3.2**

vosotros(as) you (familiar plural) **1.1**

la **voz** voice

vuestro(a) your (familiar plural) **1.3**

el **xilófono** xylophone

y and **1.1**

   y cuarto quarter past **2.2**

   y media half past **2.2**

ya already, now

ya no no longer **3.1**

yo I **1.1**

el **zapato** shoe **1.2**

GLOSARIO
inglés-español

This English–Spanish glossary contains all of the active words that appear as well as passive ones from readings, culture sections, and extra vocabulary lists. Active words are indicated by the unit and **etapa** number when they appear.

about sobre
to be afraid tener miedo **3.3**
accordion el acordeón
accounting la contabilidad
after después (de) **2.3**
afternoon la tarde **2.2**
   during the afternoon
     por la tarde **2.2**
   Good afternoon
     Buenas tardes. **EP**
   in the afternoon de la tarde **2.2**
afterward después **2.3**
age la edad **1.3**
airplane el avión
algebra el álgebra (fem.)
all todo(a) **1.3**
alone solo(a) **3.1**
already ya
also también **1.1**
always siempre **2.1**
and y **1.1**
angry enojado(a) **3.1**
animal el animal **2.3**
another otro(a) **1.2**
to answer contestar **2.1**
answering machine
   la máquina contestadora **3.1**
ant la hormiga
apartment el apartamento **1.1**
appointment la cita **2.2**

April abril **1.3**
to arrive llegar **2.1**
art el arte **2.1**
as como
   as… as tan… como **3.2**
   as much as tanto como **3.2**
at a
   At… o'clock. A la(s)… **2.2**
auditorium el auditorio **2.2**
August agosto **1.3**
aunt la tía **1.3**
awesome: How awesome!
   ¡Qué chévere! **1.3**
awful terrible **1.1**

backpack la mochila **2.1**
bad malo(a) **1.2**
   It is bad outside.
     Hace mal tiempo. **3.3**
bag la bolsa **1.2**
ball la bola **3.2**
banjo el banjo
baseball (sport) el béisbol **3.2**;
   (ball) la pelota **3.2**
baseball cap la gorra **3.2**
basketball el baloncesto **3.2**
bass el bajo
bassoon el bajón
bat el bate **3.2**
bathing suit el traje de baño **3.3**

to be ser **1.1**; estar **2.2**
   to be afraid tener miedo **3.3**
   to be careful tener cuidado **3.3**
   to be cold tener frío **3.3**
   to be familiar with conocer **2.3**
   to be from… ser de… **1.1**
   to be going to… ir a… **2.3**
   to be hot tener calor **3.3**
   to be hungry tener hambre **2.3**
   to be in a hurry tener prisa **3.3**
   to be lucky tener suerte **3.3**
   to be right tener razón **3.3**
   to be sleepy tener sueño **3.3**
   to be thirsty tener sed **2.3**
beach la playa **3.3**
because porque **3.1**
to become llegar a ser
before antes (de) **2.3**
to begin empezar (ie) **3.2**
to believe creer **3.3**
better mejor **3.2**
big grande **1.2**
bike la bicicleta
   to ride a bike
     andar en bicicleta **2.3**
biology la biología
bird el pájaro **2.3**
birthday el cumpleaños **1.3**
black negro(a) **1.2**
blond rubio(a) **1.2**
blouse la blusa **1.2**
blue azul **1.2**
book el libro **2.1**
border la frontera

boring aburrido(a) **1.2**
boy el chico **1.1**, el muchacho **1.1**, el niño
break el receso **2.2**
brochure el folleto
brother el hermano **1.3**
brown marrón **1.2**
brown (hair) castaño(a) **1.2**
busy ocupado(a) **3.1**
but pero **1.1**
butterfly la mariposa
to buy comprar **2.2**

cafeteria la cafetería **2.2**
calculator la calculadora **2.1**
calculus el cálculo
call la llamada **3.1**
to call llamar **3.1**
calm tranquilo(a) **3.1**
cap (knit) el gorro **3.3**, **(baseball)** la gorra **3.2**
careful
   to be careful tener cuidado **3.3**
to carry llevar **2.1**
cat el (la) gato(a) **1.2**
cello el violonchelo
century el siglo
chalk la tiza **2.1**
chalkboard el pizarrón **2.1**
checked de cuadros **3.3**
chemistry la química
city la ciudad **1.3**
clarinet el clarinete
class la clase **2.1**
classroom la clase **2.1**
clock el reloj **2.2**
to close cerrar (ie) **3.2**
clothing la ropa **1.2**
cloudy nublado
   It is cloudy. Está nublado. **3.3**
coat el abrigo **3.3**
   coffee shop la cafetería **2.2**
cold
   to be cold tener frío **3.3**
   It is cold. Hace frío. **3.3**
color el color
   What color…?
      ¿De qué color…? **1.2**
to come venir **3.1**

comical cómico(a) **1.2**
community la comunidad **1.1**
computer la computadora **2.1**
computer science
   la computación **2.1**
concert el concierto **3.1**
congratulations felicidades **1.3**
content contento(a) **3.1**
contest el concurso **1.1**
cool: It is cool. Hace fresco. **3.3**
corn el maíz
court la cancha **3.2**
cousin el (la) primo(a) **1.3**
crazy loco(a) **3.2**
customs la aduana

to dance bailar **1.1**
danger el peligro
dangerous peligroso(a) **3.2**
dark hair and skin moreno(a) **1.2**
date la fecha **1.3**
   What is the date?
      ¿Cuál es la fecha? **1.3**
daughter la hija **1.3**
day el día **EP**
   What day is today?
      ¿Qué día es hoy? **EP**
December diciembre **1.3**
degree el grado **3.3**
depressed deprimido(a) **3.1**
desert el desierto **3.3**
desk el escritorio **2.1**
to dial marcar **3.1**
dictionary el diccionario **2.1**
difficult difícil **2.1**
dinner la cena **2.3**
to do hacer **2.3**
doctor el (la) doctor(a) **1.1**
dog el (la) perro(a) **1.2**
   to walk the dog
      caminar con el perro **2.3**
donkey el burro
dove la paloma
dress el vestido **1.2**
to drink tomar **2.2**; beber **2.3**
   Do you want to drink…?
      ¿Quieres beber…? **2.2**
   I want to drink…
      Quiero beber… **2.2**

drum el tambor
drum set la batería
duck el pato
during durante **2.2**

each cada **2.3**
eagle el águila (fem.)
early temprano **3.1**
easy fácil **2.1**
to eat comer **1.1**, tomar **2.2**
   Do you want to eat…?
      ¿Quieres comer…? **2.2**
   to eat a snack merendar (ie) **3.2**
   to eat dinner cenar **2.3**
   I want to eat…
      Quiero comer… **2.2**
eight ocho **EP**
eighteen dieciocho **1.3**
eighty ochenta **1.3**
eleven once **1.3**
English el inglés **2.1**
English horn el corno inglés
enjoyable divertido(a) **1.2**
to enter entrar (a, en) **2.1**
eraser el borrador **2.1**
evening la noche
   during the evening
      por la noche **2.2**
   Good evening.
      Buenas noches. **EP**
every cada **2.3**
   every day todos los días **2.1**
excited emocionado(a) **3.1**
to exercise hacer ejercicio **2.3**
to expect esperar **2.1**
eye el ojo **1.2**

fall el otoño **3.3**
familiar: to be familiar with
   someone conocer a alguien **2.3**
family la familia **1.1**
fat gordo(a) **1.2**
father el padre **1.3**
favorite favorito(a) **3.2**
February febrero **1.3**

to feel like… tener ganas de… **3.3**
ferret el hurón
field el campo **3.2**
fifteen quince **1.3**
fifty cincuenta **1.3**
finally por fin **2.3**
to find encontrar (ue) **4.2**
first primero **2.3**
first name el nombre **EP**
fish el pez **2.3**
five cinco **EP**
flower la flor **3.3**
flute la flauta
food la comida **2.3**
football el fútbol americano **3.2**
forest el bosque **3.3**
forty cuarenta **1.3**
four cuatro **EP**
fourteen catorce **1.3**
free time el tiempo libre **3.1**
French el francés
    french fries las papas fritas **2.2**
    French horn el corno francés
Friday viernes **EP**
friend el (la) amigo(a) **1.1**
    to spend time with friends
      pasar un rato con los
      amigos **2.3**
frog la rana
from de **1.1**
fruit la fruta **2.2**
fun divertido(a) **1.2**
funny cómico(a) **1.2**

game el partido **3.2**
geography la geografía
geology la geología
geometry la geometría
gerbil el gerbo
German el alemán
girl la chica **1.1**, la muchacha **1.1**,
    la niña
glass el vaso **2.2**
glove el guante **3.2**
to go ir **2.2**
    to go for a walk pasear **2.3**
goal el gol **3.2**
goat la cabra
god el dios

good bueno(a) **1.2**
    Good afternoon.
      Buenas tardes. **EP**
    Good evening.
      Buenas noches. **EP**
    Good morning. Buenos días. **EP**
Good-bye. Adiós. **EP**
good-looking guapo(a) **1.2**
goose el ganso
government el gobierno
grade la nota
    to get a good grade
      sacar una buena nota **2.1**
grandchildren los nietos
granddaughter la nieta
grandfather el abuelo **1.3**
grandmother la abuela **1.3**
grandparents los abuelos **1.3**
grandson el nieto
grasshopper el chapulín
great grande **1.2**
green verde **1.2**
guinea pig el conejillo de Indias
guitar la guitarra **2.3**
gymnasium el gimnasio **2.2**

hair el pelo **1.2**
half past y media **2.2**
half-brother el medio hermano
half-sister la media hermana
hamburger la hamburguesa **2.2**
hamster el hámster
to happen pasar **2.1**
happy feliz **1.3**, alegre **3.1**,
    contento(a) **3.1**
hard difícil **2.1**
hard-working trabajador(a) **1.2**
harmonica la armónica
harp el arpa (fem.)
hat el sombrero **1.2**
to have tener **1.3**
    to have just… acabar de… **3.1**
    to have to tener que **2.1**
    one has to hay que **2.1**
he él **1.1**
health la salud
to hear oír **2.3**
heart el corazón **2.3**
Hello. Hola. **EP**

helmet el casco **3.2**
to help ayudar (a) **2.1**
her su **1.3**
highway la carretera
his su **1.3**
history la historia **2.1**
hockey el hockey **3.2**
homework la tarea **2.1**
    to be hot tener calor **3.3**
    It is hot. Hace calor. **3.3**
house la casa **1.1**
how cómo **2.2**
    How (fun)! ¡Qué (divertido)! **1.2**
    How are you? (familiar) ¿Cómo
      estás? **1.1** (formal) ¿Cómo está
      usted? **1.1**
    How is it going? ¿Qué tal? **1.1**
    How old is…?
      ¿Cuántos años tiene…? **1.3**
to be hungry tener hambre **2.3**
to be in a hurry tener prisa **3.3**
husband el esposo

I yo **1.1**
ice el hielo
    on ice sobre hielo **3.2**
in en **1.1**
instead of en vez de
intelligent inteligente **1.2**
interesting interesante **1.2**
introduce: Let me introduce you
    (familiar/formal) **to…**
    Te/Le presento a… **1.1**
to invite invitar
    I invite you. Te invito. **3.1**
island la isla
Italian el italiano
its su **1.3**

jacket la chaqueta **1.2**
January enero **1.3**
Japanese el japonés
jeans los jeans **1.2**
July julio **1.3**
June junio **1.3**

key la tecla
keyboard el teclado **2.1**
to know (a fact) saber **3.2**
   to know someone
      conocer a alguien **2.3**

lake el lago **3.3**
land la tierra
large grande **1.2**
last name el apellido **EP**
late tarde **2.1**
later luego **2.3**
   See you later. Hasta luego. **EP**,
      Nos vemos. **EP**
Latin el latín
lazy perezoso(a) **1.2**
to learn aprender **2.3**
to leave: I want to leave a
   message for… Quiero dejar
   un mensaje para… **3.1**
   to leave a message
      dejar un mensaje **3.1**
   Leave a message after the tone.
      Deje un mensaje después del
      tono. **3.1**
less menos
   less than menos de **3.2**
   less… than menos… que **3.2**
lesson la lección **2.1**
letter la carta
   to send a letter
      mandar una carta **2.3**
library la biblioteca **2.2**
life la vida **2.3**
to lift weights levantar pesas **3.2**
like (as) como
to like gustar
   He/She likes… Le gusta… **1.1**
   I like… Me gusta… **1.1**
   I would like…
      Me gustaría… **3.1**
   Would you like…?
      ¿Te gustaría…? **3.1**
   You like… Te gusta… **1.1**
to listen (to) escuchar **2.1**

literature la literatura **2.1**
a little poco **2.1**
to live vivir **2.3**
lizard la lagartija
long largo(a) **1.2**
to look at mirar **2.1**
to look for buscar **2.1**
to lose perder (ie) **3.2**
to be lucky tener suerte **3.3**
lunch el almuerzo **2.2**

magazine la revista **2.3**
to make hacer **2.3**
man el hombre **1.1**
mandolin la mandolina
many mucho(a) **1.1**
March marzo **1.3**
mathematics las matemáticas **2.1**
May mayo **1.3**
maybe tal vez
   Maybe another day.
      Tal vez otro día. **3.1**
meal la comida **2.3**
message el mensaje
   I want to leave a message for…
      Quiero dejar un mensaje
      para… **3.1**
   to leave a message
      dejar un mensaje **3.1**
   Leave a message after the tone.
      Deje un mensaje después del
      tono. **3.1**
midnight la medianoche **2.2**
Miss la señorita **1.1**
moment el momento
   One moment. Un momento. **3.1**
Monday lunes **EP**
monkey el mono
month el mes **1.3**
more más **1.3**
   more than más de **3.2**
   more… than más… que **3.2**
morning la mañana **2.2**
   during the morning
      por la mañana **2.2**
   Good morning. Buenos días. **EP**
   in the morning de la mañana **2.2**
mother la madre **1.3**
mountain la montaña **3.3**

mouse el ratón **2.1**
movie la película **3.1**
   to go to a movie theater
      ir al cine **3.1**
Mr. el señor **1.1**
Mrs. la señora **1.1**
much mucho(a) **1.1**
   as much as tanto como **3.2**
museum el museo **2.3**
music la música **2.1**
must: one must hay que **2.1**
my mi **1.3**

name el nombre **EP**
   His/Her name is…
      Se llama… **EP**
   My name is… Me llamo… **EP**
   What is his/her name?
      ¿Cómo se llama? **EP**
   What is your name?
      ¿Cómo te llamas? **EP**
to need necesitar **2.1**
nervous nervioso(a) **3.1**
never nunca **2.1**
new nuevo(a) **1.2**
newspaper el periódico **2.3**
nice simpático(a) **1.2**
   It is nice outside.
      Hace buen tiempo. **3.3**
   Nice to meet you.
      Mucho gusto. **EP**
night la noche **2.2**
   at night de la noche **2.2**
nine nueve **EP**
nineteen diecinueve **1.3**
ninety noventa **1.3**
no no **EP**
no longer ya no **3.1**
noon el mediodía **2.2**
nor ni
not no **1.1**
notebook el cuaderno **2.1**
novel la novela **2.3**
November noviembre **1.3**
now ahora **1.3**
   Right now! ¡Ahora mismo! **2.1**
number el número
   What is your phone number?
      ¿Cuál es tu teléfono? **EP**

oboe el oboe
October octubre **1.3**
of de
  Of course! ¡Claro que sí! **3.1**
office la oficina **2.2**
often mucho **2.1**
old viejo(a) **1.3**; antiguo(a) **6.1**
  How old is…?
    ¿Cuántos años tiene…? **1.3**
older mayor **1.3**
on en **1.1**, sobre
  on ice sobre hielo **3.2**
once in a while
  de vez en cuando **2.1**
one uno **EP**
one hundred cien **1.3**
only sólo **1.3**
to open abrir **2.3**
or o **1.1**
orange anaranjado(a) **1.2**
organ el órgano
other otro(a) **1.2**
our nuestro(a) **1.3**
outdoors al aire libre **3.2**

to paint pintar **2.3**
pants los pantalones **1.2**
paper el papel **2.1**
parents los padres **1.3**
park el parque **2.3**
parrot el loro
to pass (by) pasar **2.1**
patient paciente **1.2**
pen (instrument) la pluma **2.1**
pencil el lápiz **2.1**
people la gente **2.3**
phone book
  la guía telefónica **3.1**
physical education
  la educación física **2.1**
physics la física
piano el piano **2.3**
piccolo el flautín
picture la foto
  to take pictures sacar fotos **3.3**

pigeon la paloma
pineapple la piña
pink rosado(a) **1.2**
place el lugar **1.1**
plaid de cuadros **3.3**
to plan pensar (ie) + *infinitive* **3.2**
plant la planta **3.3**
to play tocar **2.3**; practicar **3.1**,
  jugar (ue) **3.2**
  to play sports
    practicar deportes **3.1**
  to play (the guitar, piano) tocar
    (la guitarra, el piano) **2.3**
player el (la) jugador(a)
please por favor **2.2**
pleased contento(a) **3.1**
  Pleased to meet you.
    Encantado(a). **EP**
pleasure
  It's a pleasure. Es un placer. **EP**
  The pleasure is mine.
    El gusto es mío. **EP**
poem el poema **2.3**
poetry la poesía **2.3**
police officer el (la) policía **1.1**
pork rinds los chicharrones **2.3**
potato la papa
to practice practicar **3.1**
to prefer preferir (ie) **3.2**
to prepare preparar **2.1**
pretty bonito(a) **1.2**
printer la impresora **2.1**
problem el problema **2.3**
purple morado(a) **1.2**

quarter past y cuarto **2.2**
quick rápido(a) **5.2**
quiz la prueba **2.1**

rabbit el conejo
raccoon el mapache
racket la raqueta **3.2**
rain la lluvia **3.3**
to rain llover (ue) **3.3**
raincoat el impermeable **3.3**

rarely rara vez **2.1**
rat la rata
to read leer **1.1**
reason la razón **2.1**
to receive recibir **2.3**
recorder la flauta dulce
red rojo(a) **1.2**
redhead pelirrojo(a) **1.2**
to rent a video alquilar un video **3.1**
to rest descansar **2.2**
to return regresar **3.1**,
  He/She will return later.
    Regresa más tarde. **3.1**
right
  to be right tener razón **3.3**
river el río **3.3**
roasted asado(a)
to run correr **1.1**
Russian el ruso

sad triste **3.1**
same mismo(a) **2.1**
sandwich (sub) la torta **2.2**
Saturday sábado **EP**
to say decir
  Don't say that!
    ¡No digas eso! **1.2**
saxophone el saxofón
scarf bufanda **3.3**
schedule el horario **2.2**
school la escuela **2.1**
science las ciencias **2.1**
screen la pantalla **2.1**
sea el mar **3.3**
to search buscar **2.1**
seasons las estaciones **3.3**
to see ver **2.3**
to sell vender **2.3**
semester el semestre **2.2**
to send a letter
  mandar una carta **2.3**
September septiembre **1.3**
serious serio(a) **1.2**
seven siete **EP**
seventeen diecisiete **1.3**
seventy setenta **1.3**
shame: What a shame!
  ¡Qué lástima! **3.1**
to share compartir **2.3**

she ella 1.1
sheep la oveja
shirt la camisa 1.2
shoe el zapato 1.2
shopping
   to go shopping ir de compras 3.1
short (height) bajo(a) 1.2; (length)
   corto(a) 1.2
shorts los shorts 3.3,
   los pantalones cortos
sick enfermo(a) 3.1
sign la señal
to sing cantar 1.1
sister la hermana 1.3
six seis EP
sixteen dieciséis 1.3
sixty sesenta 1.3
to skate patinar 1.1
skateboard la patineta 3.2
to skateboard
   andar en patineta 3.2
skates los patines 3.2
to ski esquiar 3.2
skirt la falda 1.2
to be sleepy tener sueño 3.3
small pequeño(a) 1.2
snack la merienda 2.2
   to have a snack merendar (ie) 3.2
snake la serpiente
snow la nieve 3.3
   to snow nevar (ie) 3.3
so entonces 2.3
   So-so. Regular. 1.1
soap el jabón 5.1
social studies
   los estudios sociales 2.1
sock el calcetín 1.2
soft drink el refresco 2.2
someone alguien
   to know, to be familiar
     with someone
      conocer a alguien 2.3
sometimes a veces 2.1
son el hijo 1.3
song la canción
soon pronto 2.1
sound el sonido
Spanish el español 2.1
to speak hablar 2.1
   May I speak with…?
     ¿Puedo hablar con…? 3.1
spider la araña

sport el deporte
   to play sports
     practicar deportes 3.1
sporting goods store
   la tienda de deportes 3.2
spring la primavera 3.3
stadium el estadio 3.2
stepbrother el hermanastro
stepfather el padrastro
stepmother la madrastra
stepsister la hermanastra
store la tienda 2.3
storm la tormenta 3.3
storyteller el bohique
string la cuerda
striped con rayas 3.3
strong fuerte 1.2
student el (la) estudiante 1.1
to study estudiar 2.1
subject la materia 2.1
summer el verano 3.3
sun el sol 3.3
to sunbathe tomar el sol 3.3
Sunday domingo EP
sunglasses las gafas de sol 3.3
sunny: It is sunny. Hace sol. 3.3,
   Hay sol. 3.3
suntan lotion el bronceador 3.3
supermarket el supermercado
   to go to the supermarket
     ir al supermercado 2.3
supper la cena 2.3
   to have supper cenar 2.3
surfing el surfing 3.2
surname el apellido EP
sweater el suéter 1.2
to swim nadar 1.1
swan el cisne
swimming pool la piscina 3.2
synthesizer el sintetizador

T-shirt la camiseta 1.2
to take tomar 2.2
   to take along llevar 3.3
   to take care of cuidar (a) 2.3
   to take pictures sacar fotos 3.3
tambourine la pandereta
to talk hablar 2.1

tall alto(a) 1.2
to teach enseñar 2.1
teacher el (la) maestro(a) 1.1
team el equipo 3.2
telephone el teléfono 3.1
television la televisión
   to watch television ver la
     televisión 2.3
to tell decir
   Tell (familiar/formal) him or her
     to call me. Dile/Dígale que
     me llame. 3.1
temperature la temperatura 3.3
ten diez EP
tennis el tenis 3.2
terrible terrible 1.1
test el examen 2.1
Thank you. Gracias. 1.1
   Thanks, but I can't.
     Gracias, pero no puedo. 3.1
that que
theater el teatro 2.3
their su 1.3
then entonces 2.3
there is, there are hay 1.3
they ellos(as) 1.1
thin delgado(a) 1.2
to think pensar (ie) 3.2; creer 3.3
   I think so. / I don't think so.
     Creo que sí/no. 3.3
thirsty: to be thirsty tener sed 2.3
thirteen trece 1.3
thirty treinta 1.3
three tres EP
Thursday jueves EP
time el tiempo
   free time el tiempo libre 3.1
   (At) What time is…? ¿A qué
     hora es…? 2.2
   What time is it?
     ¿Qué hora es? 2.2
tired cansado(a) 3.1
toad el sapo
today hoy EP
   Today is… Hoy es… EP
   What day is today?
     ¿Qué día es hoy? EP
tomorrow mañana EP
   See you tomorrow.
     Hasta mañana. EP
   Tomorrow is… Mañana es… EP
too también 1.1

to treat: I'll treat you. Te invito. **3.1**
tree el árbol **3.3**
trigonometry la trigonometría
trombone el trombón
true: It's true. Es verdad. **1.2**
trumpet la trompeta
truth la verdad **2.2**
tuba la tuba
Tuesday martes **EP**
turkey el pavo
turtle la tortuga
twelve doce **1.3**
twenty veinte **1.3**
twenty-one veintiuno **1.3**
two dos **EP**
two hundred doscientos(as) **5.3**

ugly feo(a) **1.2**
umbrella el paraguas **3.3**
uncle el tío **1.3**
to understand comprender **2.3**, entender (ie) **3.2**
to use usar **2.1**

very muy **1.3**
video
    to rent a video
        alquilar un video **3.1**
viola la viola
violin el violín
to visit visitar **2.2**
volleyball el voleibol **3.2**

to wait for esperar **2.1**
waiting room la sala de espera
to walk caminar
    to walk the dog
        caminar con el perro **2.3**
to want querer (ie) **3.2**
warrior el guerrero
watch el reloj **2.2**

to watch mirar **2.1**
    to watch television
        ver la televisión **2.3**
water el agua *(fem.)* **2.2**
we nosotros(as) **1.1**
to wear llevar **2.1**
    What is he/she wearing?
        ¿Qué lleva? **1.2**
weather el tiempo **3.3**
    What is the weather like?
        ¿Qué tiempo hace? **3.3**
Wednesday miércoles **EP**
week la semana **EP**
weights: to lift weights
    levantar pesas **3.2**
welcome bienvenido(a) **1.1**
    You're welcome. De nada. **1.1**
well bien **1.1**; pues **1.2**
    (Not very) Well, and you
        (familiar/formal)? (No muy)
        Bien, ¿y tú/usted? **1.1**
what cuál(es) **2.2**; qué **2.2**
    What a shame!
        ¡Qué lástima! **3.1**
    What day is today?
        ¿Qué día es hoy? **EP**
    What is he/she like?
        ¿Cómo es? **1.2**
    What is your phone number?
        ¿Cuál es tu teléfono? **EP**
when cuándo **2.2**; cuando **3.1**
where dónde **2.2**; **(to) where**
    adónde **2.2**
    Where are you from?
        ¿De dónde eres? **EP**
    Where is he/she from?
        ¿De dónde es? **EP**
which (ones) cuál(es) **2.2**
white blanco(a) **1.2**
who quién(es) **2.2**
    Who are they?
        ¿Quiénes son? **1.3**
    Who is it? ¿Quién es? **1.3**
Whose is...? ¿De quién es...? **1.3**
why por qué **2.2**
    That's why. Con razón. **2.1**
wife la esposa
to win ganar **3.2**
wind el viento **3.3**
windy: It is windy.
    Hace viento. **3.3**, Hay viento. **3.3**
winter el invierno **3.3**

with con **1.3**
    with me conmigo **3.1**
    with you contigo **3.1**
woman la mujer **1.1**
to work trabajar **1.1**
world el mundo **1.1**
worried preocupado(a) **3.1**
to worry: Don't worry!
    ¡No te preocupes! **3.1**
worse peor **3.2**
to write escribir **1.1**
writing la composición

xylophone el xilófono

year el año **1.3**
    He/She is... years old.
        Tiene... años. **1.3**
yellow amarillo(a) **1.2**
yes sí **EP**
    Yes, I would love to.
        Sí, me encantaría. **3.1**
you tú *(familiar singular)* **1.1**,
    usted *(formal singular)* **1.1**,
    ustedes *(plural)* **1.1**,
    vosotros(as) *(familiar plural)* **1.1**
young joven **1.3**
younger menor **1.3**
your su *(formal)* **1.3**,
    tu *(familiar)* **1.3**,
    vuestro(a) *(plural familiar)* **1.3**

zero cero **EP**

Índice

Créditos

Photography

1 Nancy Sheehan; 2 Nancy Sheehan (br); 3 Nancy Sheehan (tl, cl, bc); 4 Nancy Sheehan (tl); Peter Menzel (br); 5 Nancy Sheehan (t, c); 6 Peter Menzel (b); 7 Robert Frerck/Odyssey Productions/Chicago (b); 8 School Division, Houghton Mifflin Company (tl); Nancy Sheehan (tr); 12 Guía telefónica 1998, ICE Telecommunications, Costa Rica; School Division, Houghton Mifflin Company (c); 20 Nancy Sheehan; 23 SuperStock (tl); Ken O'Donoghue (c); Larry Bussaca/Retna Ltd. (br); 28 Michael Newman/PhotoEdit (tr); 34 Michael Newman/PhotoEdit (tc); Randy Taylor/Getty Images (b); 35 Michael Newman/PhotoEdit (cl); 42 DC Photos/Dee Culleny/Visuals Unlimited (bc); Visuals Unlimited (bl); 43 Reuters Newsmedia, Inc./Corbis (cr); 48 Jim Whitmer; 49 Patricia A. Eynon (cl); Reuters Newsmedia, Inc./Corbis (br); 60 Jeffery Boan/Miami Herald (tl); Paul J. Sutton/Duomo (tr); Kelly A. Swift/Retna Ltd. (cl); Getty Images (cr); Reuters Newsmedia, Inc./Corbis (bl); NASA (br); 68 RMIP/Richard Haynes; 69 Ron Thomas/FPG International (b); 71 RMIP/Richard Haynes; 72 KXTN Radio Station, San Antonio; Courtesy, ¡Qué onda! Magazine (1, bl); Bob Daemmrich Photography (cr); 73 Sygma (t); Jack Kilby/Retna, Ltd. (bl); 80 Ken O'Donoghue (background 1); 87 Fernando Botero, Los Músicos, 1979/Courtesy Marlborough Gallery, New York; 88 Michael Newman/PhotoEdit (bl); 89 RMIP/Richard Haynes; 91 Paul Barton/Corbis (tl); Jose L. Pelaez/Corbis (tr); Tim Theriault (mid cr); 95 RMIP/Richard Haynes; 96 School Division, Houghton Mifflin Company; 103 Patricia A. Eynon; 104 Bob Daemmrich Photography (r); 106 Mark Epstein/DRK Photo (tl); The Granger Collection (bl); James Prigoff (cr); Danielle Gustafson (br); 107 The Granger Collection (tr); RMIP/Richard Haynes (bl, br); 108 "The Flower Seller" (1942), Diego Rivera. Oil on masonite. © 2003 Banco de Mexico and Instituto Nacional de Bellas Artes y Literatura/Christie's Images/The Bridgeman Art Library (br); 109 Courtesy, Ballet Folklórico (tr); UPI/Bettmann/Corbis (br); School Division, Houghton Mifflin Company (bc); 110 David Sanger (tr); 111 David Ryan/Lonely Planet Images (tl); 119 David Sanger (cr); Wendy Watriss/Woodfin Camp & Associates (br); 121 RMIP/Richard Haynes; 122 RMIP/Richard Haynes; 124 Robert Frerck/Odyssey Productions (b); 144 School Division, Houghton Mifflin Company (tr); 145 School Division, Houghton Mifflin Company (r); 148 RMIP/Richard Haynes; 151 School Division, Houghton Mifflin Company (br); 152 RMIP/Richard Haynes; 158 School Division, Houghton Mifflin Company (cr); 161 School Division, Houghton Mifflin Company; 171 Robert Frerck/Odyssey Productions; 172 Doug Bryant/DDB Stock Photo (l); 173 School Division, Houghton Mifflin Company; 174 RMIP/Richard Haynes (b); 175 "El cumpleaños de Lala y Tudi," Carmen Lomas Garza. Reprinted with permission of the publisher, Children's Book Press, San Francisco, CA. Copyright, 1990 by Carmen Lomas Garza; 176 John Boyden/PhotoEdit (l); 184 Robert Frerck/Woodfin Camp & Associates; 185 Robert Frerck/Woodfin Camp & Associates; 186 Ed Dawson Photography (cr); Sean Sprague (c); North Wind Picture Archives (b); 187 Ed Dawson Photography (tr); Beryl Goldberg (cl); Sean Sprague (c); David Sanger (cr); 190 Chris Sharp/New England Stock Photo (br); 192 B.R. Spiegel Photography (c); B. R. Spiegel Photography (cr); Steven Needham/Envision (br); 193 Albert Copley/Visuals Unlimited (tr); RMIP/Richard Haynes (b); Albert Copley/Visuals Unlimited (b); 194 UPI/Bettmann/Corbis (r); 195 Ken O'Donoghue (bl); Robert Frerck/Odyssey Productions (tl, br); United States Postal Service (c); Farrell Grehan/Photo Researchers, Inc. (tr); 196 Raymond A. Mendez/Animals Animals (tr); Sharon Smith/Photonica (bl); 197 Suzanne Murphy-Larrorde (tl); 206 RMIP/Richard Haynes; 207 Robert Frerck/Odyssey Productions (t); Bob Daemmrich/Stock Boston (c); 217 RMIP/Richard Haynes; 222 Robert Frerck/Odyssey Productions; 223 School Division, Houghton Mifflin Company (bl); Steve Azzara/Getty Images (br); 226 Chris Brown & Dick Young/Unicorn Stock Photography (montage br); 227 Dave Nagel/Getty Images (cr); Scott Liles/Unicorn Stock Photography (br); 232 Scott Liles/Unicorn Stock Photography; 233 RMIP/Richard Haynes; 235 RMIP/ Richard Haynes; 238 Photo News (tr); 242 School Division, Houghton Mifflin Company; 243 RMIP/Richard Haynes (tr); 244 Robert Frerck/Odyssey Productions (1); 245 Andrew Wallace/Reuters News Media (cl); John Todd/AP Wide World Photos (cr); 247 School Division, Houghton Mifflin Company; 248 Russell Gordon/Odyssey Productions (br); 249 Bob Daemmrich Photography (t); David Simson/Stock Boston (c); Bob Daemmrich Photography (b); 252 Ken O'Donoghue (background); K. Scott Harris (t); 256 B. W. Hoffmann/Envision (tr); John Marshall/Getty Images (cr); RMIP/Richard Haynes (bl); 257 RMIP/Richard Haynes (montage r); 259 Katsuyoshi Tanaka/Woodfin Camp & Associates (tr); RMIP/Richard Haynes (br); 260 K. Scott Harris (t); 266 School Division, Houghton Mifflin Company; 277 Bruno Maso/Photo Researchers, Inc.; 278 Raymond A. Mendez/Animals Animals (l); Thomas R. Fletcher/Stock Boston (br); 279 Dennis Doyle/AP Wide World Photos (tr); RMIP/Richard Haynes (b, c); R11 School Division, Houghton Mifflin Company

All other photography: Martha Granger/EDGE Productions

Fian Arroyo 33, 45, 60, 61, 66, 70, 85, 97 (b), 130, 183, 216, 232, 243, 257, 261, 269 (b), R2; Nneke Bennett, 46, 47; Susan M. Blubaugh 95, 182, 188, 191; Fabricio Vanden Broeck 184, 185; Neverne Covington 126, 173, 189, 208, 210, 221; Ruben De Anda 98, 99; Jim Deigan 241; Mike Dietz 157 (t), 214, 217, 259; Elisse Goldstein 166, 167; Catherine Leary 51, 93, 94, 105, 128, 131, 157 (b), 179, 236; John Lytle 54; Jim Nuttle 123, 178, 267; Laurie O'Keefe 260 (br); Steve Patricia 28 (1); Gail Piazza 15, 19, 95 (t), 264, 269 (t), 275, R9; Matthew Pippin 114, 115, 200, 201, 226, 227; Rick Powell 75 (b), 104, 237, R5; Donna Ruff 77, 141; Enrique O. Sánchez 218, 219, 270, 271; School Division, Houghton Mifflin Company 62, 63, 64, 65, 75 (t), 90, 93 (t), 162, 235, 238, R1, R6, R8, R9; Don Stewart 134, 258 (l), 262; Cris Reverdy, Caroline McCarty, Jackie Reeves for Yellow House Studio 10, 11; Randy Verougstraete 37, 59